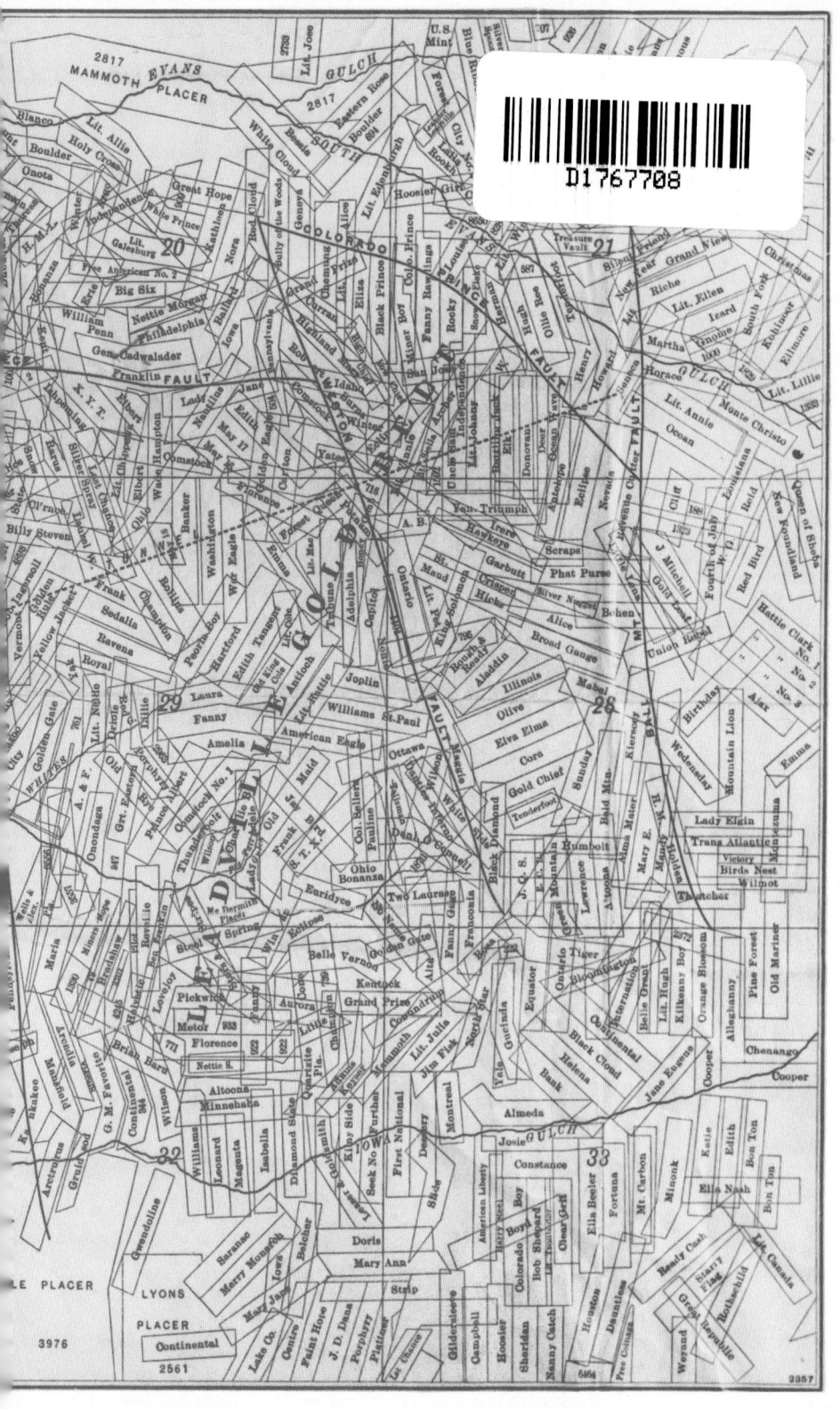

GREAT WEST AND INDIAN SERIES, VOLUME FIFTY-SEVEN

STAKE YOUR CLAIM!

THE TALE OF AMERICA'S ENDURING MINING LAWS

STAKE YOUR CLAIM!
THE TALE OF AMERICA'S ENDURING MINING LAWS

By

Charles Wallace Miller, Jr.

Westernlore Press . . . Tucson, Arizona . . . 1991

Copyright © 1991
By Charles Wallace Miller, Jr.

Library of Congress Catalog Number 91-67643
ISBN 0-87026-080-4

PRINTED IN THE UNITED STATES OF AMERICA BY WESTERNLORE PRESS

To my wife, Connie, and son, Geoffrey

TABLE OF CONTENTS

	Page
Introduction	ix
Chapter One	
A New Nation Establishes New Policies on Lands and Minerals	1
Chapter Two	
California, Popular Sovereignty, and *Laissez Faire*	21
Chapter Three	
New Rushes, New Land Policies, and a Civil War	43
Chapter Four	
The Miners Go to Washington	63
Chapter Five	
Mineral Patents and the Patent Process	87
Chapter Six	
Western Life Under the General Mining Laws	97
Chapter Seven	
The Mining Law in a Tumultuous Period	117
Chapter Eight	
Scholars and Reformers Study the Mining Law While Westerners Use It	135
Chapter Nine	
Case Law for Mines: Straightforward Despite the "Apex"	151

Chapter Ten
    The Progressive Era Finally Forces Changes   173

Chapter Eleven
    Western Mining, the Great Depression, and the
    New Deal   193

Chapter Twelve
    Wars, New Agencies, and a New Type of Rush   211

Chapter Thirteen
    Serious Movements for Reform   233

Chapter Fourteen
    Summary and Conclusions   259

Notes to the Chapters   265

Index   289

Introduction

Clark Spence, a veteran historian of the West, has identified the topic of federal mining laws as a subject almost completely ignored in the historical context.[1] Some literature is available from special perspectives, from attorneys themselves, and from the environmentalist lobby. As of 1990 no work with a genuinely historical perspective had appeared, though some of the other more specialized studies, especially two books in the 1980s sponsored by environmentalist organizations, included some background. This study is designed to fill a long identified void in the literature.

As incredible as it may seem, the pioneer mining law enacted by Congress in 1872 is still on the books today and allows mining claims on federal lands for gold, silver, uranium, lead, zinc, copper, and other minerals. Though it is true that oil, gas, coal, and common materials like sand and gravel now fall under other laws, the survival of the original mining law is still most remarkable. Initially, the mining law was an integral part of the general federal policy of encouragement of Western settlement with free or relatively cheap lands with their resources. This policy included railroad land grants, the Homestead Act of 1862, and other similar statutes. The lands distributed under the mining law were a tiny proportion of the total.

As time passed, however, the land distribution policies became outdated. Gradually Congress repealed all the statutes that provided free or cheap land and resource uses *except the mining law*. The statute first showed its unusual longevity by surviving the conservationist movement of the early twentieth century, though Congress did make major amendments in 1920. Even more amazing, the law survived the Great Depression and New Deal, which included final repeal of all the other liberal land distribution statutes (except for lands in Alaska). The law survived the "uranium rush" of the 1950s even though it cost the government dearly. The law has even survived the environmentalist movement that began in the late 1960s. In the 1970s, a Congressman from the West who proposed revisions found such an onslaught of local miners at his door that he dropped his own proposal. In October 1990 the Senate voted against a temporary suspension of part of the law but the issue is by no means dead. It is safe to say that much of the mining law will remain for some years in the future.

I will candidly say here at the outset that I view the subject as part of the "frontier school" interpretation. Adherents of this school believe that a wide range of peculiarly American institutions and attitudes stem from the fact that the nation had a vast expanse of lands that were rich in many types of resources. To some extent, then, the frontier school is a specialized geographic interpretation of history. The processes of settlement and development of untapped natural resources then had a profound effect on social and political institutions. Further, the American people developed definite attitudes on a wide range of subjects as a result of the frontier experience. Indeed, a unique psychology emerged. The effects of the developments spread far beyond the frontier itself to the long-settled regions.

Some examples of American characteristics that this school attributes to the frontier should be cited briefly. Most prevalent is the democratic spirit itself. Self-government through representative institutions, if not mass meetings, seems to have a common link to the frontier. Another important example is self-reliance, a natural outgrowth of life in undeveloped physical environments. Social equality seemed to flow from an environment in which certain skills were quite valuable, while hereditary or artificial rank was meaningless. This quality included a special recognition for the value of women's contributions; it was no coincidence that women's suffrage started on the frontier. The abundance of resources clearly produced waste. Yet the availability of resources also provided many products and jobs for areas far from the frontier itself. The frontier school stresses opportunity for the little man.

In addition to the broad, generalized definition of the frontier thesis noted above, I offer a more brief, specialized definition relevant to this topic. The frontier thesis includes a psychological outlook that the West can provide some form of solution to any problem that may emerge. This outlook extends to large scale national political problems as well as individual problems.

The primary proponents of the frontier school were historians Fredrick Jackson Turner, Walter Prescott Webb and, later, Ray Allen Billington. References to these historians are by last name only throughout the text.

Even in the early twentieth century, there were critics of certain aspects of the frontier interpretation. Legitimate examples exist of mistreatment of Native Americans. The "safety valve," the belief that workingmen in older urban centers went to the frontier in times of economic depression, can also be attacked.[2] Though critics were relatively quiet as recently as the 1960s, a new generation has now emerged. The environmentalist organizations have fitted into this recent attack. So have some historians. Certainly this is a healthy intellectual situation in a free market of ideas. I recognize that my position is not unanimously followed. Further, having personally administered the laws for the U.S. Department of the Interior, I recognize several problems in the statutes as currently on the books. This work, then, is *not* an unabashed defense of the laws in current times but reflects many grounds for defense in a *historical* context.

This work is condensed from a Ph.D. dissertation through Union Graduate School of Cincinnati, Ohio. The original title was the somewhat cumbersome *Sacred Cow in the American West; the Origin, Evolution, Administration, and Impact of Federal Hardrock Mining Laws and Policies.* Though the title is now shorter, the reference to the mining law as a "sacred cow" recurs throughout the text. I have included enough of the more general history of both politics and mining to aid the reader who may not be familiar with various events, locales, techniques, or times of development. Even so, the reader is referred to several other volumes in the notes which address these topics in more detail.

I would like to thank Union Graduate School and the members

of my committee: Dr. Marjorie Chambers, Western U.S. history specialist; Dr. Juan Garcia, historian; Mr. Robert Palmquist, Western U.S. legal specialist; Dr. Colin Greer, historian; Dr. Paul Forti; and Mr. Reginald Witherspoon. Further, I recognize the importance of records that are available at the National Archives where Mr. Jim Cassedy was crucial. The same was true at the Arizona Historical Society where Ms. Adelaide Elm was most influential. Finally, I would like to thank the U.S. Department of the Interior's Bureau of Land Management for providing a career position that led into this fascinating topic.

CHAPTER ONE

A New Nation Establishes New Policies on Lands and Minerals

When the United States first addressed the multitude of issues that it faced as a newly independent nation, Congress demanded a major proportion of the income derived from mineral production on lands owned by the new government. Ironically, the government was notoriously weak in most other important functions. However, the new Congress, operating under the Articles of Confederation, maintained jurisdiction over lands ceded by the states north of the Ohio River, which became known as the Northwest Territory.[1]

According to Article III of the Articles of Confederation, Congress retained the right of "disposal of the soil" in any matter it saw fit.[2] Thomas Jefferson left the country just as an Ordinance he sponsored was passing Congress. His measure, the Ordinance of 1784, addressed the creation of new states. The same committee of Congress that had drafted the Ordinance of 1784 proposed a land survey and distribution system the next year. Presumably, Jefferson was involved in much of the preliminary work before his departure. As far back as 1776 he had proposed a Constitution for his native Virginia that included homesteads of fifty acres for those who had no land. This policy was certainly in keeping with his well-known affinity for the independent yeoman farmer that has become a central tenet of American politics and society, and is still quite viable today.[3]

A congressional committee report of April 12, 1785, addressed the well-known features of a rectangular survey, a reservation setting aside lands for public schools, and sale of most of the lands at $1.00 per acre. The committee also recommended that a portion of "gold, silver, lead, copper, and coal mines" be reserved to the government. They left a blank space for the exact proportion. Congress voted to recommit the Ordinance to fill in the blank and make other revisions. The Committee reported back with the blank filled in as "one third of all gold, silver, lead, and copper mines for the purpose of special sale at such times and places as Congress may hereafter direct." Coal was now missing from the reservation list. Delegate James Monroe of Virginia moved to strike out all reservations. Rufus King of Massachusetts moved to second the motion. However, only one other delegate joined them, while 20 voted to maintain a reservation of one-third of most minerals. Thus it was in the final Ordinance of 1785 as enacted May 20.[4]

Should the lands be used to encourage settlement? Should they be used for revenue? Or should they be used otherwise?

The reservation of one-third of the minerals obviously reflected the revenue rather than the settlement motive that was setting a high price for farmlands as well. The figure of one-third was already well precedented even by the time of the First Congress under the Constitution in 1789. How could the otherwise ineffectual Articles of Confederation, which followed a war in protest against strong governments, produce so strong a measure? Part of the answer lies in the British legal heritage.

British law regarding mineral rights had, since the early 1600s, linked surface and subsurface ownership. This concept was well precedented in the tin mining province of Cornwall from whence it entered the Common Law. However, gold and silver, the royal metals, were reserved to the crown even if found on private lands. In the American colonies, the charters granted by the monarch reserved a one-fifth share of precious metals in several colonies with an unusual one-fifteenth reservation of copper in Virginia. New York, New Jersey, Pennsylvania, and Delaware had no reservation at all.[5]

The one-fifth figure associated with the reservation to the English crown probably reflects the policy of the leading rival among the European royal families and empires. In the Spanish colonies a reservation of the *quinto*, or fifth, was a long-standing provision of all mineral production. It should be emphasized that the *quinto* was a "royalty" (from which the word itself originated). The *quinto* was not a tax. The prevalence of silver in Spain's American colonies made this far more than an academic matter, unlike the English colonies where the only mineral product was iron.[6]

In the early days the *quinto* was more complex than the name implies. In fact, Spain used a complex sliding scale depending on mine size and metal types. In the latter part of the 18th century, Spain commissioned some major inspections and studies of the problem of stagnated mining production. The most important was by Francisco Xavier Gamboa in 1761, who advocated several reforms, including assigning the *quinto* at just that value. Belatedly, in 1783, King Charles III instituted many of the recommended changes. Production increased markedly. Some may claim that major new discoveries in remote areas of far northern New Spain (later Mexico) and the use of gunpowder contributed to production. Even these changes can be associated with the improved legal climate. Spain's example proved that systems of royalties to the government worked and, if correctly assessed, did not stifle production in an economy otherwise based on free enterprise. Independent Mexico subsequently retained the system. It is of interest to note that those who worked in Mexican mines at this time were free laborers and earned more than any other paid workers in the country.[7]

The fact that the infant United States adopted a royalty system is not surprising. There were precedents in the British legal background for such a policy, at least regarding gold and silver. However, the royalty on lead and copper as well cannot be attributed to British precedents. In actual practice in the Northwest Territory, the presence of valuable deposits of lead and copper were known in the 1780s. The Spanish precedent *may* have been of some influence in setting this course. In all probability, though, the most significant influence was the same one that established the $1.00 per acre price for lands. Quite simply, the government was more than broke due to massive debts from the Revolution.

The possibility of mines was also a prospect for income. Congress did not fully comprehend that collection of royalties presented logistical problems and, like a protective tariff, could even discourage development. Spain's *quinto* was clearly the leading example of a successful system quite evident at the time. It is ironic that the Congress of the Articles, the body that a whole school of political historians has identified as the true organ of the "Spirit of 1776," established a policy that was in theory much harsher than that of the contemporary King of Spain.

In 1787, Congress replaced Jefferson's Ordinance of 1784 regarding admission of new states. However, another meeting of delegates to a special convention that same year caused the nation's attention to focus back on Independence Hall in Philadelphia rather than the Congress then meeting at New York. (Ironically, Congress had abandoned Independence Hall in 1783 when threatened by its own unpaid soldiers, thus showing the weakness of the government under the Articles of Confederation.) A new frame of government emerged in a document known as the Constitution of the United States, which won approval of state conventions in 1788. A new government organized under this document in the spring of 1789, a government with far more legal authority than that of the Articles.

One significant point should be made regarding the remarkable convention of 1787. Delegate James Madison of Virginia undoubtedly contributed more to the Constitution than anyone else in arranging the very existence of the meeting, and in proposing a break with the Articles of Confederation. Indeed, Madison is often termed "father of the Constitution." It is interesting to note that Madison proposed that authority be granted to Congress to overturn any state law that it chose. This proposal had no chance but Article VI, Section 2 essentially gave this power to the federal court system. Madison's proposal should be remembered since it relates to the topic of the eventual federal mining law. Full discussion must wait until the narrative reaches the 1860's. The reader should keep this piece of background in mind. Madison was more successful with a proposed list of "powers as proper to be added to those of the General Legislature" on August 18. At the very top of his list was the power "To dispose of the unappropriated lands of the U. States."[8]

Ultimately the Committee of Detail incorporated several of Madison's points into Article I, Section 8, but the lands clause was significant and unique. Hence it is found in Article IV, Section 3, of the Constitution, unequivocally phrased:

A New Nation Establishes New Policies

> The Congress shall have Power to dispose of and make all needful Rules and Regulations respecting the Territory or other Property belonging to the United States...

This power did not prove controversial among the delegates so no debate is recorded on the point. The matter was precedented under the Confederation, though rather loosely.

Congress had asserted this power in the Ordinance of 1785 but by statute only. The Articles of Confederation had not even specifically stated this power, though Congress exercised it over lands that the states had undeniably ceded to its authority. Now such power was clearly set forth in the Constitution. Consequently, the new Congress repassed the Ordinance of 1787 and later revised that of 1785 to offer legal continuity.[9]

The Constitutional Convention somehow overlooked adequate protection for private property rights. However Madison himself filled this void in the First Congress when he proposed a series of Amendments, ten of which ultimately became the Bill of Rights. The Fifth Amendment concludes with a clear statement, "nor shall private property be taken for public use, without just compensation." Thus Congress had absolute power over government lands until they became private property. Then the stringent provisions of the Fifth Amendment, which includes "just compensation" for government confiscation of property, come into play. This distinction would have far-reaching implications regarding various methods of land distribution.[10]

One other Constitutional point of some significance that also is relevant to land distribution is the prohibition of *ex post facto* legislation. Simply stated, Congress cannot pass a law which makes actions illegal prior to the time of final passage of such Act.[11] The implications of this provision will be discussed in later Chapters.

Once established by the Confederation Congress and reaffirmed by the Congress of the Constitution, the reservation of one-third of the minerals to the government stood for some years. Little occurred to change this because there was little mineral development on government lands. However, there were many other domestic and international events of the last years of the 18th century and the first years of the 19th century. For our purposes, the chief result of the period was the formation of two full-fledged political parties. Western development soon played an important role, quite possibly a crucial one, in these partisan politics.

The first party, generally considered the more conservative, had formed in Congress in support of a spectacular financial plan proposed by the youthful new secretary of the treasury, Alexander Hamilton. There can be no question that the primary function of the plan was to establish good national credit in the wake of the Revolution and the Confederation's inability to pay the new nation's debts. However, the fact that holders of securities would benefit from the plan also figured into the ideas of Hamilton and his followers. This party acquired the Federalist name as taken from the supporters of the Constitution during the ratification struggle. The party that arose to oppose Hamilton was not particularly descended from the opponents of the Constitution. In fact, the primary leader of this group in Congress, James Madison, had been its chief sponsor. The Republicans, as they came to be called, essentially lost the battles on the Hamilton Plan in Congress. But by 1800 they had organized well enough to sweep the elections for both Congress and the presidency, so it might be said that they ultimately won the war. Subsequently, the Federalists gradually collapsed.[12]

Ironically, Jefferson's own party was remarkably ambivalent on the issue of lands, specifically the price to be charged for the new government's lands. Though the Republicans favored settlement, they were just as interested in establishing firm national credit as the Federalists. They saw little means of doing so except through the sale of the lands. Hence the party faced a dilemma of major proportions.[13]

In 1796 Congress finally proposed revisions to the Land Ordinance of 1785. The parties showed surprising agreement in the ultimate law that went through the legislative process. Republican Representative Albert Gallatin proposed a price of $2.00 per acre, exactly double the old price. Yet Hamilton proposed a price of only 20 to 30 cents per acre! Further, Hamilton would have essentially abandoned the time-consuming rectangular surveys, allowing early sales that favored small farmers. Some members of Congress clearly favored high prices and large block sales only, a marked advantage to the speculator. Gallatin, at least, supported small block sales, so his plan became law at $2.00 per acre. Undoubtedly, Hamilton's proposal was the best for the small farmer and frontiersman; he had greatly "out-Jeffersoned the Jeffersonians," and had done so on the issue that would become the most directly significant to them. In fact, Hamilton could take this position because, unlike most of those of his own party, he did not see profits from land sales as crucial to retiring the national debt. Instead, he had advanced his famous financial plan to accomplish sound finances and credit from other sources. One may point to earlier letters of Hamilton that suggest he wanted only controlled Western settlement at a slow rate. Yet on proposed legislation on the matter he took the opposite course.[14]

The frontier school of historians may thus cite none other than Alexander Hamilton as an example of the influence the frontier had on policy makers on the East Coast. Of course, Hamilton retained his views on many other issues related to the frontier. Yet on this issue the Republicans were less than outstanding. At the same time, the Federalists sought profits from the lands both for investors and for the government. Thus they had no desire to stop Western settlement as the British had done prior to the Revolution with the Proclamation of 1763, which helped bring on the War. Here is yet another instance showing the influence of the frontier on the political party considered the conservative one of the times. By the 1780s, the country already had considerable experience with frontier lands and was adjusting their practical realities.

On most important matters of the new nation, ranging from securities, to the bank, to manufactures, to foreign affairs, Secretary of the Treasury Hamilton essentially set policy during the Washington Administration. Only in the land matters noted above were Republicans able to set policy before their own electoral triumph of 1800. Consequently, Hamilton's views on mines are even more than interesting, considering his general image as an early proponent of what might be called big business. He discussed the topic in his Report on Manufactures of 1791, in which we can discern an evolution of thought through several preliminary drafts of the final book length document.

Some may be surprised to see that Hamilton favored a reservation even more stringent than Congress's one-third figure of the Ordinance of 1785. He wanted to reserve all of the gold and silver mines for the government, plus impose collection of royalties on other metal mines. Yet he saw coal mines as possible recipients of bounties, since they might not be profitable on their own but could well prove crucial to other new manufactures. He was not concerned whether mines were publicly or privately owned, so long as they produced. He noted one lead mine near Richmond, in Jefferson's own Virginia, which was successful under state ownership during the Revolution, but subsequently operated effectively under private owners. In other discussions of both soils and forests, Hamilton was far ahead of his time in conservationist philosophy as well. All these points, however, were simply ideas clearly subject to change, and emphatically were not policies. The only legislation in force was still the one-third reservation of the Ordinance of 1785.[15]

Hamilton's statements in his Report on Manufactures are an excellent testament that the country still had very little experience with mines at that time, though it had with lands. He implied the general lack of knowledge in the third draft of the Report when he wrote that copper... "is supposed to be abundant," and then lined out the words. Hamilton, like Congress in 1785, knew that it was present, but little more than that. However, regarding lead, he could definitely state, "This material abounds in the United States and requires little to unfold it." Overall, the final Report also implied the lack of knowledge of minerals. Consequently, these materials did not play much of a role in his recommendations for legislation.[16]

In essence, official policy regarding minerals was virtually no policy at all, even for the government's own lands. Such a lack is understandable at this period. Later times, however, would see a similar lack of policy even with much more mining development.

Thomas Jefferson went so far as to call the triumph of his party and his own candidacy the "Revolution of 1800." Yet historians have long pointed out that the Republicans retained the Hamiltonian financial system, even going so far as to organize a new Bank of the United States after the original charter had expired. Smaller issues showed similar patterns. Jefferson revealed his ideas toward mining when he drafted a Constitutional Amendment to permit the Louisiana Purchase in 1803. He would have allowed the government to undertake mining for any metal or coal, if it so chose, showing again essentially no difference from his ostensible political enemy, Hamilton. Rising tensions with Great Britain certainly influenced Jefferson. He wanted to secure metals, especially lead, if war occurred. (Subsequently, Jefferson approved the Louisiana Purchase without risking the time for the Amendment.)[17]

In 1807 Congress finally faced the first real application of the government's expressed policy to collect a portion of the mineral production from its own lands. A Lead Leasing Act was passed with very little debate. Even at that date some mining was beginning on the Mississippi Valley lead/zinc ore deposits.[18]

Accordingly, the Act authorized the government to withdraw large blocks of land in two known lead/zinc ore districts from sale to speculators or settlers. These rather large blocks were in areas that ultimately became the southeastern corner of Missouri and the extreme northwestern corner of Illinois and adjacent Iowa and Wisconsin. The more northerly district is often called the Galena mining district, after a town in Illinois named for the lead ore there. For mines on the reserved lands, the Act of 1807 provided for a leasing system. Other lead/zinc mines in what became Indiana had already passed into private ownership, through purchased by parties able to pay the price. Significantly, the government had not done much to collect its one-third royalty from lead production on these lands, but they were insignificant compared to the potential of the Galena and Missouri areas. (The scattered small lead mines in Kentucky had never fallen under federal ownership.)[19]

When faced with a genuine prospect of mineral income from its lands, the government under the Jeffersonian Republicans was willing to abandon the unrealistic one-third royalty. Yet in theory that system would have allowed private ownership of lands so long as the royalty was paid. Now the government was maintaining ownership of the land while allowing private interests to lease it for a proportion of the materials removed. Such a leasing system would arise again in the twentieth century.

Congress offered no debate on the lease system, though it may have discussed some aspects in committee that are not recorded. However, Jefferson's own views on the Act that he signed are known from a letter to his Secretary of the Treasury, Albert Gallatin, at the time of enactment. Jefferson recognized that leasing would probably not be permanent and flatly said, "We know too little" [about mining]. He then commented on why he was signing a bill on something that was so little understood:

> I verily believe that [choice] of leasing will be for the best but it will take time to find out what rent may be reserved so as to enable the leasee to compete with those who work in their own right and yet have an encouraging profit.

For the time being, he recommended "short leases," and wanted the government's share in metal rather than money. Further, he expressed great confidence in the administrators he was dispatching to the lead zones. Now dealing with mining in some volume, Republicans began to consider the activity seriously in writing policies. Hamilton in his Report on Manufactures had addressed the issue even before it emerged in actual practice. The only difference was that Jefferson was more candid about the lack of knowledge in admitting the whole system was experimental. Otherwise, leasing was certainly within the range of possible policies Hamilton had suggested back in 1791.[20]

Ultimately, the leasing system broke down for the very reason Jefferson had shrewdly identified. In retrospect, it is amazing leasing lasted as long as it did, especially in the Galena district. The ultimate collapse provides important insights into frontier conditions that related to mining.

In the early nineteenth century lead was a critical commodity in the United States for use as rifle balls. In the frontier society of the times, virtually every person over age 10 possessed a firearm. Further, the government itself demanded huge volumes of lead. It was no coincidence that the Jefferson Administration wanted payment for leases in smelted lead rather than cash. It was also no coincidence that management of leases became the work of the Army. The local officer in charge exercised near dictatorial powers.

In 1807 the United States faced serious tensions with Britain. In fact the tragic incident between the *U.S.S. Chesapeake* and *H.M.S. Leopard*, just four months after the Lead Leasing Act, brought the country to the verge of war. Though outright conflict did not come until 1812, tensions resulted in the dangerously divisive Embargo policy of the Republicans. A genuine military emergency created a viable leasing policy at first with profits for all involved, as commonly occurs during a defense build-up. Even so, the situation in the Missouri district became hopelessly tangled through a mass of disputes over the proper designation of lands as government or as private under old land grants. By 1825 the Army officer in charge, Lt. Martin Thomas, decided to concentrate his efforts on the Galena district and eventually conceded the expediency of government sale of its lead lands in Missouri.[21]

Missouri's illustrious senator, Thomas Hart Benton, introduced a bill calling for a sale of the lead mines after the election of his current friend (but former dueling opponent), Andrew Jackson, to the presidency in late 1828. Benton believed the mines were nearly worked out since Spanish activity was reported as early as 1720. Further, the bill would give the president authorization to conduct sales but would not order him to initiate such sales. Of course, Benton clearly expected Jackson to make such orders of sales, which he did. Missouri's other senator, David Barton, noted that the government lead mines in Wisconsin, Illinois, and Iowa were more than adequate for military needs. He feared that all land sales in the region would be tied up, since Missouri's lead lands were so extensive.[22]

Missouri's senators encountered some opposition. Senator John Branch of North Carolina objected to "disposing of public property in this manner." His remarks were quite prophetic. Branch went on to question the bill by asking, "Is this not the general treasure, purchased by public money [in the Louisiana Purchase]?" Despite Branch's objections, there is no recorded vote on the bill, which passed Congress on March 3, 1829, in time to avoid a possible veto by outgoing President John Quincy Adams. Andrew Jackson duly signed the bill and ordered the lands sold after he had recovered from his notoriously rowdy inauguration the next day. Missouri's senators had identified some valid points in favor of the Act. The government sold otherwise poor lands in southern Missouri at prices equal to prime farmlands elsewhere. Deep lead mines would ultimately become major producers, many years in the future.[23]

The government's interest turned exclusively to the more northerly lead district and events there generally confirmed Sen. Barton's observation as to its sufficiency. As late as 1825 the Galena district was just beginning to gain the attention of miners. Ores were plentiful at the surface and were easily removed by indi-

vidual workers or small groups. Lt. Thomas issued digging permits to miners for free, with the proviso that they sell ore only to one of eight officially designated smelters. By mid-1826, the government had issued some 350 permits. By mid-1829, this number had climbed to 4,253, hence Senator Barton's observation that Galena was adequate for the government's needs and Missouri mines could be sold. Many of the miners came from the Cornwall region of England. The Galena district was the first in the U.S. to come to know the "Cousin Jacks and their Jennies" — as the Cornish soon came to be called — but it would not be the last. People soon likened the miners, sticking their heads out of the relatively shallow holes in the lead areas, to badgers emerging from their holes. Wisconsin early acquired its nickname, the "Badger State."[24]

The smelter owner rather than the miner was the crucial figure

A New Nation Establishes New Policies 13

from the government's viewpoint. Ownership of a smelter required a bond of $10,000 and a monthly payment of lead to the government. Nevertheless, ownership proved highly profitable; the Gratiot Brothers Smelter, the largest, realized a 197.9% annual return on initial investment for a fifteen-month period in 1827-1828. Additional profits came from recovery of silver as a by-product of some of the ores. At the same time, the government received 10% of the total lead, or 268,696 lbs. from the leading smelter alone.[25]

In 1829 lead prices collapsed, primarily from the additional development that inspired sale of Missouri's mines. Also in 1829 the Army transferred Lt. Thomas, replacing him with Capt. Thomas Legate. The new administrator was personally opposed to the system so he enforced it most erratically. Even before Thomas left, authorized smelters had fallen in arrears of their lead share for 1829. By the mid 1830s they were far behind. Several unauthorized smelters had appeared. The problem of private lead lands as opposed to government lands began to emerge, just as it had in Missouri. Though the lead price rose substantially in the 1840s with record production, the complex problems caused Congress to order sale of the mines in 1846.[26]

Several modern writers have observed the success of the Thomas period and suggested that the system should have been maintained.[27] There are numerous flaws in this argument. The Thomas administration covered the first four years of mining of a totally new district in a prosperous economic climate. Even had Thomas retained his position for the ensuing decade, he would have faced divisions of land, collapse in price, and depletion of the best surface ores. The older lead mines and smelters elsewhere did not have the overhead of the lease payments to the government but their ore was of lower quality and deeper. The Galena district could compete initially despite the extra overhead because of favorable ores but that situation was quickly disappearing by the 1840s. After sale of the mines, major concerns dominated them, as might be expected with deeper deposits requiring expensive underground removal techniques. A special report to Congress revealed more problems in selling these lands than the earlier Missouri lead lands. In fact, many of the Wisconsin lands were unsold at auction and so fell open to direct purchase at $1.25 per acre.[28]

Another suggestion regarding the presumed benefits of the Thomas administration relates to the fact that he upheld an Act signed by Thomas Jefferson himself. Purportedly, the "little man" had an advantage in this system that still relied on free enterprise but with a Jeffersonian style. This argument overlooks the fact that the real winners were the smelter owners who needed considerable capital to begin their operations. The Gratiot brothers were from a wealthy St. Louis family long involved in the fur trade. It is true that the typical miner made profits comparable to the pay in many occupations of the times but there was no route to quick riches in the Galena district. Many of the lead miners went to California when the great rush occurred there.[29]

There is good evidence that Jefferson himself learned something from just the first year of the lead leasing system. In 1808 a private party offered to sell an iron mine to the government. Jefferson politely declined the offer by stating "public works are much less advantageously managed than they are by private hands." He also noted that competition brings down costs and remarked, "I have no doubt we can buy brass cannon at market cheaper than we could make iron ones." Finally, he noted that the government owned an iron mine for the arsenal at Harper's Ferry but could not even find a lessee to operate the facility.[30]

The leader of the Republicans who had advanced a position no different from Hamilton in 1803 or even 1807 apparently had revised his stand after practical experience. Jefferson's remarks in 1808 clearly reflect Adam Smith and *laissez faire* economics. Hamilton's work of 1791 was less doctrinaire and more pragmatic.[31] Of course, the fact that lead mines were on lands already owned by the government was crucial. The proposed sale of private iron mines to the government, even in a defense build-up, was a different matter. In fact, the War Department in 1808 still owned the massive iron ore deposits of the upper Great Lakes. It is true that these deposits were remote, but so were some of the reserved lead mines. Jefferson knew that the far reaches of American territory had uncharted riches, undoubtedly a factor in his position.

Hamilton and Jefferson both contemplated the topic of minerals, an interesting point of comparison since it has critical relations to both manufacturing and agriculture, the respective choices of the

A New Nation Establishes New Policies 15

two for the nation's future. Yet the near total lack of experience caused the two philosophies to start at a remarkably similar point. The government lands, be they agricultural, mineral, forest, or desert, needed some official agency for administrative functions, including surveys. Early distributions were conducted most commonly by temporary offices in locales where auctions were scheduled. In 1812 Congress approved and Jefferson's successor, Republican President James Madison, signed an Act creating the General Land Office. The agency established many local branches, wherever the government had substantial quantities of land available. Often they were quite busy, hence the term "land office business." At other times they performed little at all. The General Land Office fell under jurisdiction of the Department of the Interior upon creation of that larger administrative division in 1849. It continued as an agency within the Department until 1946 when it merged into the Bureau of Land Management. The Land Office played a crucial role on the frontier, whether local conditions were conducive to mining, forestry, or agriculture.[32]

Prices of lands and methods of distribution to settlers continued to be a major problem well into the 19th century. In 1820 Congress lowered the price to $1.25 per acre, where it stayed for some years. By the time of Andrew Jackson, the problem of squatting was rampant and Jackson was not about to use force even though Jefferson had signed a bill allowing it. It is more than symbolic that Jackson was the first president to call himself "Democratic Republican," instead of simply "Republican."[33]

Congress eventually addressed the situation in a series of Preemption Acts from 1830 to 1840. The thrust of these measures was to allow bona fide settlers the chance to purchase lands on which they could prove residency and improvements before the lands could be offered at auction. The system generally worked retroactively; the 1830 Act allowed the settlers already on the lands a period of one year to make the purchase at the standing rate of $1.25 per acre for no more than 160 acres. Subsequent preemptions followed this pattern.[34]

The Preemption Acts represented an alliance between the South and West as well as a clear victory for the Jacksonian Democrats. Yet Jackson damaged his own cause by demanding cash payments for the lands in the Specie Circular of 1836. This measure helped bring on a serious financial crisis the next year, just in time to plague the new president, Martin Van Buren. (At least one historian, Peter Temin, disputes the thesis of the harmful nature of the Specie Circular.) Despite this controversy, Jacksonian Preemption policies were important in aiding the genuine settler. Yet only a relatively small portion of the federal lands were entered under Preemption. Even after that method was in force, most land distributions, including some known to possess minerals, came from outright purchases. The fact that land purchases were still ongoing throughout this and subsequent periods should not be ignored. Ultimately the government would devise other types of preemptions that would be of utmost importance to the issue of minerals.[35]

The government had clearly adjusted its policies to reflect certain realities of frontier conditions by the late 1840s. One such adjustment was the inclusion of preemption in a system otherwise geared to land sales. The second adjustment was total abandonment of the exercise of authority regarding mineral developments. The early requirement of a one-third royalty had given way to a Jeffersonian system of government retention of the lands but with development through leasing to private parties. This was obviously for income, with settlement a secondary consideration. Yet even that reservation had collapsed under what might be described as frontier pressures. So matters stood regarding lead mines in the late 1840s.

The Mississippi Valley was not the only area of mineral development during the Jacksonian period in the young nation. The image of gold rushes is so much a part of the larger image of the American West that some may be surprised to learn of earlier rushes in the East. Gold deposits are scattered in the intensely metamorphosed rocks of the Appalachians. During the first three decades of the 19th century, gold production gradually increased in this region, particularly in North Carolina, but a full scale rush did not occur until 1829, near Dahlonega, Georgia. The production from the new zone sold to the United States mint was $212,000 in just the first year. This amount was almost double the entire Appalachian gold output sold to the mint from 1804 to 1827. Estimates of the number of men involved in the Georgia rush are 6,000 to 7,000.[36] Although the lands involved did not fall under federal land law, the mines did indirectly affect other federal policies, both short and long-term. Further, the Appalachians contributed to early general impressions of mining in an inexperienced country. Appalachian gold mining in the earliest days was almost entirely placer. At first gold could even be mined by simply scraping it from cracks in rocky streambeds. Most participants in the Georgia rush were individual white, rural adventurers, the regional equivalent of later gold seekers in the West. It was no coincidence that men with early Georgia experience later made major discoveries in Colorado and Montana. A former Georgia miner even aided in positively identifying the first California samples recovered by James Marshall at John Sutter's mill in 1848. Georgia goldfields were in a remote locale but were surrounded by more settled areas. Certainly the area had some elements of frontier life, but there were differences from the locales of later Western rushes. Most important, Georgia had been one of the original states and thus had a well-established legal code and social mores on many matters.[37]

Some of Georgia's "29ers" were slave owners who profited by using slaves in the placer mines. Usually owners worked with them, as would be expected in a mining camp that had no semblance of plantation society. No legal barrier existed to such a practice since slavery itself was quite legal. There are no reports of less fortunate miners trying to stop the slave owner from using his human property to provide extra pairs of hands to pan for gold. The general sentiment of the South in agricultural regions was much the same. Ultimately the South would fight a massive war using armies of men who owned no slaves and had no expectations of ever owning any.[38]

The Southern experience demonstrated that slave labor could be used in placer mining in a region where slavery was already established. This fact became known throughout the country since newspapers and magazines widely covered the Georgia rush of '29. The popular conception of mining before the United States had much direct experience in the industry quite commonly included an association with slavery. This conception stemmed from images from ancient history as well as a false picture of Colonial Latin American mining. (Only very recently have scholars been able to show conclusively that most Latin American mining employed free labor forces, with some exceptions in placering. T. A. Rickard, a prominent mining engineer and mining scholar, erroneously stated even into the twentieth century that Colonial Latin American mining had predominantly used slave labor.)[39]

The fact that slave labor proved profitable in placering, however, did not mean it would be successful in underground mining. Placer mining, under the open sky, with a shovel and pan, or perhaps a sluice box, is not too different a form of physical labor from many tasks in agriculture. Though the miner may get wet, the slave in a rice paddy does too. Placer mining involves no more risk of injury than raising crops. In addition, placer mining requires no more training or experience than most routine plantation jobs. Men could usually learn panning in just a few hours.

Underground mining contrasts with placering on every count. Underground mining has always required a great degree of skill and training that comes only from years of experience. Further, underground mining has always been one of the most unhealthy, dangerous occupations imaginable. If he had not already suffered a fatal or disabling accident, the typical underground miner could expect to be incapacitated by "black lung" at age 40. In the nineteenth century it has been said that the only occupation of equivalent danger was soldiering. This situation automatically excluded underground mining from slave labor. Southern planters specifically did not use their slaves for dangerous jobs like installing the ridgebeam of a barn. Instead, roving bands of free Irishmen undertook such dangerous construction tasks. The same factors that excluded slavery from factories, but made them profitable through free labor, also naturally excluded slavery from underground mining.[40]

The Appalachian gold rush influenced the federal government to undertake another initiative. The nation had a serious shortage of circulating coinage. The single mint at Philadelphia produced very modest numbers of coins that generally went to vaults for speculative purposes. In 1830 there was only one circulating coin of U.S. origin per resident. To ease the problem, the government formally recognized many foreign coins as legal tender, but there was still a severe lack of coinage.[41]

In 1838 the first United States branch mints struck their first coins. The new mints were at Dahlonega, Georgia; at Charlotte, North Carolina; and at New Orleans, Louisiana. The Dahlonega and Charlotte mints were very small and made gold coins only, hence the "C" and early "D" mint marks are highly prized by modern collectors (a later "D" means Denver, Colorado). Even so, the bulk of Appalachian gold went to Philadelphia since the branches did not open until after the Georgia rush was tapering off. Gold coins from all mints began to alleviate the country's shortage of large denomination circulating currency by the mid-1840s. The New Orleans mint was the largest branch and primarily utilized silver by-products of the Mississippi Valley, though it also received Latin American gold and silver. After the California rush New Orleans received much of that fabled output, but another branch at San Francisco (where an "S" mint mark was used) became a major institution in 1854. The three original branch mints, located in the South, ceased operations with the coming of the Civil War. The Confederacy briefly used the New Orleans mint, but Union forces recaptured it with the city in 1862 and the federal government resumed operations there in 1879. The last coins to carry the "O" mint mark appeared in 1909.[42]

The Georgia rush was similar to later Western rushes, involving a mass of ordinary citizens who quickly moved to placer locales. There is some evidence that placer techniques developed here and later spread to the West. The use of slavery in mining as well as in agriculture was part of the South's "peculiar institution," but would not go west, as we shall see. The Appalachians, combined with the Mississippi Valley, provided an important supplement to the nation's circulating currency. Further, this extra input of metals proved enough to influence the federal government to build new mint facilities. Webb emphasized such an impact of the frontier in expanding currency supplies, with resulting expansion of trade, on a world scale. Here is a good example within a more limited time and geographic frame.

Placer mining is simply a mechanical method of concentrating the gold carried by river bottom materials by allowing the great weight of its particles to sink below the accompanying sands. The simplest, though smallest scale method of placer mining is panning.
(Photo courtesy Arizona Historical Society)

Chapter Two

California, Popular Sovereignty, and Laissez Faire

As the decade of the 1840s was drawing to a close, the political leadership of the United States found it had to address a multitude of problems that accompanied the benefits of having added two massive new blocks of territory to the national domain. One of these, the result of diplomatic negotiations with Britain, includes present-day Oregon, Washington, and part of Idaho. The second resulted from the conflict with Mexico and includes present-day California, Nevada, Utah, most of New Mexico and Arizona, and part of Colorado. Now the United States would have to govern these new territories. The nation already had many years of similar experience, though, so precedents were well-established.

Yet other aspects of settlement were ready-made for trouble. Slavery had proved nearly fatal to the nation in a previous time of expansion following the Louisiana Purchase and would do so this time. With regard to mineral development, the political and legal background was ripe for a most chaotic situation, at least at the national level. The final collapse in the 1840s of the leasing system in the lead districts of the Mississippi Valley region meant that no regulations were in force to control a "mini" rush to the copper mines in the Great Lakes region. Much more significant, there were no regulations to control the first rush for precious metals on federal lands. Further, the only earlier experience with a genuine gold rush, Georgia in 1829, had involved slavery. The fact that both North and South were beginning to lose their perspective over this issue proved an additional complication to any federal policy regarding mining.

The mass of stampeders to California from the Eastern states and Europe in 1849 has obscured the fact that the first discovery at Sutter's Fort in January, 1848, provoked a local rush from California coastal areas to the gold fields before the news could leave the region. By June virtually all of the 3,000 to 4,000 persons of American background then in California were at the diggings. Most of these early miners naturally reaped more gold than the bulk of the later masses of stampeders. Further, by virtue of their early status, they established many of the legal codes subsequently used by the camps.

The miner's meeting appeared early and, as an expression of "pure democracy," wrote standing rules for mining. Many camps designated one person as the recorder of claims. Sometimes such a person also exercised judicial powers, but in other areas a jury would make legal decisions. Taking a term from California's Spanish legal tradition, the miners often called the local official the *alcalde*. In a few years, though, "justice of the peace" often replaced the Spanish equivalent. Most likely the duties were prescribed by the nature of placer mining and the presence of a mass of robust men rather than any particular national legal heritage. The meeting itself, rather than the offices it created, was the most important consideration. These meetings were the most notable examples of direct self-government in America since the New England town meetings.[1]

Unfortunately, most of the original records of the earliest local mining laws are lost. From other sources we know that the most common size of a placer claim was ten feet square. In other cases the local code simply designated the size as the area a man could cover by swinging his pick in a circle. Such a tiny size reflects growing numbers of participants, as well as obvious richness of materials and ease of removal by panning. Those first days of the rush before the advent of hoards of non-Californians caused early participants to wax nostalgic in later years. It was truly a "golden age." For the first few months crime was virtually unknown. Like all good times, that period naturally ended.[2]

The president of the United States saw fit to generate a massive rush to California. In a lengthy public message near the end of

1848, President James K. Polk openly described the gold discoveries and helped start the stampede from much of the world, partially as a justification for the recent Mexican War, partially to ensure possession. The resulting onslaught brought several new problems in dealing with California, both locally and at the national level.[3]

The newcomers of 1849 generally strengthened the character of popular democracy, within established guidelines of the previous year. A group of Oregonians proved rather influential, partly as a result of their early arrival, since they had less distance to cover. However, a case can also be made that they were "old hands" at frontier democratic experience from the "Wolf Meetings" among the settlers of the Willamette Valley a few years earlier.[4] This approach is rather fanciful, considering the relatively small number of Oregonians compared to arrivals from other regions.

Perhaps a more substantive example of the continuity of democratic participatory groups was the presence of "Mining and Trading Companies." These groups organized in the East, intending to stay together through the arduous journey and then at the mines. Some 124 such groups are definitely known to have left Boston alone during the single year of 1849, mostly by sea but some overland. There is less conclusive evidence of the presence of at least two other groups. The typical group had about 30 to 40 participants. Some groups had as few as 10, others nearly 200. Most groups, fitting the New England tradition, had a set of by-laws and met as the equivalent of a town meeting to make major decisions. The connection with subsequent miners' meetings should be obvious, though the larger populations of the camps usually absorbed these groups once they reached California.[5]

When crimes and other disputes became increasingly common as the 1840s gave way to the 1850s, the miners' meetings frequently performed judicial functions, both criminal and civil. In larger camps such meetings were impossible for any but the most important matters, so local officials accomplished these tasks. Sometimes they empaneled juries for adjudication of serious matters. The jurisdiction of some miners' meetings essentially continued for many years after California attained statehood. Hence the ideas of popularly enforced justice and trial by majority rule have become a part of frontier heritage. The background also contributed to vigilantism after duly constituted authority was present but perceived to be ineffectual. The fact that law enforcement authority combined with mining law in the miners' meeting is a testament to the impact of the participatory democracy of California. The often discussed theoretical distinction between the concepts of "democracy" and "republicanism" could be cited here. However, a more viable conclusion is simply that the differing sizes of camps, a logistic distinction, forced some to practice government by committee. In fact, California, with literally hundreds of examples, is perhaps the most conclusive proof of what might be called the "logistic explanation" that can be identified.[6]

Though the typical '49er was from a relatively humble station in life, there were numbers of more learned men in any camp. Lawyers were particularly common. It was no coincidence that California skipped the territorial stage altogether and convened a constitutional convention as early as September, 1849. The presence of lawyers in the local camps caused refinement and adjustment of the various sets of rules as even a gold rush became more institutionalized.[7]

One camp at the Forks of the Yuba was somewhat more remote than most. Consequently, the first local law appeared March 3, 1850, and is available from the diary of William Downie. Later Downie gave his name to the camp which became Downieville, California. Downie rather disgustedly noted the influence of lawyers in the writing of this code "at Mr. Kelly's cabin" where the general meeting accepted a committee report:

> First. — That ten yards be the amount of each claim, extending to the middle of the river.
> Second. — That each claim be staked, and a tool, or tools left upon it.
> Third. — That five days be allowed to prepare and occupy each claim.
> Fourth. — That none but native and naturalized citizens of the United States shall be allowed to hold claims.
> Fifth. — That the word "native" shall not include the Indians of this country.
> Sixth. — That companies damming the river, shall hold, each in-

dividual, a claim, and have a right to the bed of the river (below low-water mark) as far as it lies dry.

Seventh. — That claims be in conjunction with their dams.

Eighth. — That all matters of dispute be settled by referees.

Ninth. — That in the case of trial for crime of any kind, there shall be ten present, beside the jury and witnesses.

Tenth. — That sea-faring men in possession of American protection, shall be allowed claims.

Eleventh. — That whoever shall not be able to show his papers, shall have a fair trial.

Twelfth. — That this code of laws be in force on and after the fourth of March.

Thirteenth. — That the upper Yuba District consist of Goodyear's Bar and all above.[8]

Other local laws from this period typically called for much the same claim size, but often restricted ownership to one claim per person. Most laws were more explicit than "Forks of the Yuba" in requiring that "notices must also be posted, and stakes driven at the corners." The racial and ethnic prejudice shown in this example is actually less than many of the times. Almost all local laws had restrictions on those eligible to hold claims. Most others were more explicit in designating those considered undesirable than this camp, which specifically named Indians only. However, unlike "Forks of the Yuba," most camps allowed unnaturalized Europeans to work claims.[9]

Prejudice against Chinese was widespread, almost universal, and ultimately became a long-standing fixture in the West. Nevertheless, Chinese worked areas deemed too poor or abandoned by American and European miners. The phrase, "that's Chinamen's diggins," referred to any area that showed "poor color." Even French miners suffered in several early instances as they were driven from their claims in a number of camps. Latin Americans clearly fared better than Chinese and possibly better than the French, partly because they were more concentrated in their own district, around the appropriately named town of Sonora. A contingent of several thousand had come from the state of that name in northern Mexico. Another rather large contingent surprisingly

came to Sonora from Chile. The Chileans had mining experience in their own country and were able to join ships that docked there on the way "around the horn." The enclave of various miners of Latin American origin at the town of Sonora is particularly interesting because they organized miners' meetings, much as did the Anglo camps.[10]

The typical miner lived to work physically as much placer material as possible; there was no other way to recover gold. The camps often delegated claims on such basis. Anyone who appeared with any extra hands attached to slaves found that they were simply not allowed. Of course, few slave owners were disposed to attempt joining in a gold rush at all, much less risk their property in slaves in such a dangerous pursuit, but enough did so to find the camps' sentiment against them.

Racial and ethnic tensions were quite common in the older free states of the times, as shown by the advent of the "Know Nothing" party into the politics of the 1850s. Yet free blacks, and even most runaway slaves, apparently had a much easier time than members of other recognizable racial/ethnic groups in the goldfields. The practice of the camps moved into the state constitution. A state constitutional convention in 1850 unanimously forbade slavery but accepted free blacks, though it did debate that aspect at length. Downie reported a number of blacks working in his area, at least one of whom married and started a family. The camps had successfully excluded slaveowners along with other groups that could be openly identified by race or nationality. The slavery exclusion carried over to the state as a whole.[11] The attitude of the camps toward both federal and state policies is easy to ascertain. The preamble to the Springfield District's organic law is one of the most explicit on the matter:

> That California, is and shall be, governed by American principles; and as Congress has made no rules and regulations for the government of the mining districts of the same, and as the State legislature of California has provided by statute, and accorded to the miners of the United States, the right of making all laws, rules, and regulations that do not conflict with the constitution and laws of California, in all actions respecting mining claims; therefore we, the miners of Springfield District, do ordain and establish the following rules and regulations.[12]

Both the New England background of many of the miners in the appropriately named Springfield District, as well as the presence of the legal profession is evident. Yet the well-written code which followed this revealing preamble was voted by an 1852 miners' meeting, just as were its predecessor codes.

Implicit in the Springfield District's Preamble is the message that federal or state authority would be respected if shown. Of course actual practice might have been different, but the question had not arisen by 1852, and the miners had no expectations of any such moves by the government. There were several reasons for such marked inaction.

The leaders of the United States Army forces on the scene constituted the only semblance of federal authority in the region. Col. William R. Mason, with the aid of Lt. William T. Sherman (*the* Sherman of later Civil War fame), made a fact-finding tour in late summer, 1848. The desertion of the coastal region was striking. In the producing regions activity was already in progress on the American Fork, the South Fork, the Yuba, Feather, and Bear Rivers, and on smaller tributaries. Mason took no action at the time, presumably believing he had no authority to do so. He wrote an official report to the adjutant general in which he suggested two possible policies for federal control of the area.

One plan would have required licenses for each tract of 100

square yards for a yearly fee of 100 to 1000 dollars. A superintendent would have managed the collections. Initially, Mason personally preferred his second proposal, which would have ordered sale of the lands at auction in 20- to 40-acre blocks. This plan followed precedents of land sales by the United States prior to Preemption. Like earlier sales, it would have depended on surveys, but by that time placer gold could have well been gone. Perhaps he realized this shortcoming after more direct observation, because he later proposed that the government simply take a royalty of gold actually discovered. Again, the suggestion was for a method that had been attempted but abandoned, in this case the royalty or leasing system of the lead mines.[13]

The addition of a mass of new territory to the national domain revived a controversy which the country had previously faced but solved, at least for that time. An obscure Pennsylvania representative, David Wilmot, pushed his way into the history books in August, 1848, by proposing legislation that the new territories be free. This action antagonized the South, which had not been actively lobbying for slave status in the territories but felt compelled to defend its "peculiar institution" when challenged. Many observers were already proposing that the new territories decide the status of slavery for themselves. This concept was known as "Popular Sovereignty."

Wilmot candidly did not trust the concept, hence his proposal. He flatly stated that without clear Congressional action, "Slavery will riot in the extent of its possessions and power, and then will grow to make the South the mightiest oligarchy the world ever saw." Another representative, George Marsh of Vermont, was perhaps even more eloquent than Wilmot himself in support of the measure. Both Wilmot and Marsh questioned the argument that slavery would not adapt to the geography of the West. Marsh flatly said, "Slavery is everywhere profitable under management of a prudent master." He went on to discount economic considerations even in the freeing of slaves in colonial New England. Instead, he claimed, "Our fathers held [slavery]... contrary to the law of conscience and of God." Yet both Wilmot and Marsh explicitly denied any intent of freeing the slaves in the states where the institution already existed.[14]

Wilmot's action made many observers think they were experiencing *deja vu*. In 1820 an obscure New York representative, James Talmadge, had introduced a remarkably similar measure regarding the legality of slavery in territories then undergoing settlement. However, master politician Henry Clay of Kentucky had resolved the 1820 crisis by arranging a division of the territory in the so-called Missouri Compromise. By 1850 the Wilmot Proviso once again made this question most pertinent and possibly even more ominous than the analogous situation thirty years earlier. Now the southern states called a convention at Nashville, Tennessee, to present a united front. If the region found itself unsatisfied, the Nashville Convention could prove a tool for rapid secession.[15]

In 1850 Clay was still in Congress and still a leader. He arranged a political settlement perhaps more masterful than his own accomplishment thirty years earlier. Also lending powerful support to the settlement was Daniel Webster who was now able to reconcile his natural Northern sentiments with the need to maintain the Union. Had the South attempted secession in 1850, Northern sentiments might have been so weak that it would have simply let the South go. Even if the North had attempted military action, the region did not have the economic and demographic superiority that she would a decade later. Fortunately, North and South were generally satisfied and the Nashville Convention ended on a note of conciliation.[16]

Clay and those who followed him deserve credit for a brilliant political accomplishment that literally prevented an early Civil War. But other crucial factors in the success of the Compromises are often lost in the discussion. Five components made up the rather complex set of political deals that became the Compromise of 1850. The South obtained a stronger fugitive slave law in exchange for agreeing to end the slave trade in the District of Columbia. A secondary issue involved a boundary and debt adjustment between Texas and the United States. California entered the Union as a free state. Most optimistic toward avoiding recurrence of the problem, Congress adopted "Popular Sovereignty" regarding slavery in the New Mexico and Utah territories.[17] These last two issues had a significant impact on mining.

When Wilmot and Marsh attacked "Popular Sovereignty" in August 1848, the slow communications of the time prevented them from learning that the process was already a success. The mining camps were clearly organizing and working on that very principle. Naturally, the critics of "Popular Sovereignty" anticipated a settlement process similar to that experienced by the older states. Gold made the entire story different. Not only did California acquire a sizable population within one year of Wilmot's Proviso, the mining camps had proved themselves capable of keeping slavery out of California. And even that was not all. The mining camps themselves had gone so far as to organize a full-fledged convention to frame a state constitution which met at Monterey on September 3, 1849. California had not been through the territorial stage, so the convention did not have the customary sanction of a territorial legislature. Yet the convention had proposed a state constitution fully as democratic as any in the older states. By unanimous vote, the delegates had early dispensed with the slavery issue. The influence of the mining camps with their mass popular meetings was strongly edident.[18]

Clay praised California's proposed state constitution, including its ban on slavery, as a product of the general sentiment of the populace. Daniel Webster was even more explicit. In his March 7 speech he opened with the famous phrase, "I wish to speak today, not as a Massachusetts man, nor as a Northern man, but as an American." He then went on to note that slavery would not be viable in California or the territories for the simple reason of climate. He endorsed the admission of California as a full-fledged state despite a "degree of irregularity stamped upon her proceedings," because of most "extraordinary circumstances." The people there had spoken, first in the miners' camps, then in calling a convention from those camps, and writing a state constitution, perhaps the most popularly based in history. The people of California had exercised their "Popular Sovereignty" to write a constitution that forbade slavery. This was in marked contrast to the nation's first real gold rush in Georgia, where slavery had become a part of the process. The lesson of the mining camps and their successful control of the issue was inescapable.[19]

The same principle could apply in the territories. Utah, with its unique Mormon culture, would present no problem on that issue (though other problems were the rule). The political leaders believed that New Mexico's dry climate made her unfit for slavery. The people's own choice that had applied in California could be trusted there. (In making this judgement they overlooked the Spanish background of peonage, even in an arid region.) Overall, the principle of "Popular Sovereignty" became a guiding light in American politics. This principle would not have become so well regarded by leading figures of the 1850s without the crucial precedent of California and her mining camps. The very idea of slavery was anathema there and the miners were in a position to forbid it. Thus the power of the local people became obvious to top level policy makers.

The success of "Popular Sovereignty" in settling the slavery question in California is essential background in understanding the inaction of Congress on the other important question, the matter of ownership of the mines themselves. Once the imminent problems were settled and California was safely admitted as a free state in September 1850, Congress could look at the proposals by Army officials and others regarding the mines. Col. Mason already had proposed in broad, generalized form all three of the methods that might plausibly have been adopted in the context of the times.

California's *de facto* government had selected United States senators in December 1849, months before admission. Though perhaps unorthodox, early selection of senators was only a small part of California's unorthodox political legacy. Any state that skipped the territorial stage in government and immediately wrote a state constitution was unorthodox from its inception. The senators were controversial former Army officer John C. Frémont and flamboyant adventurer William Gwin. Frémont and Gwin had gone to Washington to await official admission of the state they were to represent. In fact, within only one year Frémont had gone from the depths of a military court-martial for mishandling orders, to begin federal authority after the defeat of Mexico in California, to election to the United States Senate. And in the interim he had made a huge gold discovery high in the mountains. Even greater acclaim awaited him in a few years.[20]

Just days after Congress formally admitted California as a state, and its new senators to their seats in September 1850, Frémont introduced a number of bills. His most interesting proposal bore the cumbersome title: "To Make Temporary Provision for the Working and Discovery of Gold Mines and Placers in California and for Preserving Order in the Gold Mine District." Frémont and Gwin claimed actual experience in California, something no other member could cite. The fact that the proposal was "temporary" undoubtedly aided it. The primary considerations were a $1.00 per month license for each miner who would be restricted to a single claim of 30 feet square. Frémont showed foresight and his own practical experience from his discovery by allowing lode mining on four-acre claims to be surveyed under orders from the Secretary of the Interior.[21]

Sen. Thomas Ewing of Ohio claimed that he supported Frémont's bill but actually had completely different purposes in mind when he suggested amendments from the floor. Ewing hoped to force all sales to the government by use of a licensing system, but had covered this motive with a diversionary discussion of claim size. Frémont saw through the amendments. He noted that Ewing's proposal had essentially been that "of old Spain... with all her laws and arbitrary powers, she was never able to make anything by that system and I do not think such a system would bring any revenue to the U.S. This plan would have the effect to make the miners hide the gold and they would never bring it forward."[22]

Missouri's legendary Thomas Hart Benton still sat in the Senate over two decades after he had arranged the government sale of lead mines in his state. Further, Benton was not above personal concern with Frémont, who was his son-in-law, and with whom he had experienced both warm and cool relations. Benton seemingly attacked both Frémont and Ewing by saying, "I am decidedly of the opinion that the United States ought not to make a revenue out of the mines; that the United States ought to content herself with getting the wealth out of the bowels of the earth itself which is now lying so useless...." Yet he concluded by endorsing Frémont's proposal simply to "preserve order." Benton figured that 100,000 permits per year at $1.00 per month would yield $1.2 million for the treasury. But that was all Benton could acknowledge as he forcefully stated, "I do not believe in nations working gold mines at all... I believe in individuals managing things of this kind, but not nations."

After Ewing admitted that his proposal would force sale of gold to the government, Benton renewed the attack. He reflected on the sale of the lead mines, which had been his pet project and which he thought a success. And "lead was a thing a man could not run away with... But gold is easily carried away, easily secreted." Also, Benton had little trust for the government agents who would purchase the gold under Ewing's proposal. The amendment went down, 24 to 12, with no discernible geographic split on the vote. Jefferson Davis of Mississippi voted along with William Seward of New York against the Ewing proposal. On most other issues of the times these two particularly were at opposite poles.[23]

Another motion from the floor had a better outcome that reflecting a growing social concern of the 1850s. Frémont's proposal limited mines to U.S. citizens. Seward, openly for equality of all in the mines, suggested broadening the permit rights to those who had declared an intent to become U.S. citizens. Several senators spoke disparagingly of Mexicans, usually in relation to the recent war and the perceived principle that the victor should take the spoils. Sen. Augustus Dodge of Iowa was perhaps most vehement in this regard. Ironically, the senators never even said the word "Chinese" on the record but only alluded to them, though in California proper they were more commonly victims of prejudice than were the Mexicans. An amendment eventually passed which allowed "persons from Europe of good character" along with American citizens into the mines, but gave no clue as to enforcement or penalties. Canadians were added in a separate motion to cover the oversight of their omission. The nativist riots against European immigrants of the mid 1850s and the emergence of a full-fledged political party on the issue were still in the future but a precursor is evident in this vote.[24]

Critics of Frémont still were not through. Senator Alpheus Felch of Michigan heartily endorsed Benton's criticisms of leasing, then went so far as to call the permits a form of leasing. Felch proposed a bill that would have essentially legalized the *status quo* with the single exception of giving the federal government a role in adjudicating between rival claimants. Felch said that his proposal was simply "to secure to everyone who takes possession of the premises the right to occupy and dig the gold till Congress shall determine otherwise." He noted that restricting mining until after survey was logistically impossible. Felch did propose larger claim sizes. Though Frémont claimed that he had been to California while Felch had not, Felch's proposal was very much like the laws that Congress would finally complete over two decades later. Indeed, the similarities are striking.[25]

For the time being, though, the Senate saw matters Frémont's way. He succeeded in adding to the bill a grant of 5% of the fees collected to the state of California. It then passed without a recorded roll call.[26]

At that time the nation had a new chief executive, the 13th, who had only been in office for a few months after the unexpected death of Zachary Taylor in July 1850. Historians have slighted Millard Fillmore in part for his 1856 campaign, on the openly nativist American party, to return to the office he had left in 1853. Even so, Fillmore signed the Acts that had made up the Compromise of 1850, while his predecessor, Zachary Taylor, had threatened to veto them.[27]

Fillmore did not pay much attention to Frémont's bill until after it passed the Senate. He was quite candid regarding his change of mind in his first State of the Union Message which went to Congress on December 10, 1850, when he stated:

> The mineral lands of California will, of course, form an exception to any general system [of land distribution] which may be adopted. Various methods of disposing of them have been suggested. I was at first inclined to favor the system of leasing, as it seemed to promise the largest revenue to the government and to afford the best security against monopolies; but further reflection and our experience in leasing the lead mines and selling lands upon credit have brought my mind to the conclusion that there would be great difficulty in collecting the rents, and that the relation of debtor and creditor, between the citizens and the Government, would be attended with many mischievous consequences. I therefore recommend that, instead of retaining the mineral lands under the permanent control of the Government, they be divided into small parcels and sold, under such restrictions, as to quantity and time, as will insure the best price, and guard most effectively against combinations of capitalists to obtain monopolies.

Fillmore also proposed creation of a new mint at San Francisco and acceptance of gold dust for payments to the government as obvious aids to the miners.[28]

When the Senate bill went to the House of Representatives the only recorded comment in the *Congressional Globe* is that it was referred to the Committee on Public Lands on January 21, 1851. The Committee never voted it out. This inaction resulted in the continued dominance of "Popular Sovereignty" in the local camps both on claims and eligibility of miners. Fillmore's ultimate opposition to the measure was probably the crucial factor. Also, Frémont left the Senate on March 3 and was no longer able to press the issue.

The fact that California was now a functioning state and took action of its own further contributed to the House's inaction, especially since states' rights was a major issue elsewhere. In early 1851 California's legislature passed an Act that formally recognized the superiority of mining camp codes to state law regarding provisions for mining claims. The precedent of this legal concession cannot be overemphasized in its long-term importance. Quite influential in the matter was Stephen J. Field, a mining camp attorney about whom more will be discussed in Chapter 9. Fillmore alluded to this legal point in his second State of the Union Message the next year when he backed off his earlier proposal and simply chose no action at all.[29]

The fact that local codes were legally superior should not imply that the state government had defaulted on involvement in mining. The contrary was true. A functioning state government now provided courts, recorders, and other officials to enforce the local codes in appropriate areas. Hence the miners' meetings and the offices they had created fell out of use as soon as state government could make its presence effective in a particular area. Generally retention of the camps' codes meant that they would stand up in court for claims filed under them, thus creating a so called "grandfathered" right. State laws included provisions for claims that were required outside of organized districts; these became more important as older areas were worked out and the claims abandoned.

With the pigeonholing of Frémont's bill by the House, Congress took only one important action that directly involved the rush. Fillmore's proposal for a new branch mint at San Francisco finally reached fulfillment in 1854.[30]

Perhaps the *laissez-faire* policy toward mining law was best from a practical standpoint at that time and in that region. Enforcement of any direct action on the miners would have been virtually impossible during the rush stage. Official U.S. Census takers could not even count them all in 1850! Efficient enforcement of monthly mining license fees would have been far more difficult. The State's official population was 92,000 that year, but a state census in 1852 found 255,000. Even the latter figure is probably incomplete.[31] The 1850 Census does deserve credit for one thing. It proved that California had many more residents than the traditional minimum of 60,000 for a new state. Hence the decennial count, coming fortuitously in mid-1850, greatly aided Congress in admitting the state and thus negotiating the celebrated Compromise.

Mining camps numbered in the hundreds, ranging in size from those of a few dozen participants to several camps that counted workers in the thousands. By the 1850s there was also a mass of camp followers, male and female. Every camp had its local law. A sizable army could not have controlled such a situation, and any money raised by leases or concessions would not have begun to defray the expenses, which would have been massive. Further, numerous other experiences with armies in mineral locales have shown repeatedly that the lure of gold overcomes all loyalties among soldiers of all nations. By contrast the Army only had to contend with 4,200 lead miners in the Galena district of the 1820s and these had drifted into the area over a four-year period.

Fillmore's proposal for sales would have taken so long for surveys that the placer gold would have been mined out long before sales could take place. Perhaps he realized this by the time of his second message. Even so, his first statement in the 1850 State of the Union sounds ominously prophetic regarding lode mining, but that stage in development would not come for a decade. In the interim, while Frémont's permit system might have raised some money for the government, despite natural uneven enforcement, it also would have had the net effect of causing earlier abandonment of worked over claims.

California's mining camp democracy had impressed such statesmen as Clay and Webster both on its own merits and by its quick, automatic, almost accidental solution to the problem of slavery in the territories. Undoubtedly, the success of California was a primary factor in Congress's decision to use the principle of Popular

Sovereignty regarding the New Mexico and Utah Territories. In 1850 Clay and Webster were still very much in charge of Congress and the Compromise that year is a massive testament to that fact. But both were elderly and passed from the scene in 1852. Ostensibly this should have made little difference. For some years Sen. Stephen A. Douglas of Illinois had been essentially an "understudy" of Clay in balancing sectional interests in Congress, most notably as Clay's chief lieutenant in the Compromise of 1850. In fact, Douglas had completed some of the more complex negotiations when Clay had essentially given up. This relation is even more remarkable considering that Clay was a Whig and Douglas a Democrat, a partisan split quite great on other contemporary issues. Douglas, however, later grossly mishandled the role he had inherited when he became too enamored of the success of "Popular Sovereignty."[32]

In 1854, Douglas sponsored the Kansas-Nebraska bill that actually repealed the earlier accomplishment of his mentor, Clay. Clay's 1820 Act had succeeded in dividing the territory acquired in the Louisiana Purchase, with the portion north of the line 36 degrees, 30 minutes becoming free, the portion south of the line slave. With the creation of territorial governments in Kansas and Nebraska, north of the line, Douglas took a bold risk. His bill opened both territories to slavery contingent on the will of local residents: "Popular Sovereignty." Douglas believed that nature itself precluded slavery in the region and that the northern settlers who would surely move there would ratify nature's decision. Instead, the result of the Kansas-Nebraska Act was tragedy.[33]

The South recognized a golden opportunity to acquire an additional slave state, with congressional representation, even if few slaves would actually live there. So she sent settlers with the intent to exert "Popular Sovereignty" for slavery despite the natural environment. The North responded and sent her own settlers plus armaments. The result was a frontier civil war, "bleeding Kansas," which became a rehearsal for the full scale Civil War of the next decade. Douglas admitted that his pet idea had produced the very result he was attempting to avoid, but it was too late. The Kansas-Nebraska Act was one of the key elements in a tragic chain of events through the 1850s that could have been avoided but that created the climate that led to secession and war in 1860–1861.[34]

The reasons for Douglas's Kansas-Nebraska Act have long been an important topic for historical discussion. The irony of the situation is fitting for Greek tragedy. The leading senator who should have been the successor to the Great Compromiser, Henry Clay, inadvertently helped to provoke the very conflict he sought to avoid. Ostensibly, Douglas was hoping to attract some Southern support for his future candidacy for the presidency. He thought the Act would be a symbol only, but Southerners took the opportunity seriously. Some historians have also tried to claim that Douglas's personal land holdings were involved.[35]

Some evidence exists that Douglas had no ulterior motives at all, that he actually trusted the idea of "Popular Sovereignty." The California experience, and the credit that the legendary figures of Clay and Webster had given it in Utah and New Mexico, weighed heavily with Stephen A. Douglas. Further, he could see for himself the positive results of mining camp democracies in California. As the Crisis of 1850 was developing, Douglas wrote a personal letter to Charles H. Lanphier and George Walker, stating that they should destroy the letter after reading. Hence the modern scholar has a powerful testament to the value of the document as reflecting Douglas's genuine sentiments. There can be little doubt as to the meaning of this passage:

> My impression is that we will all be together in favor of the admission of California as a State. I started the proposition at the beginning of last Session & then predicted that the people would decide against slavery if left to settle the question for themselves. The result has verified the prediction. Gen'l Cass expressed the same opinion I believe in his Nicholson Letter & the whole Democratic Party of the North took the same ground. The free-soilers declared that slavery would go there unless Congress prohibited it. The result has shown that we were right & they were wrong. They now have come to the support of our measure. Gen'l Cass will take strong ground in favor of the State admission of California & the Whigs & abolitions will be compelled to follow suit. The people should not be allowed to forget these things. I am glad to see that you frequently remind the people of them.[36]

Douglas's reference to Gen. Cass's letter to A.O.P. Nicholson is significant for that was perhaps the first suggestion by an important official of the plausibility of "Popular Sovereignty." Cass, a presidential candidate in 1848, had proposed the method but that was before California proved the viability of the concept. Now there was clear evidence of its success.[37]

Douglas's affinity for "Popular Sovereignty," quite evident as early as January 1850 in the Lanphier/Walker letter, probably owed much to the example of the mining camps. Initial approval of the Kansas-Nebraska Act, though most commonly associated with Douglas, also showed acceptance of "Popular Sovereignty" by a large portion of the public as well as the political leadership. Though the ultimate result was tragic, several years of positive news had encouraged the concept.

When the *New York Times* first initiated its presses in September 1851, the California gold rush was still a leading story. At the same time, the *Times* also reported a new gold rush across the Pacific in distant Australia. Several of the early discoverers, including Edward Hargreaves, the best known, had experience in 1849 California. But American influences soon emerged that were far greater than that. On October 17, the Times reprinted an article from the *London Daily Post* that led off with the headline "America Monopolizes a British Territory with Steamers from San Francisco." The text of the article included the statement that Australian "loyalty is already shaken," because

> [a] stream of republican immigration from the impurest sources in the New World will materially tend to strengthen disaffection and to loosen the bonds between the colonists and the parent state.

It was true that mining camps convened to make local regulations in Australia, much as they had in California. Any knowledgeable person of the times could see the powerful implications of these events. The practices of mining camp democracy and "Popular Sovereignty" were crossing the largest ocean and carrying American institutions to a new continent with another culture. Many publications in addition to the *Times* carried similar stories. Hence Australia's experience undoubtedly contributed to the growing allure of "Popular Sovereignty" as a solution for domestic issues as well. The inaction of the House on the Fremont Bill is probably directly related to this growing proof of the power of Popular Sovereignty in 1851.[38]

Australian authorities attempted no regulation of mines other than a license fee. Fremont should have felt some vindication from that nation's adoption of the same system he had moved through the Senate, only to lose in the House. The fact that the Australians did that much can be attributed to the geographic locale of their rush. The centers of government and population were much closer to the "diggings" in Australia than in the United States.[39]

The *Times* issues of September 20 and 21, 1851, had a combination of stories on their total of eight pages that reveal the linkage of several different themes. Douglas's speech at the New York State Fair drew full coverage. Other items included discussions of slavery and the fact that the typical Northerner clearly was not an abolitionist. Also evident were indications of the rising tide of nativism. Most important, though, the public and political leadership could read about the success of the California gold rush, see its impact even in Australia, and see one of its leading principles as a partial solution to the other dominant problem confronting the nation.[40]

Popular Sovereignty was a proven concept, under the right conditions. The primary miscalculation was in revoking a long-standing precedent of a particular area as free territory. That was the case with "Bleeding Kansas." In areas where no precedent existed, the concept worked well. Unfortunately Douglas and the nation, found out the difference the hard way. Proof that "Popular Sovereignty" could and did function was in the mining camps. Hence it was an important but generally overlooked reason for Congress's surprising silence on the matter of ownership of minerals. Douglas and those who supported "Popular Sovereignty" were loath to tamper with the outstanding example of the success of the concept the local miners' laws providing for ownership.

Yet "Popular Sovereignty" became a negative concept in the North with the experience of "Bleeding Kansas." Ironically, the 1856 nomination of the new Republican Party went to John C. Frémont, who had seen it function in California, and even owed his Senate seat to its application, but now opposed it after the Kansas experience. Frémont's mining bill of 1850 may have been more important politically than often realized since he had advocated some federal control rather than complete freedom for the miners. A *laissez-faire* position on his part might have been a problem for him when he ran for president. Though Frémont, a Southerner who got almost entirely Northern votes, lost to James Buchanan, a Northerner with strong Southern support, his candidacy alone proved a capstone to the vindication following his Army court-martial.[41]

Douglas's adherence to "Popular Sovereignty" is remarkable especially after the election of 1856. But he did not give up on a variation of the concept when it arose again in the famous debates with Abraham Lincoln in 1858 that captured nationwide publicity. By this date the problem was even more complex as the result of the Supreme Court decision in the case of *Dred Scott vs. Sanford*. The court had ruled slavery legal in all territories prior to full statehood, regardless of any action Congress might take. Presumably "Popular Sovereignty" was also a victim of the Court. Yet Douglas claimed that the principle was still viable because a locality could permit slavery only by enforcing local law and regulations for its maintenance. The seeds of this view are evident in the Walker/Lanphier Letter of early 1850. Douglas adjusted "Popular Sovereignty" to the legal climate in a speech at Freeport, Illinois, so the revised approach is known as the "Freeport Doctrine." Espousal of the "Freeport Doctrine" cost him Southern support in the Presidential contest of 1860, and hence the presidency itself. However, the "Freeport Doctrine" helped ensure that Congress would maintain *laissez faire* toward mining first by taking no action at all for several years, then by writing legislation that simply endorsed that policy.[42]

The California rush and the tumultuous decade of the 1850s provide several pieces of evidence for the validity of the Turner/Webb school. Mining camp democracy did have an important effect on national politics, both regarding the question of ownership of the mines and the use and misuse of the political concept of "Popular Sovereignty" in addressing the crucial question of the expansion of slavery. Also, the spread of mining camp democracy to a distant continent gives further support to the large scale frontier thesis as expounded particularly by Webb in *The Great Frontier*.

An interesting historical footnote to the topic of 1850s California is seen in the case of Stephen J. Field, who had motivated the first legislature to make mining district law superior to state law. Field, appointed to the State Supreme Court, decided in one case that a large private holding was not open to any other parties for mining. The particular holding belonged to John C. Frémont. Early California was like that, a giant "small town" of people who knew each other personally.[43]

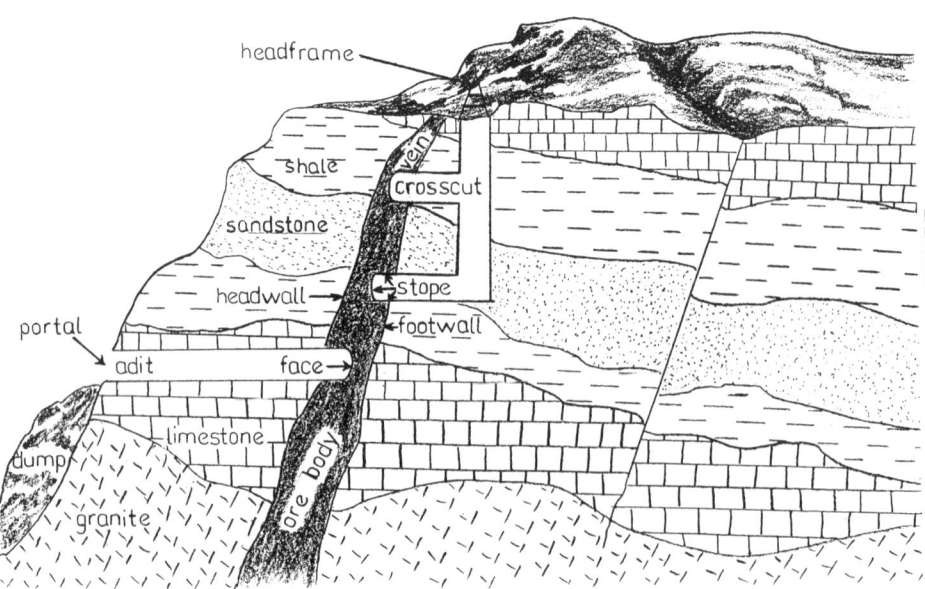

Various parts of underground mines have special names.
(Drawing by Connie Miller)

Chapter Three

New Rushes, New Land Policies, and a Civil War

> NOTICE
>
> We the undersigned claim three claims, of three hundred feet each (and one for discovery), on this silver-bearing quartz lead or lode, extending north and south from this notice, with all its dips, spurs, and angles, variations, and sinuosities, together with fifty feet of ground on either side for working the same.
>
> As Mark Twain reported posting it for himself and his partners in *Roughing It*.[1]

Mark Twain's humor hides a considerable amount of useful historical data in his classic account of his days in the West. The very nature of the notice he posted shows a different type of mining from that of the 49ers. Implicit in the more detailed description of the claim itself is a more complex geology, a more complex and costly mining process, and more complex legal considerations. By the time Twain reached Nevada in 1862, new mining rushes had occurred there and in Colorado. He simply could not resist the lure of riches and adventure:

> By and by I was smitten with the silver fever. Prospecting parties were leaving for the mountains every day and taking possession of rich silver-bearing ledges and lodes of quartz. Clearly, this was the road to fortune.[2]

This activity was aimed at lode rather than placer materials. Technical discussions of the differences could cover many volumes but Mark Twain summed it up in his characteristic style as he described his own party's prospecting:

> We never touched our tunnel or our shaft again. Why? Because we judged that we had learned the real secret of success in silver mining—which was, not to mine the silver ourselves, by the sweat of our brows and the labor of our hands, but to sell the ledges to the dull slaves of toil and let them do the mining.[3]

Heavy capital and a skilled labor force were required for much lode mining, but the discoverer of a lode of high value could do well. These facts account for much of Nevada's unique character since, from the start, she was almost entirely a product of lode mines. By the mid 1850s a few veterans of California had moved to the area that became Virginia City. They found random bits of placer gold, but it was often in the presence of "that damned blue stuff" that interfered with sluices and even panning. The "blue stuff" was silver ore from the Comstock and other lodes and eventual recognition of this fact led to the first lode rush in 1859.

At exactly the same time as California veterans were going to Nevada, the region that would become Colorado was attracting a mass of Midwesterners to the area then called "the Pikes Peak region." Colorado's rush followed a series of placer finds, some quite significant. Again miners with Georgia experience made several of the initial discoveries. Unlike California, Colorado's placer areas were not enough to support the stampeders fleeing the depressed economy after the panic of 1857.[4]

Thousands had gone overland with the slogan painted on their wagons, "Pikes Peak or Bust." Within a few months a large number returned with the added phrase, "Busted by God!" The relatively short distance to return possibly encouraged the process, in contrast to California where commitment was less reversible. Some estimates are that 100,000 made the trek in 1859 while the official Territorial Census of 1861 showed only 25,000 still remaining, though that figure was probably an under count, as with all census figures from highly transient areas. Lode discoveries eventually made Colorado a leading mining state anyway.[5]

New Rushes, New Land Policies, and a Civil War 45

By the late 1850s traditional placering was dying in California but powerful pumps were making hydraulic mining an important aspect of the scene. This region of California was the only locale having enough river water with fine gold in sands to make feasible such early hydraulic mining. This technique probably recovered as much gold as traditional placering but with far fewer participants.[6]

Also by the late 1850s several major underground mines were operating in the northern part of California's mother lode. Grass Valley had the largest number of early lode mines but Nevada City also was an important center. Small lode mines were scattered throughout the region. A series of attempts at lode mining in the early 1850s had been technical failures. Ultimately the expensive early experiments led to enough knowledge to provide some success by the end of the decade. Cornish crews, the acknowledged masters in such undertakings, soon made Grass Valley a noted Cornish center. Even so, estimates are that only one percent of gold production had been from lodes by 1860, although this figure would change markedly in a few years.[7]

The first lode laws of the areas that became Colorado and Nevada reflected the authority of the mining camp yet with far more complex legal and technical considerations than the 49ers had dreamed possible. Mining camp law emerged because both Nevada and Colorado were theoretically parts of larger entities with distant centers of government. "Nevada" was part of Utah Territory with government at Salt Lake City, while the early mines of "Colorado" were part of Kansas Territory with government in the eastern part of what is now that state. Authorities in Utah and Kansas had no experience in mining but, ironically, both regions had been embroiled in major local disputes in the 1850s. Utah had faced outright invasion by a U.S. military force over the polygamy question, while Kansas had suffered frontier civil war over slavery expansion.

The mining communities in what would become both states successfully lobbied for creation of separate territories. Congress granted Colorado's request on February 28, 1861, and Nevada's two days later. Subsequently, legislation to give both territories full statehood moved together through Congress with identical wording. Yet in many respects they were far from "twins."[8]

Nevada's celebrated Comstock Lode was so geologically confined that only two sets of local laws covered the entire deposit: those of Gold Hill and Virginia City. Several more remote Nevada districts were important, including the Esmeralda District centered at the town of Aurora near the California state line southwest of Virginia City. It was here that Mark Twain made the claim quoted above, and that Twain and two partners found a so-called "blind lead," a vein with no surface outcrop. Under local laws it could be claimed by its discoverers regardless of surroundings. Each partner believed that the others were taking the required actions to establish the claim within a ten-day legal limit. Each one, unknown to the others, had left the area on various errands. Hence an opportunity for great wealth was lost. Obviously, conformance with local laws could be crucial. (Perhaps it was just as well, since a wealthy young Twain might never have developed his storytelling.) Many other early Nevada districts vanished overnight as discoveries proved marginal but the rules of the major camps created enough examples such as Twain's forfeited "blind lead."[9]

Gold Hill, the very first on the Comstock (or Washoe) Lode, was possibly the most informal camp ever organized, since it originated from expectations of placer in early 1859. The customs of placer mining simply were inadequate when the potential of the discovery made by Henry Comstock and his partners of June 12 or 13 materialized. Unfortunately, Mark Twain himself did not describe the legal situation of early Gold Hill. A contemporary, also expert at humorous historical accounts, did fill that gap: William Wright, a young reporter for Virginia City's *Territorial Enterprise* along with Samuel Clemens. While Clemens adopted the pen name of Mark Twain, Wright used the name Dan DeQuille. In *History of the Big Bonanza; an Account...of the World Renowned Comstock Silver Lode of Nevada*, DeQuille did not spring outright tall tales, as he sometimes did on the paper, but he did make the most of anything having factual basis:

> V. A. Houseworth, the "village blacksmith," was the first Recorder at Gold Hill, and the book of records was kept at a saloon where it lay upon a shelf behind the bar. The "boys" were in the habit of taking it from behind the bar whenever they desired to consult it, and if they thought a location made by them was not advantageously bounded, they altered the course of their lines

Mining laws require a monument at the point of discovery and at the corners of claims. In arid country these are of stone but wooden posts are preferable when available. (Courtesy Arizona Historical Society)

and fixed the whole thing up in good shape, in accordance with the latest developments.

When the book was not wanted for this use, those lounging about the saloon were in the habit of snatching it up and "batting" each other over the head with it. The old book is now in the office of the County Recorder in Virginia City, and is beginning to be regarded as quite a curiosity. It shows altered dates, places where leaves have been torn out, and much other rough usage.

DeQuille noted that even unaltered descriptions were often so lacking in detail as to be useless.[10]

The actual code of Gold Hill was little better since it had been written by Californians from placer mines. The first five sections composed a basic criminal code, including mandatory hanging for murder. Another section forbade Chinese to own claims, though Mexicans were not restricted. In fact, Gabriel Maldarardo (sic) worked part of the best outcrop on the Comstock with the primitive methods still used in Mexico. The most important sections concerned spatial designation of claims on veins or lodes. First was a restriction as to the length of an exposed vein that could be claimed at 150 feet per claimant, with a double share for the initial discoverers of the Gold Hill Mining District (identified as "E. Belcher, H. Comstock, and G.W. Aurgin & Co."). However, the vein varied greatly by width; at some points it was fully 1000 feet wide, yet the claimant got the whole thing plus 50 feet working room on each side. Neighboring claimants might be entitled to far less with yet more confusion as to claim dimensions. In the Virginia District, just up the Comstock lode, the length that could be claimed along the lode was 300 feet. By coincidence, this ore was generally richer as well as being divided among a smaller number of mines.[11]

As if width were not problem enough, the ultimate in trouble resulted from rules allowing the legitimate claimant of a vein's surface outcrop to follow it below the surface indefinitely. It was this provision, rather casually adopted at miners' meetings, that prompted Mark Twain and other lode claimants to insert that part of the typical Notice stating "with all its dips, spurs, and angles, variations, and sinuosities."

The district codes at Gold Hill, Virginia City, and Aurora constituted early versions of what became famous (many would later say "infamous") as the "apex rule." The legitimate claimant of the highest point or "apex" of exposure of a lode or vein got the whole thing, regardless of its extent underground. Some precedents for the "apex rule" existed in European tradition, and historical debate long ensued as to the importance of these precedents on the laws in mining camps. Herbert Hoover, well-known in his early career as an authority on mining engineering but also on mining history, noted various possible British sources of the "apex rule." He found other sources, however, which led him to believe the rule had come directly from German mining areas.[12]

Yet alternative interpretations are quite viable. Spanish laws contrasted markedly in limiting underground extent of claims to the downward extension of surface boundaries — the opposite of the "apex rule." Further, geologists of any period would stress the myriad forms veins may take and see the obvious invitation of

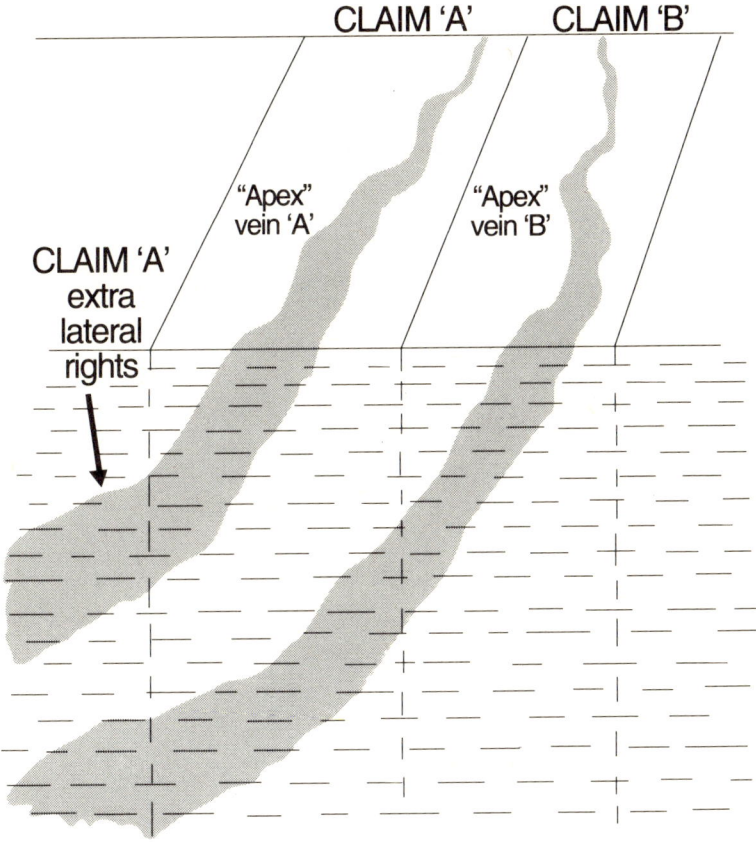

The "Apex Rule." The owner of claim A may follow vein A as far as he wants underground, even if it dips beyond the lateral limits of his claim on the surface. He has this right by controlling the "Apex," or highest point. This is also called extralateral rights. However, claimant A has no rights to vein B, even though it passes under his surface. In countries with Spanish legal background, there are no extralateral rights.

legal problems. Hubert H. Bancroft, the most famous early historian of the West, was closer to the general sentiment of the times than Hoover. The miners, according to Bancroft, felt that construction of workings at the top of the apex was sufficient justification to allow the claim to extend beyond surface limits if the vein went in another direction. The expense of headframes and other workings was enough to warrant legal adjustment to avoid their duplication. The "apex rule" might create other problems, but the frontier mind saw some very practical considerations for adopting it in the first place.[13]

When Congress finally did write comprehensive mining legislation, as described in Chapter 4, the "apex rule" became an integral part of the Acts. Historians of the matter who have tried to trace its legal heritage to Europe overlook the contribution of hundreds of mining camps that wrestled with the problem for years before Congress finally acted. The pioneers, faced repeatedly with the same problem, found there was no unorthodox solution to a matter of practical necessity. They had to "reinvent the wheel" many times but found there was no real substitute. This experience is the most important explanation of the "apex rule."

The Comstock Lode, by its very geologic nature, combined with the "apex rule" and the paucity of early records, was the "mother lode" for lawyers. The earliest, most poorly recorded claims were those at the "apex" of what might be construed as a massive vein that dipped underground for thousands of feet. It did not matter that more accurate records existed for newer claims or that federal officials and territorial government arrived in 1861. The really important claims were the earliest, which had "grandfathered" rights even under the inadequate rules in force at the time of filing. Yet several of the legal principles were not well enough documented to dissuade claimants of lands above the underground portion from fighting in court for a portion of the Comstock Lode. "Dips, spurs, and angles, variations, and sinuosities" complicated matters by providing an endless array of legal possibilities regarding rival claimants.

Only two of the original claimants held on long enough to become wealthy. The rest, like illiterate Henry Comstock himself, sold out cheaply. When capital moved in so did the best lawyers. It took a mass of lawsuits to yield, finally, a legal determination that the entire Comstock was a single lode. Hence the major mines at the outcrop had legal control to any depth. This fact plus the presence of rich zones alternating with relatively poor ones as ultimately worked to a depth of 2000 feet gave the same mines relatively long lives but with a "feast and famine" history. There would be lulls followed by renewals from the 1860s to the 1880s.[14]

The undisputed figure in finally resolving the incredible legal jumble of the Comstock was Attorney William H. Stewart. A Yale alumnus, Stewart had come to California on graduation and acquired several years of experience there. He was a fitting addition to the area that Mark Twain and Dan DeQuille bitingly chronicled. As it turned out, he purchased the *Virginia Territorial Enterprise* that employed both of them. Stewart is sometimes credited — or blamed — for forcing the resignation of the lone federal magistrate in the Comstock area in early 1861. In fairness, it should be noted that the political situation at the time involved the change from Utah Territory to Nevada Territory, a change from Democratic to Republican control in Washington, and the start of armed conflict in the East. Stewart's role was probably only contributory since there was much distrust of the particular magistrate that Utah sent to a mining region. However, Stewart won a mass of court cases, and massive fees, for the owners of what had been the original claims. By the time Stewart was through, the "apex rule" was gospel in Nevada.

Costs of lawsuits alone ran far into the millions but the Comstock was so rich that a number of family fortunes originated from it, despite the legal outlays. George Hearst founded the fortune inherited by his son of newspaper fame, William Randolph Hearst, on the Gould and Curry mine. Other great producers included the Hale and Norcross, the Savage, the Yellow Jacket, the Mexican, the Consolidated Virginia, the Potosi, which took its name from the richest mine in Latin American history, and the Ophir, which had a Biblical name. These mines were independent of each other, hence competitors, through most of the 1860s. Ultimately the Bank of California would dominate most Comstock mining. In fact, San Francisco subsequently owed more to Nevada in providing capital than it did to California. The situation would have been much different without the "apex rule."[15]

Stewart's success made him a leading figure in Nevada, though

he lost a major early start when his own mine was flooded to a cost of $1.5 million. Stewart worked even harder at his best calling, the law. His *Territorial Enterprise* forced yet other resignations of territorial judges in 1864, just as some of Stewart's lawsuits posed trouble, but again, the process of full statehood was also a factor. Stewart felt that he could take such action after the *Territorial Enterprise* collected 4000 signatures on petitions for the judges' resignations.[16] Judges realized that change in territorial status would soon affect their tenure. Regardless of prior involvement, Stewart would not be around to argue the cases before the new state courts anyway. He became Nevada's first United States senator in November 1864. In the halls of Congress he would play further important roles regarding mining.[17]

New Rushes, New Land Policies, and a Civil War 53

Stewart might be regarded as having made only one mistake. He supported a wage cut for the miners from $4.00 to $3.50 per day during an economic slump in 1864. These wages, quite high by contemporary national standards, show the wealth of the Comstock. A group of miners almost attacked him, but he reversed his stance and, within a matter of hours, convinced mine owners to restore the $4.00 wage. The incident was soon forgotten with returning prosperity and the drive for statehood, and Stewart won his Senate seat while drawing massive popular support on the matter of territorial judges.[18]

Incidents of mine salting and other scams seemed to fit Nevada's early character, though con artists still perpetrate such tricks throughout the West. Mark Twain provided the lurid details of the most common salting technique used to make a worthless property appear to have ore. In this notorious case, the perpetrator filed large silver coins into fragments, which he placed in the bottom of a mine shaft. Stock prices for the property rose dramatically until one piece of "ore" revealed the lettering "ted States of." Naturally, that stock collapsed, but salting simply became more sophisticated. A better trick was just to put filings from gold coins into shotgun shells, then fire at the supposed lode. Many inexperienced buyers believed quartz veins could carry naturally occurring ore in this manner.[19]

Unlike original records of most early California camps, which are lost to historians, Colorado's first mining camps laws are readily available. In 1859–61 the area around Central City that would become Gilpin County had nineteen districts. Others were present in the area around Georgetown that would become adjacent Clear Creek County and the massive California gulch placer area in what would become Lake County. California gulch would repeat the Comstock experience in which "that dammed blue stuff" again clogged gold pans and sluice boxes. A decade later the silver camp of Leadville would nearly equal Virginia City. In the meantime, though, placering there was far more important than it had been in Nevada.

Colorado's first local codes proved quite important for several reasons. One of the Georgians who had found success to the tune of $21,000 in 1858 was John H. Gregory. Hence Gregory Diggings, just east of the future site of Central City, acquired both its geographical and legal titles. There the "first mass meeting ever held in the Rocky Mountains" convened on June 8, 1859. Contemporary estimates of the crowd ranged from 2,000 to 3,000, virtually all of whom had arrived within the prior six weeks. A special traveller in the region gave the first speech. It was none other than Horace Greeley, the famed newspaper editor and later presidential candidate to whom is attributed the phrase, "Go West Young Man."

After further speeches, the meeting turned to its real business: writing a code. However, the eleven sections of the Laws and Regulations of the Gregory District lasted less than six weeks. On July 16 a second meeting wrote a New Code because the Committee on Codification had encountered many unforeseen circumstances. The New Code did not replace the Original Code but was an addition to it. The distinction is quite obvious. The Original Code could have been taken from California a decade earlier; it covered only placer mining. The New Code, of twenty-two more sections, addressed "Tunneling for discovery." In addition, the miners in writing the New Code also created official elected positions of a "President, a Recorder of Claims, and a Sheriff for the term of one year" as well as legal processes for adjudicating disputes.[20]

Yet even the New Code was not enough for the problems that arose with lode mining at Gregory Diggings. From February 18 to 20, 1860, the miners met again. The poor grammar and spelling of "M. Storms, Secty.," do not hide the fact that a set of legal regulations was emerging that was as sophisticated and detailed as any found in local or municipal government in the East. Further provisions in this set of codes regarded claims for "Quarts Mill" [sic] which could be "Two Hundred and fifty feet Squair" [sic]. Lode claims could run "the entire distance... for discovery purposes." Another provision of the lengthy additions stated that "the rules of Evidence as admitted in the Courts of the United States shall be adhered to and observed in the Miners Court." Clearly the legal profession had made its presence felt even at this date.[21]

The revisions of February 1860 were still not enough to meet contingencies. Subsequent meetings addressed such issues as inheritance of claims, and damages done to several mines by the Consolidated Ditch Company. This latter case is most important in demonstrating the legal power that the miner's meeting had over any particular operation, no matter how wealthy, that created problems for others.[22]

The natural unity provided by the miners' meeting is also demonstrated by some of the earliest actions of the Russell District, also named for a Georgian who made his strike a few miles from Gregory. Its first mass meeting was held on June 18, 1859, exactly ten days after that of the Gregory District, and produced a brief set of placer regulations. By October, though, the meeting had encountered enough problems from lode mines that it added a set of rules in that regard. At the same time the miners had encountered what they believed to be price gouging from the merchants of Denver and Auraria, and "[would] not submit to their dictation." So they resolved a mass boycott and fair exchange of gold dust at a rate of at least sixteen dollars per ounce. The natural strength of a unified miners' meeting was thus demonstrated.[23]

Russell District paralleled its neighbor's experience in soon writing a much more complex code but it waited long enough to get some ideas from other areas. Consequently, the code of July 28, 1860, was quite comprehensive, with a total of 75 sections showing obvious legal talent. There is no subsequent record of the mass meeting. Again, rules of evidence in United States courts applied. Detailed provisions for lodes included, in Section 63, the right of the holder of a first discovery to work across the vein of the second discovery in cases where veins cross. Another important point, in Section 64, was that "mining claims shall take precedence of all others, provided they are first recorded. No other claims shall interfere with said mining claims...." Finally, Section 67 clearly reveals the sense of equality and opportunity that many camps showed in practice: "Females shall have the same rights as males. Youths under the age of ten years shall not be allowed to hold claims."[24]

The only other district to hold an initial meeting before July 1860, when Gregory and Russell had perfected codes, was the Bay State District. The pattern here was much the same until August 6, 1861, when the meeting adopted the Gregory Laws. The same M. Storms who misspelled much of Gregory's record did the same in transferring that record to the Bay State District. Other meetings had the advantage of seeing the experience of the older ones; hence their codes were more comprehensive from the start. Most produced what were ostensibly their own codes but a few simply adopted the laws of other districts just as Bay State had finally done.[25]

A scattering of items from the later codes of Gilpin County reveal some interesting information. One large meeting, Independent District, adopted much of Gregory's law, then Cooper's District copied Independent District. Obviously a District could pull together items from others that it liked. Perhaps Cooper's District found that Independent's ban on lawyers was to its credit. Interestingly, most camps encouraged the profession but these did not. Independent District also banned "gambling houses and houses of ill-fame," a provision that Cooper's followed. Inappropriately named Nevada District had its own ban on such activities but none of the others chose to do so. Perhaps Independent District thought itself in a superior position to be rid of lawyers, prostitutes, and bartenders, but one did not have to go far to find all three. Some of the codes also contained the rudiments of criminal law but in these matters existing territorial law theoretically took precedence.[26]

Still other interesting points are found in a "press release" by the Central District that the *Rocky Mountain News* carried December 18, 1860. Unfortunately, this is one of the two districts for which the actual code is lost, but the article suggests important provisions. The miners had made an obvious attempt to become a "respectable" community by voting dry. The Central District even devised a unique mining version of the long-standing reservation of section 16 in the older states for school support. Where minerals replaced crops there was a reservation of "one claim on each lode for a school fund." These and other similar measures stemmed from an overall philosophy that the meeting clearly summarized: "We invite, and welcome to our midst, every one who comes here to get a living honestly. We shall be glad to have men with capital and machinery come among us, and equally glad to have the laborer here; but horsethieves, gamblers, grog-sellers, and blacklegs, will not find it a desirable locality to settle in." The Victorian philosophy at its highest is evident. Also prominent is a recognition of the value of both capital and labor for success at mining; this was simple frontier pragmatism.[27]

Of necessity, the various local camps wrote regulations that addressed both lode and placer claims. Colorado's first lode miners recovered only gold, hence Nevada was the early silver center, a fact that would be of some political importance. It is quite interesting that several of the very earliest Colorado mining camps did not include the "apex rule" for lode claims, but simply gave a surface limit, just as with placer. Without the massive example of the Comstock, and using simple, primitive equipment and no capital, these camps did not find the structural reasons for the "apex rule" immediately apparent. Within a short time, though, this had changed. Miners' meetings and the Territorial Assembly found it useful to add the "apex rule" within a few years. The records showing this change provide further evidence that the "apex rule" was not based on European legal tradition but was a forced reconsideration of an inescapable physical problem. The fact that most districts chose to adopt it, despite other difficulties, shows the consideration of the shaft and other equipment. Yet other districts chose the alternate. Undoubtedly, miners in Europe in the Medieval and early modern historical periods had faced similar considerations. They had made one choice in Spain, with governmental endorsement, but the opposite in the northern European mining regions.

For a time many residents of what became Colorado called themselves the "Territory of Jefferson." Regardless of name, they just wanted independence from Kansas. After Congress created the Territory in 1861, the legislature could enact various laws of its own regarding mining. Hence local codes in what became Gilpin County do not date after that time because the situation paralleled California's creation of state government exactly a decade earlier. The new government recognized existing codes but provided courts, recorders, and other machinery for their enforcement. It ordered these codes safely preserved in respective county courthouses. It provided a very well-written generalized system of statewide lode laws for areas outside organized districts. The legislature could, and did, frequently review and revise the laws. By 1864 it had designated lode claims as 1400 feet on a vein. It even went so far as to designate a portion of every vein as reserved to the state for school support and for health care. The influence of some of the early local codes is evident. Overall, the legislature's various enactments constituted a definite "freezing" effect of the local codes in the older areas.[28]

Miners' meetings were not dead, though. In new rush locales, the miners again devised local codes and even adjudicated many disputes before territorial officials arrived. The camp of Fairplay, according to some sources, adopted the name after its discovery by those forced out of a nearby camp that had large claim sizes. The Fairplay crowd decided to let all come on even if smaller claims were needed. (Other sources, though, attribute the name to a pledge for honest card games in the town.) Thus Colorado provides a marked contrast with Nevada in adjustment in territorial status. Somehow its records were much better preserved and its early mine legislation statesmanlike, whether by camp or by first legislature. Nevada had legally emerged from Utah Territory, quite painfully, and would have a similar experience on attaining full statehood, as shown by the treatment of the old jurisdictions' judges at both occasions. Colorado's separation from Kansas went much more smoothly.[29]

Early Colorado mines, placer and lode, produced only gold. Silver veins, with only one exception, were known but seemed cruelly tantalizing to the miners since they were technically unworkable with milling processes then available. Scientific knowhow would remain elusive until the early 1870s when discoveries by Nathaniel Hill finally resolved the problems. Colorado someday would equal, if not surpass, the lodes of any state, including Nevada, but she was no competitor for the Comstock in the 1860s. In fact, Colorado soon lagged behind Idaho, Montana, and even Arizona in gold production despite her early start, because these areas had larger placer deposits.[30] Yet early Colorado made an important contribution to federal mining law that is often overlooked. To understand this contribution, it is first necessary to examine the Civil War as it affected mining policy, lands policy, and the overall status of the West.

The secession of the South included a secession of its members from Congress. For the first time the Northern members, led by the new Republicans, could legislate in a number of areas in which they previously had no realistic prospect of success. Obviously the nation faced a war and Congress naturally addressed that concern. Yet political leadership for the primary military concerns came from the new president, Abraham Lincoln. Hence Congress was able to devote a surprising amount of its time to issues indirectly

related to the war effort, and to issues seen as significant to anticipated postwar developments.
  The output of the mines existing at war's outset went to the North. Most transportation routes assured that outcome but the sympathies of most producing states were also with the Union. Just enough Confederate sympathizers were present in the mining communities to make the early days of the war interesting, but were not enough to present a real threat. The creation of the Territories of Colorado and Nevada, as noted earlier, was intended to keep those areas within the Union fold. Both could have become states as well at the same time but only Nevada chose to do so. She wrote a lengthy state constitution that went to Washington by telegraph, at a cost of $3500, in time for Congress's approval. That was the Nevada style. (There was considerable concern that Lincoln needed every last bit of support, including that of the new state, for reelection in 1864, but he won handily.) Colorado rejected the opportunity by voting down its proposed Constitution by over 3 to 1 because it included automatic election of the new officeholders. A grass roots trick that Nevada would have relished was thus the undoing of the Republican pro-statehood gang in "straightlaced" Colorado. Full statehood there waited another dozen years until another closely contested presidential race finally allowed her entry.[31]
  Militarily, Confederates could not threaten any important mining areas except Colorado. A force of Texans invaded present-day New Mexico. Authorities there, though pro-Union, could not raise forces of sufficient strength to stop the Texans. Colorado's territorial governor, William Gilpin, had barely taken office when the prospect of invasion threatened his jurisdiction. He raised an effective fighting force and sent bills for supplies and pay totaling $400,000 to Washington. As a result he lost his office and saw the military refuse to honor the bills. The force he had raised maintained its organization despite lack of official support and moved into New Mexico to defeat the Texans at Glorieta Pass. After this demonstration of the validity of Gilpin's timely preparations, the military paid the bills after all. Further, Colorado found itself taken much more seriously in Washington, a fact that would prove important to some crucial future policies.[32]
  New strikes, virtually all placer, occurred in the early 1860s in

what is now Idaho and Montana. Congress wanted to keep output in Union hands as well as to encourage possible new states in a geographic area of obvious potential for the North and the Republican party. In 1863 Congress created one territory that covered the entire region but divided it into Idaho and Montana the next year.[33]

That part of established New Mexico Territory that would become Arizona had some elements of Southern sympathy. A Union force from California led by Col. James Carleton entered the area in 1862. The immediate military goal was not security of mines, but clear control of an area in which Confederate sympathizers conceivably could offer a challenge, both locally and from New Mexico itself. With Carleton's forceful military occupation, and a temporary thwarting of hostile Indians as well as Confederates, miners soon moved into the area. Almost all went for placer gold at three locales: on the Colorado River near Yuma, near Wickenburg, and near Prescott, which later became one of the territorial capitals. The famous Vulture mine near Wickenburg, a major gold lode operation, also originated in this period. Since the area was militarily secure, Congress designated it a territory separate from New Mexico in 1863. In other regions the government had reacted to the advent of mining, but in the case of Arizona the government's own action had, almost by accident, created a major mining area.[34]

After military rule ended in Arizona, the territory attempted to establish a uniform code for mining in an effort to replace the miners' meetings. The new system required registration of mining claims by the counties. In addition to recent placer claims of the newcomers, some lode mining in the southern part of the territory represented long-standing Spanish presence. Thus in Pima County the parties who filed the initial group of claims, dated early 1866, bear such names as Gonzalez, Alderete, Gallardo, and Herreras. These miners assigned such names as San Juan, Guadalupe, and Veta Chiquita to their claims. Most of the documents were in English but claims in Spanish were also filed in the Pima County Courthouse.

Soon the Pima records also contained claims titled Last Chance, Southern Belle, Julia, and Constitution, as prospectors more inclined to use such names moved down from other areas. Filers of early claims included John Clum, later famous as editor of the

Tombstone Epitaph, and Charles Poston, the first territorial governor, who helped separate Arizona from New Mexico. However, the Spanish background in mining there was quite important and often overlooked, partly because it did not inspire "rushes" but was more directed at copper ores with silver as a by-product. Neighboring New Mexico had similar longstanding mines of Spanish/Mexican origin near Silver City. That locale has tried to assert her position as the only mining center prior to United States control of the Southwest. Considering the history of mines near Tucson, Silver City's contention is simply untrue.[35]

In sum, the Civil War allowed the legal organization of four territories and one full-fledged state with mining as an economic base. The output of the mines was unquestionably a great aid to the Union.

The year 1862 saw three land distribution acts that showed the full strength of the new Republican majority in Congress. A number of grants for "internal improvements" had been made over the years. First canals, then some railroads received lands as an incentive to construction. Finally, dreams of a transcontinental line could be fulfilled. Such a measure had previously been stalled over the question of route and obvious regional favoritism. The Union Pacific and Central Pacific companies would realize the purposes of the Act in 1869 but could not even begin construction until after the war. Here was a clear example of forward thinking in an optimistic vein. Subsequently, several other transcontinental routes would also obtain massive grants.[36]

Federal land policies had helped support education since the Land Ordinance of 1785 reserved Section 16 in each township. The Republican Congress passed a major new education act, named for Rep. Justin S. Morrill, that provided land grants for colleges which taught "Agricultural and Mechanical Arts." Every state would eventually get at least one land grant college. The lands themselves were in Western states and territories.[37]

The common man of agrarian background had long been the largest customer of lands, whether bought directly from the government or other parties. Now the Homestead Act allowed him 160 acres free if he first lived on it and improved it for five years. Thus was combined the principle of preemption for the actual settler with an outright subsidy for the figure most fitting the Jeffersonian ideal, the yeoman farmer. Ironically, although the Jeffersonian and Jacksonian parties had never gone this far in land policies, the descendant party of their opponents did just that. The Homestead Act helped form a Republican majority. Over the years other acts that might be considered geographic variations of Homestead allowed other methods of free use of land with possible ultimate acquisition. A Timber Cultures Act and a Desert Land Entry Act simply adjusted requirements and acreages for different regions.[38]

During the ensuing years the lands distributed under the Homestead Act would total over 270 million acres. The Morrill Act provided 11.2 million acres. And the Pacific Railroad Act (with an 1864 Amendment) provided 34.5 million to the two companies alone. In short, Congress was giving land to any and all recipients: large corporations, states, and individuals.[39]

As finally developed during the Jacksonian era, land sales with the Preemption amendments were still primary policy prior to 1862. After that date land became a free commodity, governed by time for development, not monetary payment. Certainly, this fact is a very powerful consideration in any study of the period.

Chapter Four

The Miners Go to Washington

After all the years of inaction, Congress finally adopted a federal act for lode claims in 1866. In 1870 it did the same for placer and in 1872 it revised certain provisions of both earlier Acts. The first Act was the most important from the historical perspective since it finally set a direction. The same William Stewart of lawsuit fame from the Comstock, now Nevada's senator, led the immediate debates favoring the bill. Indiana Representative George W. Julian contested the measure with his own proposals regarding mining laws. There has long been a wide range of historical interpretation of this confrontation and these two individuals. Yet a number of other figures were just as important as these well-known antagonists. Further, the political confrontation evident at the time of the Act of 1866 had been developing for some years. A rather detailed look at the period prior to the legislation is essential to genuine understanding of the Act.

Aside from California, the mining regions could not send full-fledged members to the House and Senate since they were not in states but territories. Congress did allow each territory to send an elected delegate (rather than a representative) to the House of Representatives. The territories had no direct voice at all in the Senate. The delegates to the House could engage in debates and introduce legislation, but they could not vote on legislation, even if it was their own. During the early 1860s five territories that ultimately became mining states sent delegates. Nevada's representation lacked continuity with a change of members in 1863. Delegates from Arizona, Idaho, and Montana drifted in sporadically as the respective territories gradually held elections. Only one territory, Colorado, sent a delegate, Hiram P. Bennet, who served long enough to provide genuine leadership on issues relevant to the entire region.[1]

Although a native of Maine, Bennet typified the Colorado resident of the times, aside from his profession. He had studied and practiced law in Missouri and Iowa before moving on to Nebraska in the tumultuous 1850s. After rising to the position of Speaker of the House of the Nebraska Territorial Assembly, Bennet joined many others from the Plains and Midwest in moving to Colorado during the overplayed mining rush of 1859. Denver's first newspaper editor, William Byers of the *Rocky Mountain News*, assured his victory in being elected the territory's first delegate to Congress. In a campaign coinciding with the start of the Civil War in 1861, he won heavily since his opponent was a rumored secessionist. Bennet stayed in Washington until 1865 and subsequently was active in Colorado politics for many years. Indeed, he became something of an elder statesman.[2]

Bennet had little more than arrived in Congress when he alone succeeded in getting a unanimous resolution through the House that was a clear precursor of the ultimate mining legislation. The House realized the matter was of some importance despite the years of inaction. Bennet's resolution read:

> That the Judiciary Committee be instructed to inquire into the legality and propriety of legalizing all consumated litigations under miner's and place courts in Colorado Territory which were had and done therein prior to origin of said Territory by Act of Congress February 28, 1861.[3]

Bennet did not attempt to write a general law regarding the mining camp rules throughout the West at the time. He was concerned for Colorado which was in a stage of legal hiatus after a dispute between Kansas Territory and proponents of Jefferson Territory. The Judiciary Committee did not immediately report out anything but if it was not fully aware of the situation, this resolution restored the matter to Congress's attention after the long period of *laissez faire*.

The Miners Go to Washington 65

Bennet addressed several other matters of importance to Colorado and the West in general. He suggested various surveys, both of the geography of the region, and for aid in developing minerals. Congress would follow his suggestion after the war with such successful expeditions as those of Powell and Hayden; indeed, a permanent agency, the U.S. Geological Survey, would emerge from these early attempts.[4]

The size of the Comstock's silver production alone demanded establishment of a new branch of the mint. The miracle was that Carson City provided the site rather than Gold Hill or Virginia City. Bennet introduced a bill to establish another branch mint at Denver. Some question arose as to the comparability of production between the two areas. Bennet responded that Colorado's output of minerals was comparable to Nevada's but over a larger area. Further, Nevada was relatively close to San Francisco, but Colorado miners had to cross hundreds of miles to reach a federal mint. His arguments prevailed and Congress established both mints in 1862. Later Bennet proposed yet another mint for Boise, Idaho, but that facility was never built. U.S. Assay offices at Boise and other temporary locations, though, were almost as important as mints since they did buy ore from miners.[5]

The mints established during the Civil War became important parts of the overall mining scene in the West. The new facilities at Carson City and Denver purchased ore and manufactured bullion bars in the early days. By the late 1870s the Carson City mint made some silver dollars but only for a few years; hence the "CC" mint marks are valuable to collectors. Denver's facility ultimately became the best-known and largest U.S. mint but it made only bullion bars during its first four decades. Coins with the "D" mint mark did not appear until 1906. From that year forward, the "D" mark has been on far more coins than any other mark, even including that of the main mint at Philadelphia. Bennet undoubtedly contributed as much or more than any single federal representative in Colorado's history in initially obtaining this facility.[6]

In yet another matter, Bennet showed commendable foresight. In early 1864 he requested hearings on "a law to restrain the wanton destruction of buffalo...." The Committee on Territories did investigate the matter but legislation was tragically delayed for many years. Bennet, representing the West, had tried. The Congressional majority, virtually all from the East, were the ones who took no action.[7]

Finally, Bennet saw a most pressing need. On March 18, 1864, he asked unanimous consent simply "to introduce a bill in relation to mines and minerals on the public domain." It was no longer just a matter of his own territory, but of the entire West. Bennet's bill contained the primary provisions that later became federal law: recognition of local and state laws regarding claims and allowance of future claims on federal lands. The House consented to introduction of the bill. A major confrontation still lay ahead.[8]

Exactly one month after Bennet introduced his measure, New York Representative Fernando Wood also produced a bill. Wood remarked that Bennet's bill had gone nowhere. He related the mines to the then ongoing debate on "derangement of finances" from the Civil War. Debate had just concluded on a proposal to reduce paper money. Though the proposal lost 40 to 60, the matter of currency was obviously quite important. Wood simply suggested that the president seize the mines in Colorado and Arizona until Congress could legislate for their disposal.[9]

At first, Wood claimed his bill was intended to combat a problem with "speculation" and mining fraud. Other members immediately questioned him. Rep. Thomas B. Shannon of California pointedly asked why Wood had omitted Nevada and Idaho from his proposal. Wood claimed that the perpetrators of frauds then operating in New York were dealing with properties only in Colorado and Arizona. Rep. John Kasson of Iowa thought coal in Washington Territory should be recovered by the government since private parties were claiming it as well.[10]

Wood cited a recent request by the Commissioner of the General Land Office who was frustrated by lack of guidance from Congress on the matter, especially in light of Homestead and other land distribution measures. He became more candid about his real reasons for the proposal. He believed that it was "incumbent... to protect all the property which the Government actually possesses," because "there are interests of the Government in these mines and in the mineral lands almost enough to pay the public debt."[11]

Bennet responded that title to the lands was not affected by private citizen's workings but the Government received the benefit of gold and silver produced for currency. At that time some five-sixths of the circulating gold came from Western mines. Further, he noted that most of the business activity in New York to obtain financing for mines was completely legitimate. Some of the best citizens of Colorado had gone to New York to obtain capital. He summarized his own position by concluding:

> The gentleman talks of putting the occupants off these lands. This cannot be done. The only thing that should be done is to pass some liberal statute to aid the occupant, or else to let him entirely alone to work out his own salvation. A reasonable tax would not be objected to in these war times by the miners, but it should be accompanied with statutory protection to the miners in his possessions. With the same propriety the gentleman might propose to drive the settlers off the agricultural public lands because they are producing corn and wheat as to drive off those who are producing gold.[12]

Yet Wood still wanted action because he felt that after any delay at all, the mines "will be exhausted." He wanted immediate action, not even referral to committee.[13]

Representative Elihu Washburne of Illinois attacked Wood on the simple practicality of his proposal. He pointedly asked,

> What is it that he expects the President to do? Is he to raise a force and go into the mines and drive the miners off? We all know that in Colorado, Nevada, and California the settlers go upon these claims and hold them by virtue of the laws of the Territory.

Washburne likened the situation to the earlier settlement of farm lands by squatters who could claim preemption rights. His own background included experiences in the Galena mining area of Illinois, which he thought quite similar to the current status of the West. The military had accomplished nothing there but had cost tax money in trying. He went so far as to predict a second outright "Civil War at once in the West" if Wood's proposal was adopted as proposed.[14]

Wood backed off somewhat on this challenge. He clearly did not want the president to fight another Civil War but thought some measure could reduce taxes for the Eastern states. Ultimately the

House voted to table his resolution. The policy of *laissez faire* thus continued.

As a result of the House proposals at both extremes by Wood and Bennet, the matter was now becoming imminent. The fact that the North was clearly winning the war undoubtedly also figured in the background. In the Senate, Zachariah Chandler of Michigan introduced a mining bill on April 26.[15]

The very next day in the House the matter regarding revenues arose once again, but this time in more subdued form. The same prominent Vermont representative who had sponsored the Land Grant College Act, Justin S. Morrill, was in charge of devising an income tax. He proposed a surprisingly complex code that included a mass of provisions for virtually every business and occupation then imaginable. The matters of taxes on mines naturally arose. Morrill's proposed code included a $10 license fee on every company and 5% *ad valorem* on output. California Representatives William Higby and Thomas Shannon objected to the fee as potentially damaging to the prospector, who might be construed a miner, yet had little or nothing and made no direct production. Representative Thaddeus Stevens of Pennsylvania lauded the gold miners but compared their situation to those in the East who produced coal and iron with a royalty to private landowners. Stevens flatly stated, "I am sorry our friends from California do not appreciate the liberality of the Government." The House then defeated the amendment that Higby and Shannon had proposed.[16]

Bennet also proposed an amendment that would have set the tax rate at only 3% of net mine income, rather than 5% of gross. The House defeated his measure also. The West did achieve one victory in the tax code. Delegate William Wallace of Idaho noted that the Pacific Coast was "flooded with paper money" and it would be unfair to deny the miners use of it, even if they did produce gold and silver. The tax code specifically demanded payment from the mines in gold or silver. This was the only form of business subjected to such a criterion in the entire code. Wallace's proposal to allow payment in paper money passed without opposition.[17]

The matter of mines in the tax code was of more legal significance than might be presumed at first glance. In general, Western mines were treated no differently than Eastern operations. Mines on public or private lands were subject to the same taxes. A flat per cent applied to any material produced, be it iron, coal, limestone, granite, silver, or gold. However, the code as finally written did include a provision for forfeiture of claims for non-payment of either the fee or the tax. In so doing, Congress, almost by accident, implied an approval of mining claims and the authority of state, territorial, and local codes providing for their existence. In fact, the tax code was very short-lived after the war. Enforcement machinery was lacking in many areas, including the forfeiture of claims. Yet this measure did mark the first legal recognition of the existence of mining claims by the Congress.[18]

Up until mid-1864 Bennet had carried most of the battle of protecting mining claims in Congress. The matter had arisen in the House but not the Senate since the 1850s. Finally the natural leader on the issue in the upper House proposed legislation on the matter. Senator John Conness of California might be considered the archetypical figure from that state at the time. An Irishman, he had immigrated to New York at age 12. When news of the great rush arrived in 1849, he was one of the first to go to California. Interestingly, Conness had no political or legal background but made his way up in California government to the Senate in 1856. Conness's two bills proposed "the survey and sale of Mineral lands, and to extend the right of preemption thereto." Many problems could be anticipated in conflicts between mining claims under local law and other land entries like homesteads, under federal law. Yet just how should claims be sold? This part of Conness's bill was unexpected.[19]

In early 1865 after the Second Session of the House had organized, Bennet again proposed a land preemption measure. Rep. William S. Holman of Indiana wanted to exclude mineral lands from such status. Bennet protested that his proposal was primarily aimed at those lands. The objection stalled the measure for the time, and the end of the war and related items further delayed consideration. In the meantime, Nevada's flamboyant William Stewart arrived in the Senate.[20]

Various matters relating to mines again arose in the Second Session, which began in late 1864. California Representative Cornelius Cole was intent on establishing a Mining Department; Congress finally referred the proposal to the Committee on Public Lands. It was only natural that Cole and Bennet joined to request an appropriation for a mining survey. From the House floor they produced a letter from the Commissioner of the General Land Office who supported the request for $25,000, but suggested certain uses for the data. The Commissioner noted that "one billion dollars have already been extracted without a dime of revenue to the Treasury." After the war was over, the mines could be "giving support to multitudes of individuals," and also "relieve the nation and diminish taxation."

Cole and Bennet certainly opposed the latter statements, but they introduced the entire letter anyway to endorse the survey request. The matter of final federal recognition of mining claims was becoming imminent. Bennet saw the survey as a lead toward "the legislation which will be demanded at the hands of Congress at the next Session." Conflicts involving homesteads and mining claims were anticipated with a mass of postwar migrants to the West. By then Bennet would be gone from Congress but his forecast proved accurate. Indeed, these were his last recorded words in the House. In the meantime, the body voted $15,000 for the survey.[21]

The anticipated mining legislation in the next Congress took a while to make much appearance. Stewart managed an early technical victory by placing an amendment in a bill creating the federal courts in his own Nevada. According to Stewart's amendment, federal courts had to adjudicate disputes between miners if such cases came on appeal from state or mining district courts. Federal judges could not automatically dismiss such cases by noting that the United States was the actual owner of the lands. Even so, this measure must be regarded as "legally precarious." An act to clarify several crucial points was necessary.[22]

Senator John Sherman of Ohio formally submitted a mining bill, designated as S. 257, in April 1866. Previously Sherman had supported sale of the mines, but no longer. Essentially S. 257 was a preemption bill only for lode mining claims, but it did include a 3% tax on total output.[23]

In the legislative process involving S. 257, the full cast of players showed a variety of political talents. Stewart's motions and speeches on the floor were impressive, but others did much behind the scenes. California's John Conness chaired the Senate Committee on Mines. The matter dragged on for several months but the Committee ordered its report published on May 28, 1866. The fact that the report did not actually appear in the *Congressional Globe*, the official record of the debates of Congress, has led some historians of the mining law to neglect it and its author in finally bringing the issue to a head. However, members of Congress at the time were quite familiar with Conness's report which concluded:

> The miners' rules and regulations are not only well understood, but have been construed and adjudicated for now nearly a quarter of a century...By this great system established by the people in their primary capacities, and evidencing by the highest possible testimony the peculiar genius of the American people for founding empire and order... *Popular sovereignty* is displayed in one of its greatest aspects, and simply invites us, not to destroy, but to put upon it the stamp of national power and unquestioned authority.[24]

There was that very phrase "Popular Sovereignty," the concept that had once cost Stephen A. Douglas his presidential aspirations, and had even been a background factor in bringing on a Civil War. Yet now that the tragic conflict was over, the stigma attached had dissipated and the general idea was quite viable since it was demonstrated as successful in mining camps if not in Kansas. Now Congress could at last recognize it.

Another point that Conness's report stressed was that the Mining Districts

> become the means adopted by the people themselves for establishing just protection to all... The local courts, beginning with California, recognize those rules, the central idea of which was priority of possession.[25]

True, there were claim-jumpers in the mines. But that could be expected regardless of the legal status. There were claim-jumpers on agricultural lands, and even in townsites. Mining camps had themselves policed the problem, and for the most part, done so successfully. They were the people most affected and best situated to handle problems, rather than some more distant organ of federal or even state authority. A Senate Committee had endorsed "Popular Sovereignty" as well as "first come, first served" regarding mining. The report is clear evidence in support of the frontier school. As incredible as it may seem, the report actually changed Conness himself; in earlier sessions he had favored some degree of government profit from the mines, though he had always favored preemption. Conness must have reconsidered the principle of "Popular Sovereignty," both in the abstract as well as in practical reality in the mining camps. He definitely stressed these concepts above all other considerations when he endorsed the Committee's final report.

With the Conness report in hand, the Senate proceeded to debate the matter in June 1866. Senate Bill 257 included the following points:

Lands were opened to all U.S. citizens and to aliens who had declared an intention to become citizens to lode mining claims.

State, territorial, and mining district laws were recognized in most regards but the "apex rule" was written directly into the bill as applying at all times.

Claims could be no more than 300 feet on a vein, only one claim allowed per vein except an extra to a discoverer (thus following most early mining district laws for lode claims).

Full patent (the legal grant of ownership given by the government, not to be confused with the protections given to inventors) was available for a fee of $5.00 per acre.

Patent rights for a fee made this a preemption measure, but that legal recognition could come only after any problems with conflicting claims had been locally adjudicated.

Agricultural and mineral lands were distinguished, hence the mining law and homesteads applied to two different types of lands.

Rights of way for roads, ditches, and canals could be granted over mining claims.[26]

Stewart himself added a provision from the floor designed to eliminate fraudulent patents. The claimants would have to make improvements of a value of $1000 as verified by the surveyor general to obtain patent. Then Stewart delivered his forensic finest in a long speech more designed to draw attention from the newspapers in his home state than to sway any of his fellow Senators. Stewart praised the West, mining and miners, and the existing system of law by the miners themselves. He even remembered California's impact on Australia. However, he opposed all forms of taxes on the mines.[27]

During the course of the debates, Sherman asked that the 3%

tax that he had proposed be raised to 5%. Yet after several other members pointed out enforcement problems, he changed his position and opposed any tax at all. The government already collected five-eights of 1% on all output of stamp mills. That income might be jeopardized by another tax on the mines themselves.[28]

The most serious opponent during the Senate debates of June 1866 proved to be George Williams of Oregon. Williams was not an opponent of the miners, nor was he ignorant of the issue, despite the allegations of Stewart. In fact, he emphasized that his last case before leaving law practice to come to the Senate was a major mining case. Williams simply did not want any type or form of sale of the mines, even if it meant continuing *laissez faire*. The vote on Williams's motion to drop all sales of mines was the only one recorded on the Act. The sale provision stayed in by a vote of 21 to 10 with 18 absent. The matter was by no means finished and all knew it. Stewart himself acknowledged that revisions would be needed as problems became evident.[29]

Previously, the most divisive debate on the issue, between Bennet and Fernando Wood, had not been in the Senate but in the House of Representatives. At least one opponent still wielded considerable power there and was in a position effectively to block legislation. Representative George Washington Julian of Indiana had a pet proposal of his own and, as Chairman of the Committee on Public Lands, thought he could promote it over the Senate bill. Julian would first survey the mining lands, then offer them at auction. He would give those already on claims a first chance to buy but he admitted his proposal was primarily for revenue. Further, he wanted "orderly settlement of the public domain." Julian's ideas went into H.B. 322, "For Survey and Sale of Lands... Containing Gold, Silver, and Other Valuable Minerals." Julian was able to get his own bill out of his committee while bottling up the Senate bill, but the net result appeared to be no accomplishment at all.[30]

The members of both houses from the West realized they had the votes but Julian could prevent their bill from reaching the floor, if they played the game his way. A bit of legislative "sleight of hand" won the point for the West. Conness had as his counterpart in the House of Representatives a fellow veteran of the original California rush, who was Chairman of the Mines Committee.

Above left: *Colorado delegate Hiram Bennet, statesman and proponent of comprehensive mining legislation in the early 1860s.* (Courtesy Denver Public Library) Above right: *California Senator John Conness, a primary figure in the passage of the Mining Laws.* (Courtesy National Archives) Below left: *Nevada Sentor William Stewart, traditionally credited with sponsorship of the mining laws, was no more important than several other legislators.* (Courtesy National Archives)

This crucial figure, William Higby, quietly reported a simple measure for the "protection of ditches and canals" as used in California placering on June 13. The measure, designated H.B. 365, seemed innocuous enough, and went to the Senate on voice vote.[31]

Julian should have been more skeptical. Higby tried to bring up S.B. 257 on July 3, only to see it referred to Julian's Committee. The Senate then simply attached the text of the Mining Bill to H.B. 365, the "ditches and canals" bill. Since the Senate had recently passed the Mining Bill as S. 257, it made this adjustment by simple voice vote on July 22. Now the full House would have to act on it as an amended bill that they had already passed. The strategy thwarted Julian. He attempted to add his own bill for sale while stressing the Constitution's clause for Congressional control of lands, but the matter passed by voice vote. Higby naturally led the Western side in the floor debates. Julian could not get even a roll call. Although President Andrew Johnson had enough troubles with Congress, this was not one of them and he signed the bill into law.[32]

Perhaps James Madison rolled over in his grave. The reader will recall from the first chapter that Madison had favored the power of Congressional veto of state legislation as part of debates at the Constitutional Convention of 1787; now Congress allowed state legislatures, and even local meetings, to write laws regarding the federal government's own lands. Yet Madison himself had successfully adjusted his views to new times and conditions over the years. Congress could defend itself by saying it was doing the same.

In discussing the Mining Act of 1866, historians have given a variety of appraisals. Carl Mayer and George A. Riley in *Public Domain; Private Dominion* (1985) have perhaps been most critical, and stated that the Julian proposal would have been advisable even then. However, William S. Greever in *The Bonanza West* (1963) was generally positive. An official history by a Public Land Law Review Commission (1968) with the relevant chapter by Robert W. Swenson took something of a middle ground.

Regardless of different positions on the value of the final Act, many historians have attributed the legislation to Stewart with the ominous note that he was a "silver king" himself who had labor problems in his mines. Yet discovering any connection between this measure and labor policies taxes the imagination. Even Russell Elliott, who wrote a biography of Stewart criticizing many of the Senator's actions believed the Act was beneficial.[33] As for Stewart's single-handed role, the matter had been ongoing for several years with a variety of crucial supporters. Colorado's delegate Hiram Bennet, certainly not to be mistaken for Stewart, had promoted the measure long before the notorious Nevadan even entered the Senate. When Congress finally did act in 1866, two Californians, Senator John Conness and Rep. William Higby, contributed as much or more than Stewart. The legislative stratagem that brought the bill to the House under a different title should not be judged harshly. In fact, proponents of the landmark Civil Rights Act of 1964 used a similar technique to bypass powerful Southern committee chairmen who opposed that bill.

What about those who had opposed the West? Did Fernando Wood and especially George Washington Julian propose alternatives that might have been more favorable to the "little man" in getting mining property? Such a thesis simply does not stand scrutiny. Julian was very much a part of several of the largest and most controversial railroad land grants ever made by Congress. Julian openly favored immediate transfer of all mines to complete private ownership rather than continued government control of the lands. Julian based his proposal on the experience involving the Missouri and Wisconsin lead mines.[34]

As noted earlier, the lead mines ended up in the hands of major developers anyway. Julian's proposal would have given small miners and prospectors the first chance to patent their own discoveries, but only for a price that would have driven them off the discoveries. Without the purchase price, the lands would have been open to bidding, a certain method of consolidation by the major companies anyway, though the treasury might have benefited to some minor extent. Julian's own mining proposal, had it become law, would have prevented the orderly Western development he expressly desired. The consolidation of claims necessary for successful large scale mining on the Western frontier would have produced considerable chaos and violence, possibly more than actually occurred.

In previous periods, the concept of "orderly development" certainly did not imply any system that favored the "little man." In the early days of the nation when speculators competed with genuine settlers for land titles, the speculators had demanded "orderly development." So it was with Julian's other major contribution, railroad land grants. A comparison can be drawn between Julian's ideas and those of British authorities at the close of the pre-Revolutionary era. To promote "orderly" settlement of the trans-Appalachian West, the British issued the Proclamation of 1763, which temporarily forbade settlement beyond the crest of the mountains. The Proclamation proved most unpopular to masses of the "little men" of those times and contributed to the sentiment that produced the Revolution.

Suggestions that the military might have moved into the mines and confiscated them are ludicrous. True, large armed forces stayed mobilized after the Civil War, but the short shrift that Congress gave to brief suggestions of this nature show there was absolutely no sentiment for such actions. Congress was then at the peak of its power in the entire history of the country. It was practicing what is known as "Radical Reconstruction" against the South. All of the figures discussed above were involved in Reconstruction as well. By 1868 they were able to impeach president Andrew Johnson. Hence Congress's will was the way. Congress did not want to seize the mines even though it was willing to send armies to the South.

Another suggestion in hindsight is that establishing a leasing system by 1866 might have been the best solution. However, Julian himself opposed the idea on the basis of the failure of the Mississippi Valley lead mines.[35] The point is moot because there was no sentiment for leasing at all in Congress of this period. Even if there had been such sentiment, however, administration would undoubtedly have fallen to the General Land Office, which would have taken much the same attitude that ruined the practice in the Galena district. A good administrator might have made some difference, but such a figure was rare in all aspects of land policy in this period. Leasing would, however, become viable in a more politically and economically mature stage of Western development.

At the time of the 1866 Act, the Republican party dominated American politics, the Democratic party being largely excluded from government through the political exclusion of the South. The different proposals of Stewart and Julian did not represent a "big man" versus "little man" split or any partisan split, since both were of the Republican party. The split shows many more characteristics of a division between East and West.[36]

The Eastern states were more concerned with Reconstruction than with mining, but in the West the Act of 1866 was the big story. Byers, the editor of the *Rocky Mountain News*, summed up the matter for the region by writing that the bill then moving through Congress was "coming nearer the wants of the mining States than any of the many bills heretofore proposed." He believed that "the best plan for acquiring permanent title is the perplexing question," which the bill did address. Even so, the contrast of $5.00 per acre with the agricultural preemption rate of $1.25 was "unfair" since the miner should have "equal advantages." From the modern perspective the difference seems trivial but many families spent five years and more to prove homesteads which they could have bought for $200, if they had had that sum. Despite this question, Byers proclaimed Sherman's bill far superior to Julian's. Colorado had followed the precedent of 1850 California in electing senators even though the territory had not yet achieved full statehood. Byers commented that, "Our own Senators-elect [sic] have lent aid on the bill. They think it is nearly or quite what people of Colorado want." Byers praised California's Higby in obtaining the bill, while lamenting the lack of representation from the West.[37]

Colorado waited another full decade before she could seat her senators because President Andrew Johnson vetoed the act providing admission. The action was undoubtedly a career saver since he came within one Senate vote of removal from office in 1868. Colorado got the mining bill anyway, despite her lack of votes in Congress. Ironically, her own territorial legislature had just passed an act similar to the federal one but vein claims in Colorado could be up to 1400 feet long. Hence the federal law as written was much more limiting of claim consolidation than some laws of the mining states and territories themselves.[38]

Stewart had been quite correct in anticipating that various revisions would be needed in the Act of 1866. Jefferson and Hamilton had both indicated that mining was a little-known field in their time and, in some respects, it still was three quarters of a century later. Placer mines were quite different from lode and were not addressed in the Act of 1866. Other problems, not foreseen by legislators, were almost sure to arise.

The House Committee on Mines saw the lack of legislation on placer mines as the most pressing need for changes. The Committee sent a bill to the floor on March 17, 1870, to fill the legal gap. The voters of California had retired Representative Higby since his success on the last bill, but yet another veteran of California of '49, Aaron A. Sargent, now took up the task. Even as the bill emerged from committee, Julian replayed his old role by vigorously protesting both the current bill and its predecessor. Yet this time there was a difference. The Committee which examined the measure did not include him. The bill passed the House by voice vote.[39]

In the Senate, Stewart was naturally on the Committee and reported out the results of a conference with the House on June 28. California's Cornelius Cole, who had aided Bennet in the 1864 debates with Fernando Wood in the House, had moved to the Senate. Cole, also a Committee member, stated he had not signed the report only because he favored a claim size of ten acres compared to the twenty acres allowed under the bill. Even so, he was quite diplomatic in his position. Stewart made a most unusual observation about the bill. Many small placer miners in California's Mother Lode region had stayed on their claims long after gold was depleted. This bill would allow them to patent the lands they had lived on for two decades, having adjusted by farming. It was for that reason that the price per acre was set at $2.50, as compared with the $5.00 per acre for lode claims. Traditional agricultural preemptions had always cost $1.25 per acre, so the miner who had turned to farming was not in a particularly advantageous position from the Act of 1870. There is little question that Stewart and the Senate believed the new law would benefit the retired placerer, even though the next Act, only two years later, would effectively repeal such use of worn-out mining claims.[40]

The only recorded opponent of the Placer Mining Act debated in the 1870 Senate was James Harlan of Iowa, who did not want mining claims that were larger than agricultural claims. Under the bill, an association of up to eight persons could claim up to the 20 acre limit for each person, for a maximum of 160. A key distinction was that placer claims had to conform to the grid survey system while lode claims followed the natural shapes of veins. Harlan believed the bill would allow "men of wealth to monopolize the mineral lands." However, the Act passed by voice vote.[41]

The Act of 1870 could have favored the rich had it been enacted in 1850, but only if the Miners' Meetings had allowed claims of the maximum size as ultimately allowed under federal law. There would have been absolutely no chance of that occurrence and Congress recognized the fact. By 1870, much larger placer claims were required for any successful gold production at all. This was true in California, where hydraulic mining with powerful pumps was recovering fine gold on long-worked lands. It was also true in those areas of Arizona, Montana, Idaho, and Colorado that had seen placer rushes as recently as the early 1860s. Easily worked placers simply did not last long. Subsequently, the only placer rushes in U.S. territory would be in Alaska, where miners' meetings would still give the "little man" some chance.

Further problems in the mining laws required yet another adjustment. Though the Senate had passed such a bill to address some inconsistencies in 1871, the House never got around to debating it in the First Session of the 42nd Congress. In the Second Session, on January 23, 1872, yet another Californian took a leading role. Representative Aaron Sargent, a Massachusetts native who went West in '49, presented a bill designated H.B. 1016 from the Committee on Mines to the full House. Montana Territory's newly elected delegate, William Horace Clagett, probably had some input on the Committee, though as a delegate rather than a full representative, he could not be an official member of any committee.[42]

Clagett would one day become the best-known of all mining attorneys in the country. Indeed, his earlier career was remarkably similar to that of Colorado's capable delegate, Hiram Bennet, of a decade earlier. Clagett originally came from Maryland but had learned law in Iowa. He went to Nevada in 1860 just in time to meet Mark Twain and become a character in Twain's *Roughing It*. He also met Stewart. As with so many in the mining West, from the depths of the tunnels to the Congress of the United States, Clagett moved through an amazing sequence of classic locales. Between 1860 and 1899, when he passed away in Spokane, Washington, Clagett practiced law and politics at several Nevada towns, including Virginia City; Helena and Deer Lodge, Montana; Denver, Colorado; Deadwood, Dakota Territory, and in the Coeur d'Alene of Idaho. He was president of the Idaho Convention, which wrote the first constitution needed for statehood in 1889. He probably contributed more to neighboring Montana, however, during the stint as delegate to Congress.

Clagett introduced the bill that ultimately created Yellowstone National Park, as well as a multitude of measures for Montana's early growth. His forensic abilities earned him the nickname "the silver tongued orator." Clagett's background was Democratic but he changed to Republican in the earlier part of his Western career. Democratic Montana defeated his reelection despite his great contributions. Ultimately he became a Populist, in time to support another "silver tongued orator," William Jennings Bryan, for president in 1896. All along he took a multitude of "little man" mining cases. He continually supported the mining laws, both as delegate and subsequently as the leading attorney who had to deal with them. Ultimately, he died poor.[43]

Unfortunately, Clagett did not use his "silver tongue" on the floor of Congress regarding the Mining Bill. The debates among some other members show the issue had matured since 1866. These were quite brief, especially considering the earlier exchanges between Bennet and Wood which produced no legislation at all. The importance of the Act of 1872 should not be seen as any less. This Act legally improved the earlier ones enough to cause the "Sacred Cow" to survive.

The Act of 1872 sailed through smoothly for good reason. As its House sponsor stated, the bill "does not change in the slightest degree the policy of the Government in the disposition of the mineral lands. Changes relate to the legal questions involved." In the House, Colorado's delegate Jerome Chafee added a single amendment from the floor to allow the surveyor general to designate boundaries for patents. Otherwise, sponsor Sargent summed up the net effect of the matter, the "legislation of 1866 imperfect," but the basic principles had been sound. "This bill simply oils the machinery a little." However, the bill did include language that repealed all of the 1866 Act except recognition of state, territorial, and local laws, and the president's power to send officials to the areas as needed. As a result of the repeal, Representative Charles

Willard of Vermont added a stronger clause protecting existing rights. Final passage by the House was through voice vote.[44]

Action in the Senate was just as easy, though delayed until the Committee could report on April 16. Senator James Alcorn of Mississippi presented H.B. 1016 while praising his Committee, since he had "learned something" in process. His own state had no mines at all, undoubtedly the reason the other members asked him to present the measure. Alcorn stated the principal purpose was control of land titles to be set up by Congress. Ironically, the only animated debate — over lode claim dimensions — was between Westerners who generally favored the measure, Nevada's Stewart and California's Cole. The Act of 1866 had promoted many false names on lode claims so they could be consolidated. Now the size was set at 1500 feet and the number of claims any party could hold was no longer limited. The wording stayed unchanged. Senator Samuel Pomeroy of Iowa wanted to put the money paid for patents into a special fund, but withdrew the proposal. A voice vote sent the bill with the Committee's adjustments of language back to the House, which concurred by voice vote on April 29. President Grant signed the bill on May 10, 1872. It remains the basic mining law to the present day.[45]

Perhaps the most significant single observation about the Act of 1872 is that it specifically states that federal lands are *"free and open"* to mining. Hence the Act literally confers a *right* to mine. To do so a miner does not even need a mining claim; the value of that record is to protect against rival claimants and provide the initial step toward patent. Further, the Mining Law originally gave any parties working a claim the right to live on the claim and to remove other natural materials (such as timber) for development of facilities. There can be no better testament to the liberal attitude of resource distribution of the times. True, ultimate patent was a costly proposition, but the great majority of miners worked for years without worrying about that option, as discussed in later chapters.[46]

Compared to the Act of 1866, and even that of 1870, the Act of 1872 is more legally refined. The change in lode claims could now account for all types of deposits, not simply classic epithermal veins. If a vein were present, the claim should follow it up to 1500 feet. A limit in width to 600 feet was clearly an improvement over a total lack of any limit in the 1866 Act. End lines of claims now had to be parallel. The rules of local mining districts still stood but were subordinate to federal law as well as state and territorial law. The "apex rule" continued but now applied to all veins that might have a top within the surface limits of a particular claim, not just the primary vein as the 1866 Act had provided.

Several sections in the Act of 1872 gave more specific and detailed procedures for record keeping and patent applications. For patent a claimant had to certify having made $500 worth of improvements and had to pay for an official survey. To hold claims prior to patent, the claimant had to certify $100 work per year. The fees for patent remained $5.00 per acre for lodes, $2.50 for placers. A claimant had to clearly "monument" the area on the ground and post legal notices there as well as registering them with local authorities. Cases of lodes on placer claims, a situation previously in legal limbo, could now be patented as part of the placer lands at lode fees. The Act specified that intersecting lodes went to the earlier (senior) locator of the area of the intersection. Claims and patent applications under the old laws still stood but those filed after the date of approval, May 10, 1872, fell under it. Claims were valid only on "valuable" mineral lands. Many years of court cases would finally establish working rules around this single word. One result would be repeal of the use of worn out claims for farming since no "valuable" deposit remained. However, the distinction between mineral and agricultural lands remained; presumably such a retired placer miner could still obtain his lands through other methods, at cheaper cost.

The Act gave tunnels some recognition (if there was a genuine discovery) and created a designation of claims for millsites of no more than five acres which could be on lands lacking a "valuable" mineral deposit. A millsite had to have some association with claims on undisputed mineral lands. (Though the 1866 Act had not specifically mentioned millsites, some patents had been granted for them in association with lode claims as various local laws had allowed. Now the rules were more definite.)

The Acts of 1866, 1870, and 1872, all closely related, are often called the General Mining Law. This title is frequently used interchangeably with the term "Act of 1872" or "Mining Law of 1872" in the industry, though in a strictly legal sense, some provisions of the earlier Acts still applied after the enactment of the 1872 law. For simplicity, the terms General Mining Law, Act of 1872, and Mining Law of 1872, are used interchangeably throughout the balance of this paper. The full text of the Act of July 26, 1866 is in 14 Stat. 251, the text of the Act of July 9, 1870 is at 16 Stat. 217, and the text of the Act of May 10, 1872 is at 17 Stat. 91 (Stat. refers to the U.S. Statutes).

The Act of 1872 facilitated the recording of claims in many lesser-known areas too small to have miners' meetings. The Act also encouraged claims for materials of many varieties not generally associated with classic mineral rushes. Major oil companies legally used mining claims to develop several important fields in the early 1900s. In other cases, various parties used mining claims to develop stone, sand, and gravel. In 1873 Congress made coal subject to the provisions of the Mining Law of 1872. The same year Congress made a regional exception to the mining laws; the presence of iron ore deposits in the upper Great Lakes prompted removal of Minnesota, Wisconsin, and Michigan from application of the 1872 Mining Law. There is reason to believe this was a mistake, as described in the next chapters.[47]

Critics of the Act of 1872 have observed that Congress gave a subsidy for a mining tunnel in the Comstock as promoted by financier Adolph Sutro. However, they failed to connect that legislation with the Act that provided the system of recording mining claims, except for noting that both were passed in 1872. The tunnel was not as successful as Sutro had convinced Congress it might become, but it was of some value. Had it been initiated earlier it would have been much more successful. In calling for it, Sutro had the safety of the mines as his primary consideration. He actually swung a pick in its construction. Sutro's idealism in seeing the tunnel as a public-spirited measure for draining all the mines, as well as providing an emergency escape route, was not lost on the public. Later in life Sutro himself became a Populist mayor of San Francisco. Sutro "unloaded" his interest in time to save himself, since his tunnel company was too late to turn the profits it might have a few years earlier. Even so, he was a man of vision and perseverance.[48]

The Acts of 1870 and 1872 are themselves indicative of the rise of the "sacred cow" status Congress had recognized in 1866. If the

Act of 1866 had not been what the times required, significant opposition would undoubtedly have arisen. It did not. Further, Western leaders would not have taken a risk of possible defeat by proposing revisions in 1870 and again in 1872, since they had their most basic points in the 1866 Act. True, the Acts may be associated with such men as Stewart as well as Presidents Andrew Johnson and Ulysses S. Grant, who are not generally known in positive lights in other regards. The so-called "Gilded Age" had people of all descriptions, in and out of the halls of Congress. Even those from the mining states were not necessarily flamboyant con artists. Hiram Bennet represented a mining frontier far different from contemporary Virginia City, Nevada. Further, Bennet's Colorado reflected the values of the Midwest rather than the second generation mining rush that was Nevada. Such positions as early Conservationism show Bennet was very much a statesman. Yet he had laid years of preparation for the crucial first Act of 1866. William Horace Clagett may be regarded as a similar figure. Both Colorado and Montana would ultimately develop larger mining cities similar to those of Nevada, but not at the time the three Acts were under consideration. California's John Conness, a classic example of a man risen from the social bottom to the top, also clearly sought to represent all of his constituents, not just the most prominent.

In summary, it might be observed that the Act of 1866 saw some attempts to impose Eastern values on the West, but that the West triumphed. The subsequent Acts show mining was an area in which the East had allowed the West to write its own ticket. Hence the "sacred cow" was already established. Yet at that time such a result was not necessarily negative. Webb himself observed that many of the land allotment laws reflected too much imposition of inappropriate Eastern values. Homestead, the example most relevant from his own background, had cruel tricks for the unwary. The limited size was just too small for successful agriculture on the plains. And the grid system also placed an unrealistic burden on the farmer. Interestingly, the General Mining Law as it existed by 1872 had resolved both of these problems. Claim shapes followed the natural shape of the object of work — the veins to be mined — at least for lode claims. Further, limits on the number of claims had ended so long as the claimant could pay filing fees and perform the annual work. Thus the mining laws permitted consolidation of claims but included some realistic limiting factors for those times. Later circumstances would be another story, but for the time being the General Mining Law represented the best of what Webb and other proponents of the frontier school saw in a legislative outcome of Western values.[49]

Lode mining requires considerable capital to provide the equipment necessary to remove large volumes of overlying materials from ore deposits still in place within the earth. Even epithermal deposits, usually veins which formed relatively near the surface, require some underground mining. The structure above a mine shaft which supports a large bucket or elevator is called a headframe.

(Photo courtesy Arizona Historical Society)

Chapter Five

Mineral Patents and the Patent Process

The General Land Office had been giving other types of land patents for some years so it adjusted to mineral patents fairly readily. Ironically, the very first patent granted under the Act of 1866 was not for gold or silver but for mercury. In fact, the Monterrey Quick Silver Mining District had naturally established special rules for that substance since it was the primary ore mined near the California coast. Representatives of the San Francisco branch of the Land Office surveyed 6,000 feet along a vein stained red from cinnabar ore, the primary source of mercury. The application, by four individuals, represented a consolidation of claims as allowed under local laws. In addition to the survey of June 3, 1867, the General Land Office's staff members wrote a brief report describing the deposit and verifying that shafts of more than $1,000 in value were in place.

With a complete file in hand, the Washington office approved mineral patent number 1 on July 14, 1868. The application materials became part of the government's permanent collection of records. A final document for the patent, laboriously handwritten and including a colorful plat of the property, went to the claimants, with a copy, also handwritten, going into the first bound volume of the new set of mineral patents maintained by the Land Office. The file for patent number 1 also contains a letter from the Land Office to Senator John Conness of California noting the occasion, certainly an indicator of the political interest and the relevant party in the administration of the new mining law. No other similar high-level interest appears in the early patent files.[1]

[87]

The Land Office team, even including the surveyors, had only minimal instructions as to the patent process. In fact, the printed guide from Washington was only ten pages plus the text of the Mining Laws. The checklist of items the inspectors used to consider an application is revealing. Similar lists are virtually unchanged even in patents of the present day since the Acts of 1870 and 1872 basically followed the method described in the original Act of 1866.[2]

The items that must be presented to the government are:

1. The application form itself.
2. Copies of the original claim location notice and, if used, any diagrams as filed with the local official.
3. A copy of a newspaper advertisement announcing that patent application has been made and describing the location. Further, the publisher had to certify that such advertisement had appeared at least one time per week for ninety days.
4. A statement that a Notice saying the claim was under patent application had been posted on the land itself.
5. A statement that the Notice of patent application had been continuously in place for at least ninety days.
6. A statement that the Notice of patent application had been on public display at the nearest branch of the General Land Office (this, at least, was the responsibility of the official, not the claimant).
7. A copy of the local miners' laws (if applicable) and a certificate of compliance with such laws.
8. An affidavit of citizenship of the applicants, or a declaration of their intent to become citizens.
9. The report of the government surveyors and their field notes.
10. Receipts for the required fees for the land itself, the application, and the survey.
11. A certificate from the county clerk or other appropriate local official that no suit was pending, or that a final judgment was on the record if such suit(s) had been filed.
12. An abstract of title if the parties applying for patent were not the original claimants. Such abstract had to cite a chain of official documents showing an unbroken record of ownership.[3]

Obviously much of the intent of Congress in establishing these requirements for patent was to bring out all potential challenges

Mineral Patents and Patent Process 89

prior to the final grant. Patents could and would be overturned but usually by action of the government, not by rival claimants.

The first four volumes of the permanent patent records provide a convenient frame for comparative studies. These volumes include patents under all three Acts: 1866, 1870, and 1872, and allow some analysis. The volumes have a total of 425 entries, including some cancellations still of value for scholarly purposes, and represent almost exactly the first four years of the system, from mid-1868 to mid-1872.[4]

Patent number 5 for a gold mine near Mariposa, California, is listed as having been canceled by government action in 1895 but the cause is not in the records. Another patent, number 56, on the Knickerbocker Lode in the American Flat District in Storey County, Nevada, bears the note of cancellation but was reissued as patent number 134. One other lode and two placer claims in the first four volumes were apparently canceled at the time of final review rather than at a later date, but no further record is in the files.[5]

The first placer patent bears number 205 and went to the Helena Water Company in the Oro Fino Gulch District of Lewis and Clark County, Montana, Territory, on April 4, 1871. California's first placer patent, number 227, went to Luigi Misene, Stefano Zerga, and Stefano Cassassa in one of the classic locales of the great rush of two decades earlier, the Ionaville District of El Dorado County. These claimants were still mining but may also have been taking advantage of the Act of 1870 to purchase the land for farming. Senator Stewart had emphasized such action as a legitimate use of the law. The Act of 1872 soon repealed this application of mines to farming. However, most patents for placer claims do appear to have been for mining. Despite the cheaper fee of $2.50 per acre, it was no bargain when compared to the genuine methods of entry for agricultural lands. Indeed, the list of items required in submitting an application for a placer patent included a statement that there were no known lodes in the area. Further, the final document as granted to the owners of placer claims includes a clause allowing physical access to the land by the owner of a lode claim if necessary to pursue the vein underground. In other words, placer claims are subordinate to lode claims under a kind of legal extension of the "apex rule."[6]

As the number of mineral patents grew, a variety of problems arose. The Reese River District in Lander County, Nevada (county courthouse at Austin), is much less known than many other areas, but its total of forty-six patents represented more than for any other single district in the first four volumes. It was only natural that the first conflict between two claimants who both ultimately received some of their respective claims would occur in this district. Patent number 6 went to the Old Colony silver lode. When the owners of the neighboring Savannah Lode filed their application shortly thereafter, the survey revealed part of it in conflict with a patent already in place. Nevertheless, the claimants received patent number 55 to the portion not in conflict, with a resulting gap on the plats. Needless to say, this would not be the last such overlapping conflict in which a claimant received less than the acreage he or she had requested. Some highly developed districts would have patented claims broken into as many as eight separate pieces because of overlying prior patents.[7]

The General Land Office soon learned to send the survey crews to areas where a number of applications were pending at once. This common sense practice saved unnecessary travel and made resolution of possible overlaps somewhat easier. Of course, claimants had to wait longer for the final certificate, but that was part of frontier life. The first four volumes thus show many sequences of patents granted from the same areas, often for claims that were literally adjoining each other.[8]

In the procession of patents, the first listings from the Comstock do not appear until numbers 61 through 64, when the surveyors examined the adjacent Chollar Potosi, Hale and Norcross, Savage, and the Gould and Curry. Subsequently only two other patents appear in the first four volumes from the Virginia District on the Comstock. One of these was a small lode located in a space overlooked between two of the larger ones. Though several other large mines in the Virginia District ultimately went to patent, the owners were in no particular hurry. The nearby Gold Hill District accounted for fifteen patents but they still reflected the limit of 150 feet along the vein, as local laws provide. Hence their plats are long and narrow when compared to those of other areas.[9]

Within a few years of the Act of 1866, the Bank of California, under financiers William Ralston and William Sharon, successfully bought out many of the major Comstock mines. This development had nothing to do with the Act being in place, though some historians, including Mayer and Riley, have claimed otherwise. In fact, the Bank's control only lasted until 1875. Ralston's mismanagement caused the collapse, plus the loss of his personal fortune, and possibly his drowning under circumstances that might have been suicide. The bank had also opposed Sutro's tunnel but on that score, too, it lost.[10]

It is impossible to justify the whole complex set of mining laws as simply a move to protect the Comstock. Of 121 patents in Nevada as reported in the first four volumes, the Gold Hill and Virginia Districts together accounted for only 21. There were 7 more elsewhere in Storey County. Most of the rest of Nevada's total were in Lander County and another important but little-known district in White Pine County (courthouse at Ely), quite distant from Virginia City.[11] A few were in Mark Twain's Esmeralda District, near Aurora, also some distance from Virginia City. Consequently, the owners of the more remote patented claims are not the famous figures of mining. Yet they were not the ordinary prospectors who had made the discoveries. They were essentially small businessmen.

The situation was somewhat similar in the patents granted in Colorado, as shown in the first four volumes. It is perhaps quite symbolic that the first patent granted there was in April 1869 to Henry Teller, for a gold mine on the Peck and Thomas Lode in the Gregory District of Gilpin County. Teller ultimately did become a mining magnate and a prominent United States senator from Colorado. (Teller should not be confused with H.A.W. Tabor, a somewhat later mining magnate and short-term U.S. senator from Colorado.) The records of Teller's Peck and Thomas Lode include an abstract of title showing the claim had changed hands several times between its discovery and Teller's purchase. This is just what the mining law was designed to encourage: discovery by a prospector, intervening owners, and development by a party with sufficient capital. All benefited.[12]

Colorado from the beginning had a mass of smaller lode mines as compared with other areas. The first four volumes of federal patents reflect this situation and the resultant diversity of ownership. Almost all the claims were in the various districts of Gilpin

County, as noted in an earlier chapter, or neighboring Clear Creek County, since other noted locales in the territory were not yet to the stage of development that produced patent applications. The total of 157 lode patents was the highest of any state or territory. Henry Teller owned ten and his brother William had four, certainly no undue concentration. Few other parties filed for patent on more than one claim, which often included a millsite, depending on local district laws.

A rare personal look at the application of the Act of 1866 is provided by Irving Stanton, the local registrar of the General Land Office at Central City, Colorado, who issued almost all of the patents from that state in the first four volumes. Stanton wrote directly to the commissioner of the General Land Office in Washington in late 1869. He saw the filing of adverse claims as a serious problem that delayed the process. Of 100 applications then pending, fully half were tied up in local court. Stanton suggested administrative hearings before the local office, similar to those in contested agricultural cases. Further, federal recognition of miners' meetings "virtually annuls the Territorial Statute." However, that was a relatively trivial matter, as Stanton saw it. For federal policy changes, he suggested recognition of mill sites. He concluded with an illustrative statement for his locale and the nineteenth century in general:

> It is well known that when the Act of July 26, 1866, first became a law and before it was fully understood and appreciated, there was strong opposition to it in the mining districts of Colorado but the opposition has entirely disappeared and I do not now know of a single person who is opposed to it, but on the contrary every one favors it and claimants are very generally disposed to avail themselves of its benefits.
>
> I think with Amendments something like those herein suggested two or three years would suffice to dispose of the valuable portion of the Mineral lands of this District.[13]

Stanton's observations show that the overall policy was to distribute the lands as quickly as possible, but to eliminate contests before going to final private ownership. As noted in the last chapter, Congress itself soon began debating various amendments that re-

Mineral Patents and Patent Process 93

sulted in the Acts of 1870 and 1872. The latter gave federal status to millsites, as Stanton had recommended. Also as he suggested, the territorial assembly made amendments the very next year, and most subsequent claimants chose to file under those revised rules rather than mining camp regulations. Territorial law did have one point in its favor: a better basis for enforcement of conflicts involving claims prior to full patent. In fact, more favorable claim dimensions on the surface were the only grounds that an applicant might cite for choosing local laws. Some miners' meetings allowed claims along veins twice as long as those allowed under territorial laws. Even so, most patent applicants still chose to file under the territorial laws.

The patent process naturally required some capital but was by no means an option for the rich alone. The purchase price itself was $5.00 per acre for lodes under the Act of 1866, charged on application. A claimant also paid $30 for the survey by government officials, and $5.00 more for certification of the required $500 in improvements. These costs remained much the same into the twentieth century. One modest miner/businessman, Frank Rearden of central Colorado, estimated that a patent application he filed as late as 1900 would ultimately cost $605, much the same figure since number 1. Considering wages of $3.50 per day for the more fortunate miners, such a cost required some production, even well into the twentieth century. Still, the full patent option was advisable if there was chance of conflict with other claimants, as was frequently the case.[14]

Figures from the first four volumes show relative activity of newer areas as well as the older ones. Montana had 27 lode patents and 16 placers. California had 45 lodes and 48 placers. Utah had 10 lodes and Oregon had 2 placers. Among the Colorado total of 156 and Nevada's 121 there were no placer patents at all though there had been initial rushes for this type of deposit in both states. Almost all lode patents were for gold and silver, though four were for cinnabar and one was for copper. Clearly, there was no rush to patent "used up" placer claims. (The above totals include cancellations simply to show activity by area.)

The numbers of patents proliferated as the years wore on. By late 1877, the General Land Office had finished volume 30. By late 1880 the Office was into volume 54. The records of 1881 show that patents were no longer laboriously handwritten but placed on printed forms with blank spaces filled in. Certainly this was a relief not only to Washington personnel but many county recorders who had to recopy patents, including the plats, into their own records. Early applications had been for one patent at a time but as the industrial age progressed, some applications were for a number of adjacent claims owned by the same party. By 1908 the numbering sequence that had started so neatly had long since become broken, but the Office had filled 461 volumes with a total of well over 47,000 patents. Unfortunately, by that date the colorful plats were long gone and the blanks on the forms were filled in by typewriter. The year 1908 marks the greatest aesthetic loss because the agency went to a different filing system and the series of volumes of final patents ended. Subsequent mineral patents are interspersed among all other land patents so comparative studies are administratively impossible.

As soon as the Act of May 10, 1872, was on the statute books, the General Land Office reworded the phraseology as written into the patent documents themselves so as to reflect the change in status of the "apex rule." Patents under the 1866 Act clearly granted subsurface rights beyond the claim's surface boundaries but only to the primary vein used to designate the claim. The patents granted under the 1872 Act allowed the owners to follow into the subsurface "out side the vertical sidelines of said survey" any vein that topped within the claim's limits on the surface. The General Land Office made the shift immediately, even for claims in the legal process prior to the Act and simply awaiting final approval. The first to reflect the Act of 1872 was patent number 357 from the American Flat District of Storey County, Nevada. This provision as well as the definite five acres allowed to mill sites under the Act of 1872 observably encouraged claimants to ignore local district laws. By filing under state or territorial laws they generally had nearly full use of the liberal terms of the federal acts. The official at Central City, Colorado, who had noted the early priority of district laws, soon found himself reviewing almost all applications under territorial law instead. Most Colorado claims became uniform at 1,400 feet long, the maximum allowed under territorial laws.[15]

Several other points from the patent files are of interest. Many local court judgments are included, showing various types of con-

Mineral Patents and Patent Process 95

tests were common. Most of these involved surface boundaries. Applicants for patent were often foreign-born, so many files contain naturalization papers. Though a party only had to declare the intention to become a citizen, some contests hinged on whether such legal declaration was on record at the time a claim was on file.[16]

As noted earlier, the government canceled some patents, even in the earliest days. The records are too sparse in most of these cases to determine fully a cause for such action, but one case does have considerable documentation, though it is from the early twentieth century. V. A. Johnson filed the Way-Up lode claim near Lewiston, Idaho. In a 1902 investigation, Sidney Miller of the General Land Office found no evidence of workings. Instead, Miller determined that the claim was designed to control access to Crystal Lake. The claimant contested the decision but eventually lost in a 1906 ruling. The investigations conducted on mineral patent applications thus seem to contrast markedly with cursory actions given to other types of land distribution governed by the same agency. This case has an unusual amount of documentation because the party attempted to gain a full patent. Generally, those who filed nuisance claims for various purposes lacked the audacity to go on to the next step, much less an appeal. Nuisance claims were relatively common but the General Land Office became skilled at ferreting them out, at least under mining laws, if not other land distribution measures.[17]

Parties legitimately attempting to mine met all the requirements on the checklist upon payment of fees, and could thus expect a patent. In the early days the government generally accepted such evidence of valid discovery on a claim, unless it had reason for skepticism. It was not until the 1940s that officials took samples and wrote a more professional mineral report to justify the contention that a valid discovery was made. Even so, the costs of patent generally ensured sincerity on the part of applicants, until inflation made a mockery of the prices specified in the Acts, a situation not evident until after World War II.[18]

Today county courthouses throughout the West have a variety of records relating to the entire patent process. There are copies of the original claims, copies of annual assessment work, copies of transfers of ownership of claims prior to the status of full patent, and copies of the approved patent documents. The final documents bear the name of the president, but usually are signed by an aide. Once the General Land Office sent the final document to the applicant, it was his responsibility to see that the local recorder also made a copy. Naturally, most parties did so rather quickly, but some neglected to do so either by accident or perhaps purposefully to avoid local taxes. Presumably the federal document already in possession was enough to guarantee against a contest. Thus copies of patents still drift into county courthouses many years after the date they were issued in Washington, usually when a resale is pending.[19]

Overall, the patent process was simply homestead adjusted to the rugged country where wealth would come from mining instead of agriculture. The Turner/Webb school has given considerable support to homestead and similar practices as an integral part of development of the West. The General Mining Laws belong in a special subgroup of the same broad category.

Chapter Six

Western Life under the General Mining Laws

The late 1870s and early 1880s saw a succession of major lode rushes across the West. In several cases, the prospectors who actually discovered the districts reaped massive profits, along with those who "grubstaked" them. Naturally, the early developers of these districts became magnates.

The single year 1877 saw the discovery of three classic lode districts: silver at Leadville, Colorado, and Tombstone, Arizona, and gold at Lead, Dakota Territory. At Leadville, two prospectors, August Rische and George Hook, backed by storekeeper H. A.W. Tabor, received over $300,000 total for the sale of their claims. Though there had been some placering in the area for many years, it took longer to recognize finally the value of "that damned blue stuff" than at the Comstock. Tabor, by himself, patented the discovery, the Little Pittsburgh mine. Subsequently he sold it for $1 million, then made more on other claims.[1]

At Tombstone, a colorful prospector and "jack of all trades," Ed Schieffelin, entered remote Apache country despite warnings that all he would find would be his own tombstone. Thus he named the first of several silver discoveries that brought him a modest fortune: Tombstone. He sold the claims but kept on prospecting.[2]

At Lead, in the Black Hills of Dakota Territory, a single Precambrian gold deposit was the discovery of a team from George Hearst's company, subsequently reorganized to become Homestake Corporation. Such a discovery team forecast prospecting in the next century. Here Hearst made even more than he had at the

Ed Schieffelin, the discoverer of the Tombstone claim.
(Courtesy Arizona Historical Society)

Comstock, especially since Homestake soon gained control of the entire deposit, relatively easy to consolidate.[3]

Two Alaska prospectors, Richard T. Harris and Joseph Juneau, discovered placer and lode gold at the site of the city named after Juneau. The grubstakers, merchants in Sitka and San Francisco, also profited. A moderate-sized rush resulted. Mining camp law was all that existed in Alaska since Congress had intentionally withheld application of the land laws after its purchase from Russia in 1867. The lack of surveys as well as lack of officials to process any types of patents in the remote region caused Congress to fall back on well-precedented inaction. So Alaska was in much the same legal situation that California, Nevada, and Colorado had seen prior to the Act of 1866. Before the rush to Juneau there had been some sporadic placer mining and development of one lode mine near Sitka, the center of what little authority then existed in the territory. Subsequently, a series of placer discoveries would finally bring massive rushes to the neighboring Canadian Yukon and to Nome and Fairbanks around the turn of the century. The legal vacuum would remain the same until the massive rushes. Even then, a host of new problems would arise with local law and officials.[4]

In the early 1880s yet another prospector, Noah Kellogg, made the first discovery in what became the extensive Coeur d'Alene region of Idaho that eventually included several districts. Kellogg received a good sum for his claims, but lost a portion to the grubstakers after attempting to exclude them from their share. Frontier courts undoubtedly heard a variety of fascinating cases.[5]

The 1863 discovery of silver (with deeper copper) at Bingham Canyon, near Salt Lake City, Utah, had unusual social effects. The U.S. Army officer in charge of the region, Patrick Connor, hated the polygamous Morman culture. He saw the rush as a means of weakening the dominant group in Utah, so he did all he could to encourage mining. Even so, the followers of Brigham Young were too committed to their faith to defy their leader's admonitions against joining the miners. Instead, they profited by selling their traditional farm produce to the new settlements. Mining did aid Connor by bringing many non-Mormons to Utah over subsequent years.

Some of Connor's own soldiers made discoveries at what became

Park City in the Wasatch Mountains in 1868. A few years later an ordinary miner from Bingham Canyon, Tom Kearns, also prospected there. His discoveries made him a leading mining magnate, one of the most dramatic examples of a typical working man transformed into a millionaire. (Later Park City joined several Colorado towns as old mining locales which had good skiing.)[6]

Mining laws provided a dramatic means for common men to go literally from "rags to riches." Henry Comstock had blown his chance, but enough others made fortunes to draw even more into hardrock prospecting.

Several of these developments had further importance regarding mining law. In Leadville, the State of Colorado had a single mining district nearly equal to the celebrated Comstock. Further, a group of flamboyant millionaires emerged, colorful enough to rival the Virginia City crowd. However, no single person or company, not even Tabor, controlled the district. Instead, a mass of lawsuits served to spread a good part of the wealth. Geologically, the most important ore deposits at Leadville were mesothermal replacements of materials in late Paleozoic limestones. This fact alone proved significant. While the major Comstock mines had fought successfully for their "apex" rights, the opposite happened at Leadville. Many small veins were identified along fault lines at Leadville, but the situation was so complicated that years of litigation ensued. Cases at Aspen, another nearby silver camp long before the skiing era, had the same result since some ores there were in an unusual mass of glacial debris rather than in more easily recognized and worked vein type of deposits.[7]

Similarly, Tombstone never fell under any dominant concern, though one mine, the Grand Central, was undeniably the largest. The Coeur d'Alene had no dominant concern, but it was geographically dispersed enough that particular towns within the larger district became company towns. Such communities were unusual in precious metal mining areas, though they would be common in a later age of industrial metals.[8]

How large were the later discoveries in comparison to the earlier ones and to each other? As a reference point, the Comstock had averaged $12.1 million per year the first dozen years. Then, in 1873, the Comstock produced $35 million, but soon tapered back to the earlier range. By way of comparison, all of Colorado had produced

The original claim as filed by Ed Schieffelin at Tombstone.
(Courtesy Pima County, Arizona, Recorder)

$7.5 million in 1864, a figure that fell to $1.8 million in 1867. New milling techniques developed by Nathaniel P. Hill subsequently allowed some mines to reopen and production stood at $6 million by 1871, roughly where it remained toward the end of the decade. In part, these milling techniques account for the numbers of early Colorado patents discussed in the previous chapter. Then spectacular Leadville alone brought $11.5 million in 1880. Tombstone averaged $3 million a year in its first decade. The Coeur d'Alene region yielded $10 million in 1890.[9]

What were the secondary impacts of such masses of ore flowing from mines? Again using the first major lode mining state, Nevada, as the standard, official census returns show it had a slight edge over Colorado as late as 1870. That year Nevada had 42,000 to 40,000 for Colorado. Even before Leadville, Colorado's growth in the early 1870s was remarkable. Agriculture in the eastern part of

Colorado mining magnate H. A. W. Tabor who had been a rather simple store owner before he patented the Little Pittsburgh mine and helped start a lode rush to Leadville. (Courtesy Denver Public Library)

the state and what can only be described as early tourism in the mountains, with spectacular scenery and hot spring resorts, had promoted growth to 196,000 by 1880. Leadville alone had nearly 15,000. Nevada's total then stood at 62,000. Yet Colorado was not finished. Her population reached 413,000 in 1890, while the borrasca of the Comstock caused Nevada to fall back to 47,000. And that was before Colorado found Cripple Creek, the most fabulous district in the United States.[10]

Part of Colorado's continued success of the 1880s resulted from a series of discoveries in the remote San Juan Mountains of the state's southwest corner. By the mid-1870s the Ute Indians ceded the area in a treaty and prospectors could enter. (The Utes remained peaceful, in contrast to the Sioux, who had claimed the Black Hills which were opened to prospecting at about the same time.) The San Juan Mountains, so spectacularly scenic, hosted many diverse ores while making them quite difficult to remove. Instead of such relatively large centers as Virginia City, Leadville, or Cripple Creek, the San Juans forced the development of several medium-sized mining camps with many smaller ones scattered between. The best-known are Silverton, Ouray, Creede, and Telluride, the latter again famous because of its revival as a resort and skiing center.[11]

The development of Telluride was a direct result of development of the Smuggler mine, located on a mountainside above a natural townsite in a magnificent glaciated valley beyond the San Juans. In fact, the Smuggler was the most famous early mine in the region. Yet some might charge that the developers of the Smuggler had engaged in a claim jump. Two parties had originally filed claims on an easily recognized quartz vein, but each had erected corner markers to include about 2,000 feet along the lode. As noted earlier, claims legally have a limit of 1,500 feet in length. A third party, J.B. Ingram, observed this situation and noted the lack of vigor one of the parties was showing in developing the claim. The lack of interest went so far as failure to file the affidavit of annual assessment work legally required to hold the claim. Ingram in 1879 filed his own claim of some 1,054 feet right out of the middle of the vein, taking the "extra" 500 feet that each of the other parties had marked. His action stood up, through a patent granted the next

A panorama of Leadville at its height by pioneer photographer L. C. McClure. In the background are Mts. Elbert and Massive, the tallest in Colorado. (Courtesy Denver Public Library)

year. With more capital for more active ore removal, the Smuggler mine produced millions. Its owners later bought out what was left of the adjacent claims. Indeed, on foreign investment markets the name "Smuggler" became virtually synonymous with the entire San Juan region.[12]

Ironically, the Smuggler lode was a "traditional" quartz vein, and not a telluride vein such as would later make Cripple Creek famous. However, the original name of the nearby town, Columbia, proved confusing to postal authorities, who had to decide

whether to send handwritten envelopes to "Columbia, Cal.," or "Columbia, Col.," both mining camps. Somehow the name changed from Columbia to Telluride. Beside the Smuggler, several other important mines were working in the area by the 1880s, most notably the Tomboy.[13]

The progress of any mining at all in the San Juan region is a testament to extreme ingenuity and perseverance in developing transportation. The best-known figure in these endeavors was Otto Mears, who built wagon roads over high passes, then backed narrow gauge railroads (3 feet between railheads, as compared to 4 feet, 8½ inches for standard gauge). Like Sutro, Mears was a visionary man partly of Jewish heritage. And like Sutro, some of his projects proved technically successful but not financially rewarding for investors. Even so, Colorado, the highest of the mountain states, with the "toy trains" that added so much to its character, was the leader in precious metal mining well into the twentieth century. No single corporation, however, dominated the mines or other aspects of the state.[14]

Other mining regions were similarly competitive except for Lead, South Dakota, which became Homestake's domain. Even the Comstock regained a more competitive status after the Bank of California collapsed, though a group colloquially called the Bonanza Four attempted to gain control. Somehow, that group simply did not display the ruthlessness often associated with other "robber barons" of the era, perhaps because it was obvious that the Comstock was declining, though still valuable.[15]

In other regions of the country and in other industries, the age of monopolies was clearly a fact of life. Some blatant examples were the major steel companies in this period, which consolidated the best iron ore lands in Minnesota, Michigan, and Wisconsin into a far more solid block than later concerns could consolidate other industrial metals in the West. Congress had intentionally repealed the 1872 Act for these states simply because of the iron ore; was that to aid the giants or to try to protect against them? The records of the General Land Office's branch at Duluth show that major companies quite successfully used homestead, preemption, and direct purchase capabilities under other federal laws to accomplish acquisitions in the 1880s. Fraudulent homesteads were commonplace; lumber companies also used them to secure the best forest lands.[16]

The Mining Law of 1872 gave the "little man" at least some opportunities he would not have otherwise had as a prospector, placer miner, and shallow lode miner even in districts where the size of deposits would ultimately require larger concerns. It is difficult to imagine any mining laws that could possibly have been more favorable to the "little man" than the Acts of 1866, 1870, and 1872, given the physical constraints of mining in many locales. To stake a claim under any of these Acts, all the individual needed was the nominal county filing fee! Without the General Mining laws, major developers could have bought mineral lands under the Timber and Stone Act of 1878 for $2.50 per acre, or used dummy locators for fraudulent homesteads to acquire the mining lands, just as steel companies did in the Great Lakes region. Had the Julian proposal passed instead of the 1866 Act, Western mining would have followed much the same course as mining on federal lands in other regions.

The Timber and Stone Act gave large concerns a great opportunity to exploit another type of resource. The standard tricks of dummy locators, with exercise of preemption, helped some companies consolidate masses of forest lands. Thus the nation lost many forests of common types of wood as well as much of California's unique coastal redwoods. It was an era of arrogant rising corporations, including railroads, grain elevators, and various other industries, yet in some areas the "little man" had a much better chance.[17]

Claim jumping was widely practiced, but if the "little man" could do so against a giant, he became a local celebrity. Quite commonly the Land Office issued patents for claims that were broken into two or more separate areas by overlying claims of earlier dates. Records in the richer districts show this problem on almost every map. While Leadville was at its peak in the early 1880s one mine hired armed guards to prevent jumping. Several enterprising individuals legally jumped another mine with $15,000 worth of improvements, not to mention the ore, because prior claimants had neglected to file the annual assessment form under state law.[18]

Many legal claim jumps were attempted over annual assessment, some much more successful than others. Colorado provides yet another excellent example. In the early 1880s the state changed the legal date for filing the assessment document from the anniversary of filing the particular claim to a uniform date of January 1. Miner Will C. Ferril and his partners had neglected to file the assessment form but planned simply to relocate the claim as soon as legally possible, at 12:01 a.m. They waited on the unidentified claim, while watching potential jumpers prowl the area with lanterns. At the appointed time they placed new markers and a notice on the claim and celebrated by discharging their weapons, causing the prowlers quickly to disappear. Even so, jumpers successfully relocated several mines in the area, as observed the next morning.[19]

In short, the Mining Acts actually allowed the "little man" to turn the tables on major operators. In other cases big companies fraudulently used land entry methods to acquire resources.

Though claim jumping often simply pitted one little man against another, there was no lack of attempts to jump the major mines. These incidents resulted in occasional violence, but even in the frontier West the usual outcome was litigation. An excellent example is provided by historian Roger McGrath, who documented many violent incidents over an extended period at Mark Twain's Aurora, Nevada, and a later mining town, adjacent Bodie, California, from the 1860s into the 1880s. Yet he found only two episodes that might be called armed confrontations related to claim jumping, though shots were fired in other incidents. In the first incident, two small groups contested the extent of land involved in sale of a claim. One fatality resulted. In the other, large groups were involved in a case also involving management opposition to labor. Even so, the parties soon decided to allow judicial settlement of the matter, a testament to the power of the customary use of the courts.[20]

News of discoveries naturally prompted many others to go to mining areas to attempt to duplicate the good fortune of the most publicized prospectors. By late 1879, just two years after Ed Schieffen's discovery of Tombstone, a group of brothers arrived from Kansas, Texas, and California, and began to file claims within a matter of days. At the time, they had to go all the way to Tucson to file. They recalled an earlier place of residence by giving the claims names like "Dodge" and the "Long Branch," after the famous saloon in Dodge City, Kansas. However, they did not immediately find enough ore or other sources for what they considered a reasonable living. In Kansas and other locales they had been involved with law enforcement, so they drifted back into that type of occupation since Tombstone had far more problems than even contemporary Colorado mining camps. Thus Wyatt Earp and his brothers became U.S. marshals. They enlisted help from an old acquaintance, "Doc" Holliday (who also owned at least one mining claim), and became involved in the celebrated gunfight of October 1881, which had a number of violent repercussions over ensuing months. Legal actions also resulted. Two of principals of these much-studied events provide excellent examples of people affected by the mining law.[21]

Wyatt Earp spent only twenty-seven months at Tombstone, in a lifetime of nearly eighty-one years. He had never killed anyone during his days as law officer in Kansas, and never did subsequent to his Tombstone experience. However, he acquired a massive reputation during that tumultuous period. He also acquired a new wife, Josephine Sarah Marcus. Josie had come to Tombstone as part of a stage show troupe at age 19. She had grown up in San Francisco in a German-Jewish family. Ironically, her good looks had initially attracted the attention of Johnny Behan, the local sheriff who became a political opponent of the Earps. Behan's alliance with notorious rustlers, though, was probably the most significant factor in bringing the tragic reign of violence. Several other forces were also part of the background of a frontier settlement that literally became a city within a matter of weeks, with plenty of potential for trouble.[22]

Ultimately it was too much even for the Earps. One brother, Morgan, died and another, Virgil, was injured. In mid-1882 Wyatt took his new wife out of the danger zone and moved to Colorado, where he prospected in several areas and filed more mining claims. Josie learned to go with him. Yet the couple's social life even included H. A. W. Tabor and his new, young wife, "Baby Doe," who was involved in one of the most publicized "society scandals" of the century. Josie and Wyatt probably related well with the Tabors since their own situation was similar.[23]

Early 1884 found them in Idaho's Coeur d'Alene just after word arrived of prospector Kellogg's good fortune. Here too, Wyatt filed several mining claims. Eventually he and Josie spent time in Texas and in San Diego, California, and thus were not actively prospecting in the late 1880s and early 1890s. Even so, they had a number of adventures.[24] They could never avoid mining for long, as we shall see.

Only a few prospectors could make the big strike. Some, however, might find something of value. A good example is provided by claim records filed in Cochise County, Arizona Territory. Tombstone had been part of Pima County since its discovery, so Schieffelin had filed his initial claims at Tucson. With the resultant rush, Tombstone and a large surrounding area that had been within Pima County became a new entity, Cochise County.

The new county recorder formally wrote the first copy of a "Notice of Location" on March 2, 1881. By May 17, 1881, he had filled a 640-page volume of "Notices," almost all one per page. It

385

General Land Office
No. 4369

Mineral Certificate
No. 108

The United States of America

To all to whom these Presents shall come, Greeting:—

Whereas, In pursuance of the provisions of the Revised Statutes of the United States, Chapter Six, Title Thirty two, there have been deposited in the General Land Office of the United States the Plat and Field Notes of survey of the claim of the Ouray Mining Company and J. B. Ingram upon the

Smuggler Lode

accompanied by the Certificate of the Register of the Land Office at Lake City in the State of Colorado whereby it appears that, in pursuance of the said Revised Statutes of the United States, the

Ouray Mining Company and J. B. Ingram,

did, on the twenty third day of December, A. D. 1879, enter and pay for said mining claim or premises, being Mineral Entry No. 108, in the series of said Office, designated by the Surveyor General as Lot No. 283, embracing a portion of the unsurveyed public domain, in the San Miguel Mining District in the County of Ouray and State of Colorado in the District of Lands subject to sale at Lake City, containing seven (7) acres and twenty-five hundredths ($\frac{25}{100}$) of an acre of land, more or less, and, according to the returns on file in the General Land Office, bounded, described, and platted as follows, with magnetic variation at fourteen (14) degrees fifteen (15) minutes East, to wit:—

Beginning at Corner No. 1, a Post four (4) inches square, in mound of stones, marked "Cor No. 1" on one side, and "Sur No 283" on the opposite side, from which Locating Monument No 3, a Post six (6) inches

> United States of America, have caused these Letters to be made Patent, and the Seal of the General Land Office to be hereunto affixed.
>
> Given under my hand, at the City of Washington, the thirtieth day of November in the year of our Lord one thousand eight hundred and eighty, and of the Independence of the United States the one hundred and fifth.
>
> By the President: R. B. Hayes
>
> By Wm H. Crook   Secretary
>
> S. W. Clark   Recorder of the General Land Office.
>
> Recorded Vol 54 Pages 385 to 390 inclusive

Final patent of the Smuggler mine near Telluride in the San Juan Mountains of Colorado. Rival parties could take advantage of each other on legal points during the claim stage, as happened regarding this mine, but the patent provided much better legal protection.

(Courtesy National Archives)

had taken the Pima County recorder a full decade to collect a similar number, showing the extent of prospecting activity in a mineralized region but prior to a genuine rush. The bulk of the Cochise County claims had two, three, or four locators. The names of women appear on a surprising number of the notices. In some cases, the same individuals had several claims, but no massive concentrations by large companies appeared at that stage. Considering Tombstone's total population of only two to three thousand, it is safe to say that virtually every adult in the area had a share in at least one mining claim. (In Arizona, Pima County retained its original records with Cochise County picking up only at the time of its creation, thus complicating matters. By contrast, in Colorado new counties inherited records for areas that became their jurisdictions after separation from parent counties.)[25]

Yet another indication of the situation at Tombstone in fall 1881 is found in the patent application for the Good Enough claim. None other than Ed Schieffelin had filed this claim along with the Tombstone itself, then sold it to the Tombstone Mill and Mining Company, which applied for the patent in May 1881. That fall the company's attorney, Robert Blutelier, wrote directly to the commissioner of the General Land Office, N.C. Farland, as follows:

> There is an entry in your department of a mine near Tucson, Arizona. Good Enough mine they desire a patent for the reason that other parties are sinking a shaft just outside of their survey: and extracting the ore from their mine the applicants desire a patent at once to prevent by injunction the outside parties from extracting their ore.[26]

Here, despite the lack of punctuation, was the best analysis of the legal value of securing a patent instead of simply working a claim. This letter is dated October 25, 1881, just one day before the famous Earp-Clanton shoot-out (which had no obvious connection). Ironically, there was probably equal cause for such a result in the mining case. The General Land Office was well aware that a formal protest to the patent was already on file from the Way Up Mining Company, the very party allegedly stealing the ore. The Commissioner took until November 28, when he issued the patent to the Tombstone Mill and Mining Co. In the end the record showed that firm to have a conclusively better documented relation to the claim that Ed Schieffelin had originally filed.[27]

Tombstone itself provided only a portion of the overall activity in the extended area of southeastern Arizona. Cochise County alone has 6,218 square miles, somewhat more than the state of Connecticut. A number of other silver towns also flourished but disappeared, lacking much of the romantic draw of Tombstone that would help preserve it as a tourist center. Among the classic "ghost towns" in southeastern Arizona alone are places with the fascinating names of Contention City, Dos Cabezas (Spanish for "two heads," from two huge lumps on the nearby mountains), Paradise, and Total Wreck. Others had more conventional names. Remnants at twenty-one such sites can be visited today in southeastern Arizona, over fifty throughout the state, and many more elsewhere in the West. A very few ghost towns had economic bases other than mining but these were quite rare. Obviously the Act of 1872 provided the legal basis for the existence, no matter how temporary, of these communities. When the mines reached borrasca, the inhabitants generally drifted to other locales in the West. Hence the mining laws clearly served their purpose, development of a permanent population in the region, though the mines themselves naturally played out.[28]

Central Colorado, as another example, had the great mines at Leadville, as well as a mass of smaller lode operations. Records of Lake County, Colorado, provide excellent figures for comparison of that region, which had its second rush at the same time as Tombstone's first rush. The first volume of claim records covers 1865 to early 1879 and lists some 4,297 entries. Most of these were filed under the Colorado law of mining claims but a few were filed under surviving district laws. During the hectic period of February 13, 1879, to November 29, 1879, the county recorder filled a second volume with 3,201 entries, almost all of which were initial lode locations with only a scattering of relocations, placer entries, and mill sites. The great majority were in the immediate Leadville area, but some were in outlying districts. The impact of the silver discoveries that made Tabor should be obvious. Despite the mass of claims in any particular area, relatively few actually went on to patent. Records at Lake County through the 1880s show a total of only 374 mineral patents filed, mostly for acreage far less than the maximum legally allowed size.[29]

Many outlying claims in Lake County and surrounding locales were at extremely high elevation on some of the most lofty peaks in the United States. In fact, some mine portals can still be seen above 14,000 feet elevation on Mts. Lincoln, Bross, and Democrat, in the Ten-Mile/Mosquito Range between Leadville and Fairplay, and on appropriately named La Plata ("silver" in Spanish) Peak south of Leadville. These were mostly small operations compared to those at Leadville, but a few could be called medium-sized. Together they provided a respectable volume of ores both of silver and gold. There are no remnants at all of several towns that once existed on the east side of the Ten-Mile/Mosquito Mountain Range. One miner worked a claim by himself high on Mt. Democrat and was observed to accumulate a large stash. The man was a loner; no one even knew his name or much about him except that he lived in a well-built cabin and was black. His disappearance was just part of his general character.[30]

Another unusual solitary high altitude miner staked claims at an elevation of 13,400 feet near the top of Mt. Antero in the Sawatch Range south of Leadville. This miner was not as reticent as the one on Mt. Democrat. He recorded claims in 1884 under the name Nathaniel D. Wanemaker. Under the Act of 1872 "valuable deposits" could be located by filing mining claims. Wanemaker had despaired of finding silver but on Mt. Antero he found gems. Mt. Antero, named after a wise Indian chief of the Ute Tribe, provided many semi-precious stones, especially blue aquamarine. Wanemaker had the mountain pretty much to himself for some years. He lived in a stone cabin and recovered about $600 his first year. Eventually, others moved in and gems from Mt. Antero became rather well-known, with production running into thousands of dollars per year.[31]

Yet another early case of "valuable" materials that bore no resemblance to gold or silver also came from a remote part of Colorado. As early as 1873, geologist Sylvester Rich described an unusually pure deposit of marble on the western side of the Elk Mountains. The next year George Yule found the deposit that bears his name: the Yule marble. This material is a genuine marble in the geologic sense; it is a section of the Leadville limestone formation subsequently changed by the tectonic action of mountain building. In fact, many materials sold commercially under the name of "marble" are simply ordinary limestones. The Yule marble is the hardest and purest known. Finally in 1885 several individuals set about developing the material. John Osgood raised capital while others filed mining claims under the Act of 1872. By 1895 the builders of the new state capitol at Denver used the marble in its construction.[32]

Certainly Wanemaker's deposits of gems as well as the Yule marble qualified as "valuable" under the Act of 1872, but the government would eventually begin to look more skeptically on other cases that were atypical to the Western United States. Eventually, a set of case law would define the issue but that would take many years.

While miners were getting used to the General Mining Laws, they also found it necessary to get used to some new technical methods involving mining. Previously, the trade depended on *Black Powder and Hand Steel*, as historian Otis Young observed. Both of these components disappeared from almost all mines during the 1870s. Alfred Nobel's famous invention, dynamite, finally caught on in the mines after some early samples had given it a reputation as unreliable. Power drills replaced the dangerous hand held jacks. In hitting the jack with a sledge hammer by the light of a flickering candle, there was a good chance of serious injury. Drills appeared in Colorado in 1869 and on the Comstock in 1872, just in time for the next stage of deeper mining that would have been impossible with older methods.[33]

Regarding equipment, one final tangential observation is in order. Webb in *The Great Plains* notes several inventions that made settlement of that region possible. These included barbed wire, the windmill, various plows, railroads, and the revolver type of pistol. Such technical adaptations to a harsh environment finally allowed settlement and development by Europeans. A similar but perhaps less dramatic situation existed with mining in the West. The older methods proved sufficient for some early settlement, but the advent of dynamite and power drills furthered a more stable industrial base. Some larger mines used small electric locomotives to move ore cars when these became technically feasible in the 1890s. In fact, the first alternating current electrical generators in the country served the remote San Juan region of Colorado. The cost, however, was prohibitive to many smaller operations, which relied on simple hand pushed ore cars. After 1910, carbide lamps replaced candles for illumination, and further aided technical development. Overall, mining was in a very dynamic stage in the evolution of its methods, both technical and legal.[34]

Chapter Seven

The Mining Law in a Tumultuous Period

The crucial date in United States history, according to Turner, is 1890. The director of the Bureau of the Census, in the final report of the count of that year, officially proclaimed that the frontier had ended. Turner emphasized this fact in his famous paper at the Chicago World's Fair in 1893. Of course, such a division is arbitrary, since frontier conditions remained for many years in isolated parts of the West. Further, frontier conditions still persisted into the late twentieth century in portions of Alaska where the government opened some areas to homesteading as late as the 1980s. Even so, some demarcation is useful.[1]

During the 1890s a number of problems emerged that appear to be characteristic of a maturing nation rather than a country still having a frontier. A severe economic depression hit in 1893. Though known by the nineteenth century term "Panic," the length and degree of this economic downturn clearly qualified it as a "depression" in the twentieth century sense. Modern economists have determined that it was fully as serious as the better-known Depression of the 1930s, though it did not last quite as long. As in other times of economic trouble, many labor disputes arose in the 1890s. Several tragically violent episodes had marked labor relations since a massive railroad strike in 1877, but these had been in the more developed regions. A new group of labor strikes affected Western mines as well as urban areas of the East and Midwest in the 1890s.[2]

During the latter part of the nineteenth century, gold and silver became significant issues in national politics. Great detail is not necessary here but the importance of the issue cannot be overemphasized. In 1873 Congress quietly passed the Coinage Act, which ended purchases of silver by the mint and allowed it to produce only token amounts of new silver coins. Soon after passage of the Act, farm crop prices collapsed throughout the country. Farming groups and their political representatives "discovered" the Coinage Act as the source of their problems and called it the "Crime of '73." Instead of restricting purchases and coinage of silver, debtor farmers in the South and the Great Plains demanded Congress enact "free and unlimited coinage of silver."

If the amount of "new" currency proved substantial enough, the "free silver" process would inflate the currency enough to improve crop prices. Inflation would also allow them to repay debts with money of less value in real buying power than their initial loans. All parties involved in silver mining, management and labor alike, also favored "free silver." Those opposed to the proposal included creditor interests. Though the opponents are usually associated with banking and commercial interests in the East, any creditor who stood to lose from inflation was likely to be an opponent. This group favored gold as the only monetary standard. Somehow the gold supporters acquired the name "sound money men," an unearned title that served them well. By the 1870s California had little placer gold left, and even lode mines were playing out. There were no prospects for new discoveries of gold of any magnitude. Consequently only a small number of mining interests favored that metal as compared to interests involved with silver throughout the West.[3]

By 1878 silver interests had secured passage of the Bland Allison Act, which provided for some silver purchases and restored some production of silver dollars. The measure fell far short of producing noticeable inflation. Economic prosperity returned without the impetus of "free silver" in the 1880s so the issue became temporarily dormant. In 1890, though, a glut on the silver market led to Congressional passage of the Sherman Silver Purchase Act, a measure designed to aid the mining industry more than to create inflation. In 1892 the Populist Party, an agrarian third party in the debtor farmer states, called for "free silver" as one of several remarkably farsighted planks in its platform. The Populists' ideas became

The Mining Law in a Tumultuous Period 119

increasingly widespread as the 1890s wore on. Congress repealed the Sherman Act just in time to be blamed for the depression that hit in 1893. As a political issue, it was the "Crime of '73" all over again but fortified by current hard times. The debtor farmers once again suffered the most of any national constituency.[4]

A former Populist, young William Jennings Bryan of Nebraska, used "free silver" as his sole issue in gaining the Democratic Party's presidential nomination in 1896. In one of the most famous speeches in American History, he literally swung the convention to his own nomination, concluding with the immortal line, "You shall not press down upon the brow of labor this crown of thorns, you shall not crucify mankind on a cross of gold!"[5]

Unfortunately for Bryan, the issue that brought his nomination was inadequate in a general election. Groups that opposed inflation in 1896 were not just the eastern financiers. Urban workingmen, small businessmen, and even farmers who were not debtors opposed inflation simply to protect their own earnings and savings, as modest as they might be. Many Democrats defected to Republican William McKinley, the victor.[6] The depression and the story of "free silver" are obviously important background for any study of mining in the 1890s.

Specifically, silver prices had run at 94 cents per ounce in the late 1880s, rallied to $1.04 with the Sherman Act in 1890, but collapsed to 63 cents by 1894. Many mines closed across the West. One well-known "roaring camp," Creede, Colorado, began in 1890 with the discovery of the Holy Moses mine, so named because of the prospector's cry when he recognized a rich vein of silver ore. The Sherman Act gave it a good start but Creede virtually collapsed with the panic in 1893, thus making it one of the shortest lived of the major rushes. A local hoodlum, "Soapy Smith," who ran the town's "rackets" moved on, but would turn up in another interesting locale.[7]

At the same time that the economy was severely contracting, an influx of immigrants further increased the nation's labor pool just when many jobs were disappearing. The newer immigrants generally found they could qualify only for lower paying mining jobs, even when the economy was prosperous. The "Cousin Jacks" in earlier times had filled a variety of the typical jobs, but by the 1890s they had become the mining elite. American-born miners were not as widely regarded as the Cornish because they tended to

The official portrait of William Jennings Bryan, a.k.a. the Silver Tongued Orator and the Boy Orator of the Platte, for 1896 Democratic Convention. (Courtesy Nebraska Historical Society)

move more often. Even so, they generally commanded better jobs than other groups. The Irish held the lower jobs. By the 1890s, many immigrants from Southern and Eastern Europe were also competing for these jobs. The situation paralleled much of the Eastern experience in both mining areas and the pattern of urban development.[8]

Labor problems of the times obviously do not directly relate to mining laws. Yet they are important background to understanding the survival of the Acts of 1870 and 1872 through an otherwise tumultuous period. The position of the labor organizations and some leading figures in the movement reveals the sentiment toward mining laws.

Even before the economic collapse of 1893, a labor strike in the Coeur d'Alene region of Idaho set the tone for the severe problems of the rest of the decade. In early 1892 mine owners attempted to divide the work force into two different pay groups of $3.50 and $3.00 per day. A resulting walk-out dragged for months. The owners attempted to bring in nonunion workers. By July a pitched battle resulted in five fatalities and the dynamiting of a stamp mill. The National Guard finally stopped the violence but the situation was so tense they had to stay for months. In the end owners got the wage differential for job categories, but the miners saw a weakening of company stores and bunkhouses. The final collapse of the economy — and silver — the next year delayed further unrest, but the Coeur d'Alene's problems were not over.[9]

The "free silver" supporters saw the West as the key region in improving the entire economy. They correctly identified the region but did not realize that major gold deposits still remained to be discovered. When these came into full production, they not only provided jobs for the miners but inflated the currency even without "free silver." The most important mining district in the 1890s proved to be Cripple Creek, Colorado. When the '59ers had sought gold in Colorado, they simply did not know what they were looking for. Neither did fully three decades of later prospectors. A set of volcanic deposits on the "back" side of Pikes Peak from Colorado Springs had long shown just enough placer gold to attract occasional interest. The area was less than 40 miles from a major resort center with a full railroad terminal. Technically the ores are epithermal, but lack the characteristic quartz veins of other gold deposits then well-known throughout the West. Veins are present in the Cripple Creek district but are telluride ores, which are quite different in appearance from quartz. Cowboy Bob Womack finally made the first discovery in 1889 while others with little or no mining experience made several major strikes. In fact, those who had experience, either practical or scientific, were disadvantaged by the "wrong" knowledge during the initial years.[10]

Cripple Creek, then, proved to be the developing camp during the otherwise depressed 1890s. Since it was a gold rather than a silver district, prosperity was assured. Gold, fixed at a price of $20.67, naturally attracted the attention of investors, especially since almost all other prices were falling abruptly. Cripple Creek proved of great importance for the mining economy of the West since many miners moved there from silver areas.

The name of one early claimant is almost synonymous with Cripple Creek, just as Tabor was at Leadville. Winfield Scott Stratton filed his notice on July 4, 1893; hence he named the claim the Independence. The assays proved phenomenal and ultimately Stratton's discovery gave the district its impetus. Stratton had worked as a skilled carpenter in Colorado Springs during winters, while he studied mining and metallurgy at both Colorado College and the Colorado School of Mines. He spent many summers and an estimated $20,000 in prospecting before the Independence discovery. Stratton was clearly in a league with Tabor as a "rags to riches" story, but differed in another regard. As might be expected from his personal style, careful mining and management of assets marked Stratton's business procedures, in contrast to Tabor's style. Stratton left an estate of nearly everything he had recovered; Tabor had lost everything within just a few years.[11]

Cripple Creek was able to avoid many of the lengthy court battles of Leadville and the Comstock. The legal principles of the "apex rule" and other aspects were now established so that suits generally went no further than the local courts. However, Stratton himself contributed to the smooth legal situation. He carefully hid the true wealth of his mines and quietly bought up surrounding claims, both legitimate and frivolous. Stratton allied with the owners of the rich Portland mine, who had found a tiny area covered by no other claims and hit fabulous ore. With Stratton's shrewd policy, he and the Portland owners found themselves unchallengeable in the immediate area.[12]

The mines at Cripple Creek were not the only ones with unusual volcanic ores. Several smaller mining towns, as well as the city of Victor, almost as large as Cripple Creek, developed within a few years, all within an ancient volcanic crater. By the peak year 1900, the U.S. Census showed the district had a population of over 50,000, probably an undercount as with most mining areas. Official production was over $18 million that year, with much more "high graded" by the miners and quietly removed in lunch boxes.[13]

During development, Stratton became well-known as a very kindhearted mine owner. He contributed heavily to local projects in Cripple Creek and Colorado Springs. At first he even regretted that his gold mines were working at a disadvantage to the more numerous workers elsewhere in silver mines, though ironically Cripple Creek proved big enough to aid the economy both regionally and nationally. Stratton favored "free silver," the political idea incorporated into the Democratic Party Platform in 1896. Other mine owners, notably the Woods brothers, also had good reputations among workers.[14]

As early as August 1893, the Cripple Creek miners had organized and joined the Western Federation of Miners (WFM). This union was only two years old but had quickly emerged with the onset of economic depression. Yet there were more workers available than even booming Cripple Creek could absorb. Total production had gone from $557,000 in 1892 to $2 million in just one year but the population had quintupled, from 2,500 to 12,500. In January 1894 some owners demanded a ten-hour day, citing the prevailing economy. Stratton and the Portland owners were major figures but the district had at least 28 millionaires, not to mention smaller operations. Hence owners more favorable to labor could do little to influence other owners, though they did not suffer personally in most of the disputes since they maintained eight hours. The union struck for 130 days and physically occupied several major mines, forcing the governor to intervene with armed forces. Though there were several confrontations, explosions, and instances of taking hostages, no fatalities occurred. Ultimately, the union did obtain the eight-hour day at $3.00 per day throughout

Winfield Scott Stratton, a "little man" who made it big with the discovery of long unrecognized gold telluride ores at Cripple Creek, Colorado. Development of this area helped end economic hard times throughout the United States. (Courtesy Denver Public Library)

the district. Only two union men served jail time. Overall, this was a victory for labor. Cripple Creek became far more productive within a few years, enough to affect the entire economy as noted earlier. However, the Cripple Creek victory led the union to overextend itself in subsequent moves.[15]

In 1899 the Coeur d'Alene erupted again when the WFM attempted to unionize one major mine, the Bunker Hill and Sullivan. Again, there was a violent confrontation between union and nonunion miners and the dynamiting of a mill. Again, the Idaho governor, now Frank Steunenberg, suppressed the strike with military forces and a declaration of martial law, which did not end for two years. The State successfully prosecuted several union men involved in various incidents, but others escaped. The union was severely weakened. The miners did go back to work. This was no small accomplishment considering the context of low silver prices that continued for years into the twentieth century. The aftermath of bitter feelings should not be overlooked in the violent story of the Coeur d'Alene of the 1890s.[16]

Prosperity had generally returned by the start of the twentieth century, yet labor problems did not end. The pattern evident in the Coeur d'Alene then returned to Colorado. The WFM now had as a goal the elimination of all non-union labor. A series of episodes at smaller camps in 1901 led to a semblance of victory for the union, now led by President Charles H. Moyer and Secretary William Haywood. Tragically, there were several fatalities at Telluride.[17]

By 1903, the union was again focusing on the Cripple Creek area. The Portland Mine was already completely union, thus providing inspiration that the entire district might become a closed shop of the WFM. Sporadic violence came to a head in June 1904, when an explosion killed 13 non-union miners. The governor called up the militia and ultimately deported the most identifiable union figures; some 91 went by train to the Kansas state line. WFM President Moyer, already in custody at Telluride, faced formal charges on the explosion. Though the case against Moyer was too weak to prosecute, well-known hoodlum Harry Orchard was clearly implicated as having set the explosion from a neighboring mine. The WFM suffered a severe loss of credibility in Colorado and the 1904 elections produced a marked conservative reaction. There had been some public sympathy for labor, but violence combined with the WFM's growing espousal of socialism and opposition even to other unions proved counterproductive in the end. Significantly, even at the height of the 1904 crisis at Cripple Creek, both mine owners and the state government welcomed unions other than the WFM.[18]

After the debacle at Cripple Creek, the focus of labor problems returned to Idaho, but not in the form of a strike. Former Governor Steunenberg, who had earlier broken a strike in the Coeur d'Alene, opened his front gate on December 30, 1905, and died in another dynamite trap. Authorities apprehended none other than Harry Orchard shortly afterward, and found incriminating evidence in his hotel room. Orchard implicated the leadership of the WFM, including Moyer and Haywood. These men were still in Colorado and legal extradition was impossible. Idaho authorities, however, arranged a kidnapping, placing the suspects on a train late at night.[19]

This high-handed action by authorities in literally railroading the defendants out of Colorado made the case a cause célèbre. Contributions flowed in from all over the world. Colorado's officials remembered Cripple Creek and other losses of life when they allowed removal of the defendants. But public support reversed. "Big Bill" Haywood's 1907 trial attracted Clarence Darrow for the defense, William Borah for the prosecution, and a mass of reporters. The State produced no evidence to corroborate Orchard's testimony, and the jury acquitted Haywood, though they believed he was probably guilty. Moyer also "walked," in a later, less publicized trial.[20]

Though the union was broken in both Colorado and the Coeur d'Alene, Haywood emerged, for the time being, as a folk hero. Ultimately he defected to the Soviet Union, having proclaimed himself a supporter of the Revolution there. Today, Communist party tour guides show his tomb, along with that of one other American, John Reed, as those of fellow partisans who have received the Soviet's highest honor.[21]

The decline of labor in the early twentieth century was part of a return to prosperity. The advent of the new gold into the economy strengthened a recovery that began in the late 1890s. Bryan's assumption that "free silver" could elect him in 1896 had been as flawed as the belief that gold and silver necessarily represented separate socioeconomic groups. Cripple Creek finally showed its potential with improved milling processes that allowed more recovery. The Klondike rush to Canada's Yukon sent the bulk of its gold to the United States beginning in 1898. The Klondike helped stimulate further discoveries in neighboring Alaska where some activity was already occurring. And in Australia and South Africa other major ore strikes helped ease the problem on a worldwide basis. A final discovery at yet another "overlooked" locale, Tonopah/Goldfield, Nevada, in 1902, helped preserve prosperity until World War I. Though "free silver" is a major topic in U.S. history, the reason for its demise as a political issue so soon after the election of 1896 is equally important and much less-known.[22]

Recent economic problems made the Alaska/Yukon rushes even more popular than they might have been in other times. The great majority of stampeders faced severe hardships, including an unbelievable "staircase in ice" across Chilicott Pass. The presence of Canadian Mounties and firm requirements that each person carry certain supplies undoubtedly saved many lives. This policy contrasted with those in neighboring Alaska, as well as earlier rushes in the U.S.[23]

Several old hands from previous mining locales showed up in the Alaska/Yukon rushes. "Soapy" Smith tried to corner the "rackets" in Skagway Alaska, the terminal of the Klondike trade, much as he had done in Creede, Colorado. At Skagway, though, the locals finally tired of the situation. A vigilante group formed and dispersed the thugs. Smith himself died in a shoot-out.[24]

Josie and Wyatt Earp also found the far north irresistible. Though they got as far as Alaska on the way to the Klondike in 1897, Josie's pregnancy precluded going on to Skagway (and probably precluded a confrontation with "Soapy" Smith). Josie miscarried around the time of their return to San Francisco. The next season they tried again, on the all-water route to the mouth of the Yukon River in southwest Alaska, then to Dawson in the Klondike. The fact that this was well known as the "rich man's route," in contrast to trails from the vicinity of Skagway, indicates much about the Earps' status at that time. Even with the fast route, they arrived too late in that best-known year of 1898 to participate. They spent the next winter back in Alaska at a small town on the Yukon.

They finally found success the next season, making far more than most other gold rushers at the port of St. Michael, where Wyatt sold cigars and beer. The latest rush to diggings at Nome, however, was again an irresistible draw.[25]

Nome repeated many other mineral rush experiences, yet it had some unique circumstances, notably that ocean beach gravels had gold. Congress had finally made some provisions for filing Alaskan mining claims in the Act of 1898, and had extended the Acts of 1870 and 1872 to the region in April 1900. Yet belated application of the General Mining Laws still made no provision for ocean beach placers, basically unprecedented. A miners' meeting once again became an important entity in the history of the American frontier as it wrote local regulations allowing claims 1360 feet long and 660 feet wide to recognize this situation.[26]

At Nome, Josie and Wyatt Earp made yet more money from a saloon/nightclub named the Dexter. Wyatt made special trips to secure fancy furnishings. Just as at Tombstone, he confronted a problem in local corruption. Now that he was well-to-do, though,

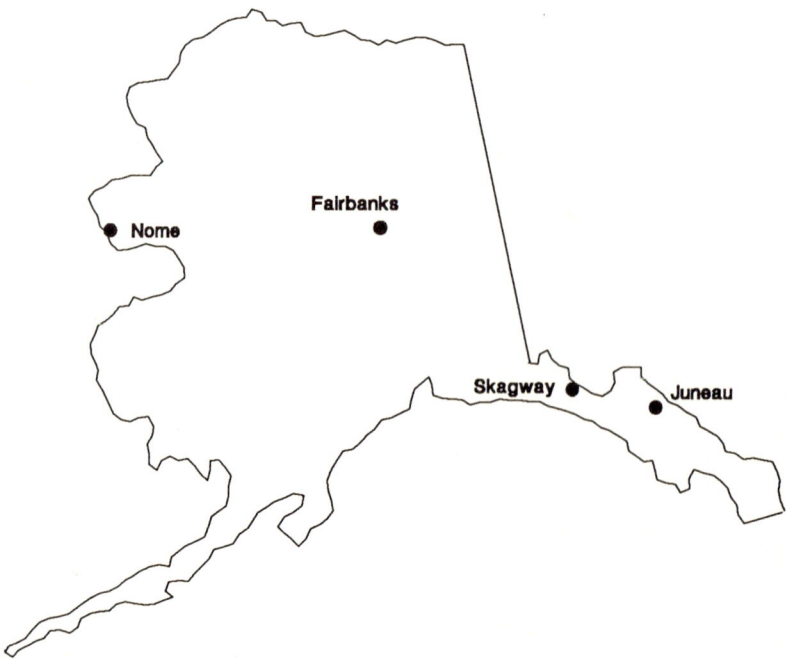

his actions differed greatly. A group known as the Spoilers included a crooked U.S. magistrate, Arthur E. Noyes. The group would identify valuable claims, and have "dummies" jump them. When the conflict went before the judge, he would appoint a supposedly disinterested "holding party" until final adjudication. In the meantime, the temporary holders would deplete the claims while the matter languished in the courts.

Wyatt saved two friends from losing to the Spoilers by providing a security bond for their claim. The judge then decided the initial fee of $10,000 in gold was too little so he doubled the bond. Wyatt came up with the rest, but sent a message that "if we find it necessary to raise anything more, it's going to be on hemp!" No further raises followed. By 1901, Nome had finished its roaring early days. The Earps got bored and ended their Alaskan stage. About the same time the Spoilers lost influence, though the leaders avoided prison. During the months it operated, the ring had even been able to use the U.S. Army to its purposes. Yet a group of concerned citizens, including Wyatt Earp, forced the changes and true justice in Nome, without bloodshed or vigilantism.[27]

Nome and another major Alaskan mining district, centered at Fairbanks, rank among the greatest gold producers in United States history. At Fairbanks, the gold was placer but buried in ancient river deposits more than one hundred feet below barren younger gravels. Hence Fairbanks depended on larger capital for its operations. (Only California and Cripple Creek had produced more by volume up to that time than either Nome or Fairbanks.) With these additions to the currency supply, the first years of the new century would naturally be prosperous.[28]

One other gold operation of the 1890s merits special mention. This was the Camp Bird Mine in the remote San Juan Mountains between Ouray and Telluride, Colorado. Irish immigrant Thomas Walsh had prospected, mined, and practiced carpentry across the West for years. In the Black Hills he let some of the most valuable gold claims slip through his fingers, yet incredibly he made a major discovery elsewhere. From some modest success at Leadville, he acquired enough money to open a mill at the appropriately named camp of Silverton, Colorado, also in the San Juans. The silver price collapse of 1893 practically ruined him, but in owning a mill he was in an unusual position to know the values of many local ores. He started looking for gold content and quietly buying claims that seemed to have more of that metal than silver. In 1896 he acquired what would become the Camp Bird mine. Walsh was a popular employer who provided superior lodging and good wages for his workers, since the remote mine was high in the mountains. He faced none of the labor problems of the early twentieth century but pocketed 59% of the gross of the mine anyway, a figure that reveals the highly rich ore there. Ultimately he toured Europe, met royalty, and acquired the Hope diamond, which now rests in the Smithsonian Institution in Washington, D.C.[29]

Despite the depression of the 1890s, a growing demand emerged for one other metal beside gold. This was copper, essential to a newly emerging stage in the industrial age. The electric power industry thrived despite the depression and created a market that maintained the price of the "red metal" at a stable level of approximately 11 cents, until 1899 when it went to 17 cents. The increase was a harbinger of yet greater demand to come with the automobile age.[30]

During the 1890s the primary Western source of copper was Montana, though the Great Lakes region was still the leader. In the Great Lakes land laws were not a factor, but they clearly were in the West. The primary mineralized zone in Montana was in the vicinity of the town of Butte. A famous "war" developed there between the two major producers. The larger of these, Amalgamated, ultimately became the Anaconda Corporation. Amalgamated found that a smaller competitor was far more imaginative in its practices.

F. Augustus Heinze an independent operator, made the most of his role as a David confronting a Goliath. He filed literally hundreds of suits against Amalgamated and won many by "owning" a local judge. Heinze did have the advantage of being an expert geologist and knowing the Butte region thoroughly. The Act of 1872 gave him another opportunity. He discovered two tiny triangles of land between three huge Amalgamated mines to which no claims at all were on file, so-called "orphaned fractions." Heinze claimed the triangles and sued all of Amalgamated's mines on the grounds that his claims were the "apex" of the entire zone! He achieved an early victory before his "owned" judge, William Clancy. However, Amalgamated finally won the matter by closing the mines and letting the workers know in no uncertain terms that Heinze was fully responsible with his frivolous suit. Heinze backed down. Nevertheless, this case shows the problems that can arise from overlooked areas in major mining districts, as well as some legal mischief aided by the "apex rule."[31]

Anaconda finally took complete control of Butte's copper in the early 1900s. The company then dominated Montana politics until after World War II, a circumstance that reflected, in part at least, the conflict with Heinze. Company towns, stores, dormitories, and so forth emerged as in coal mining areas of the East, but such domination would appear only in copper areas in the West. During the war there is little question that miners and ordinary people benefitted from the competitive situation. While tragic labor violence marked the nearby Coeur d'Alene, Butte's unionized miners found good wages, good hours and no need to strike. In fact, some miners worked jobs in mines of both companies, which they could do on different shifts since they had shorter hours. Heinze portrayed himself as the friend of labor and, aside from the triangular claim incident, successfully maintained the image. His underlying motives may be questioned, but the result was beneficial.[32]

It was only natural that the issue of "free silver" would generate support for the General Mining Laws. If the goal was to produce as much as possible, all measures to do so were welcomed. In fact, the Democratic platform of 1896 included the following passage:

> The Democratic Party believes in Home Rule, and that all public lands of the United States should be appropriated to the establishment of free homes for American Citizens. We recommend that the Territory of Alaska be granted a delegate in Congress and that the general land and timber laws of the United States be extended to said Territory.[33]

The party obviously still believed in frontier solutions to the problems of the times, even though the Census Director and Turner had declared the frontier ended. Though the passage does not directly mention the Acts of 1870 and 1872, they can clearly be inferred as part of the "general land and timber laws" that were useful for "free homes for American Citizens;" so useful that they should also be encouraged in Alaska. The Democrats lost on free silver itself, but Congress did extend the land laws (including homestead as well as mining) to Alaska in 1898 and 1900.

Yet the Acts of 1870 and 1872 related about as much to policies espoused by the Republicans as by the Democrats. Mining claims could cover silver or gold mines. As it turned out, the gold mines proved sufficient to end the depression on their own. Though this outcome was basically unexpected in 1896, the convention platform emphasized the "free homestead policy of the Republican Party." Both parties favored use of the frontier, and public lands, to end the depression. In addition, Republicans also favored admission of Alaska. A minority report in the convention, written by Colorado Senator and mine owner Henry Teller, endorsed "free silver." This little-known attempt shows that both parties had elements favoring both metals.[34]

Even labor organizations and their leadership endorsed the Acts of 1870 and 1872. "Big Bill" Haywood had prospected and owned at least one mining claim in Nevada when he was young. He had regularly done the annual assessment work for several claimants yet neglected his own, acquired as a gift from another prospector. He frequently walked past the claim, the Caledonia, wondering if he would ever find time to develop it. Instead, he let the assessment work lapse, thus legally abandoning it. Other parties restaked it and found sufficient ore to develop a working mine. Haywood himself worked there for a time. (One could speculate about Haywood's subsequent life had he become an entrepreneur.)[35]

Though Haywood ultimately became a Communist, he always favored the independent prospector, probably from his own experience. Hence he urged maintenance of the mining laws. Further, he espoused a plan whereby unions would acquire and work their own mines. The best way was to find new mining claims rather than buy developed mines (though he favored that when possible). Mining claims thus could be the basis for a utopian system of communal groups attempting to fulfill some of the basic tenets of Marxism. Haywood did not go into much detail for such organizations but he did form a basic concept.[36]

Undoubtedly the typical miner, unionized or not, favored the Acts of 1870 and 1872. In fact, he likely had a few claims of his own. Any experienced miner was familiar enough with valuable ores to believe he could always prospect, even if he could not find a

The Mining Law in a Tumultuous Period   133

job in a larger mine. And many did just that. The advent of the industrial age simply broadened the types of materials that might be "valuable." Now the prospector could use the claims system for even more chances at the big strike, even though larger firms were the only ones that could ordinarily develop industrial metals. The prospector, at least, could bargain among many potential buyers.

The mining experience of the 1890s, and mining law in particular, relate to a key part of the Turner/Webb thesis. An early, controversial point of the thesis stated that the frontier provided a "safety valve" during times of economic hardship. When Turner originally expressed this idea, he presumably was thinking of Eastern cities and supposed that otherwise volatile populations were redirected to the frontier. Subsequent historical research showed that the frontier drew most migrants during times of prosperity and that few came from urban areas anyway. Even so, Turner's supporters had, by the 1920s, advanced an alternate thesis that the frontier provided a psychological safety valve during hard times simply by being there, since it gave a potential outlet to those who might otherwise have been socially disruptive.

Duane A. Smith has rightly called the larger mining towns *The Urban Frontier*. The communities were surprisingly similar to Eastern cities in many ways. The depressed 1890s provoked labor unrest in mining towns just as in Chicago or other areas that suffered strikes. The advent of mining for copper, an industrial metal, instead of gold and silver, was also part of the urbanization and maturing of the region. The West, however, had its own outlets for much of the displaced energy of the depressed 1890s, since gold mining rose so markedly just as silver collapsed. Cripple Creek, the Klondike, Alaska, and even Tonopah/Goldfield, Nevada, after 1900, qualify as examples of a "safety valve" in Turner's original interpretation, but within the West. True, there were serious strikes, but the situation would undoubtedly have been much worse without the new districts. The success of organized labor at the rising gold camp of Cripple Creek, as contrasted to its failure in the declining silver area of the Coeur d'Alene, shows that the simple presence of labor unrest is not a sufficient identification of the problem. The outcome of such unrest merits observation.

Further, the possibilities of new discoveries always provided a psychological "safety valve" in the sense used by Turner's later supporters. This aspect took on more meaning when the miner himself had a claim or two stashed in some remote locale. In fact, such ownership often differentiated the miners who had been in the region for some time — the Americans, Cornishmen, and even the Irish — from the newer immigrants. Noted mining engineer T. A. Rickard, himself of Cornish birth, made this point in discussing the strikes. He commented on the predominance of Eastern European names in unions and of English-sounding names among the more skilled miners who opposed unions. Presumably a few years of assimilation into American culture, and of becoming familiar with the concept of mining claims, would change the outlook of the newer immigrants. Rickard's observations show that urban problems of the rest of the nation were catching up with the West. However, much of the frontier spirit remained there, even in the 1890s, which included a psychological "safety valve" in the form of speculative mining claims. The West still had enough undiscovered resources in the early twentieth century to emerge from a depression. This fact may even be sufficient to question both the director of the Census and Turner in placing the end of the frontier at 1890.[37]

Chapter Eight

Scholars and Reformers Study the Mining Law While Westerners Use It

The typical Westerner undoubtedly favored the Acts of 1870 and 1872. There was a good chance that most residents of any Rocky Mountain states held some mining claims, or at least a partnership in some claims, regardless of his or her primary occupation. Yet Congress had previously revised the laws and always recognized the possibility of having to do so again. As early as 1879, some sentiment for amendments developed among the mining community itself. The primary bone of contention was the "apex rule." The professional community of mining engineers, aided by some firms that had lost suits on apex cases, exerted enough political pressure to bring some consideration for a change. President Rutherford Hayes appointed a Commission on the Public Lands, which recommended repeal of the "apex rule." Significantly, the Commission made no proposal to end the system of claims. Yet the idea of tampering with the otherwise popular law was too much to overcome. The Acts of 1870 and 1872 were a "sacred cow" within seven years of their completion.[1]

Over the ensuing years, members of both houses proposed bills that would have abolished or at least simplified the measure. Stewart himself proposed modifications in 1888, 1893, and 1894. By those late dates, he could not even amend the Act that he had supposedly written (though others were also involved, as we have seen). The fact that Stewart repeatedly attempted such amendments is a strong point in his defense against such academic critics as Mayer and Riley (whose book, published by the Sierra Club, is cited in the Introduction and Chapter 4). However, the populace of the West expressed different sentiments.[2]

When the Progressive Era, or Age of Reform, got under way in the early twentieth century, a variety of governmental entities studied almost every conceivable institution in existence. It was only natural that a variety of officials once again looked at the mining laws. President Theodore Roosevelt appointed a commission of "big name" mining engineers to recommend changes. This commission, which included John Hays Hammond, James Douglas, and Daniel Barringer, unanimously favored removing the "apex rule." Congress itself then studied the matter and issued House Report No. 639 in 1914. The primary purpose of this report was only to call for yet another commission to study the matter, but it did briefly mention three important legal changes. First, the report suggested repeal of the "apex rule." Second, the report suggested ending mining claims for oil, gas, coal, and phosphates. Third, the report suggested a separate recording system whereby the government itself would keep records of mining claims, as well as continuing the requirement for records in local offices. Though Congress took no immediate action, the importance the matter held at this time should be noted. Powerful forces opposed changes, even in the most trouble-ridden part of the Act of 1872. Some of these forces are obvious from the previous chapter; others might be inferred in the rest of this chapter. However, court decisions, discussed in Chapter 9, are probably the most important reason for the Acts of 1870 and 1872 being the "sacred cow" evident by the twentieth century.[3]

At the same time the "apex rule" was raising questions, the general topic of mining law attracted the attention of scholars. The initial California gold rush was so remarkable that it had acquired a romantic image as early as the 1880s. Several influential figures had experience in the original rush, among them U.S. Supreme Court Justice Stephen Field, and journalist Henry George. By that period the academic world was beginning to take notice of the event, and Western mining in general, as a significant historical force. As with any historical topic, a variety of interpretations soon emerged regarding mineral rushes and the social systems they spawned.

The first detailed, scholarly study of mining law is a major part of Charles Howard Shinn's *Mining Camps; a Study in American Frontier Government*. This important work appeared in 1884 but the story of its author is particularly revealing. As a child, Shinn left Texas with his family and settled in California in the mid-1850s. In his late twenties he worked for the *San Francisco Bulletin* as a reporter. Then he belatedly went off to college across the continent at Johns Hopkins University in Baltimore, Maryland. The faculty members who influenced him rank almost as a Who's Who of noted literati of the times. In the Preface Shinn cited the following figures at Johns Hopkins: President D. C. Gilman, Dr. H. B. Adams, and Dr. Richard Ely. He also cited Dr. Josiah Royce of Harvard and others. Shinn applied the historical principles he had learned at Johns Hopkins to the most uniquely Californian institution that he knew, the mining camps that had practiced "popular sovereignty" and "pure democracy."[4]

Definite influences from Dr. Herbert Baxter Adams and Dr. Richard Ely can be discerned in Shinn's writings. Adams had been particularly masterful at disseminating the "germ theory" of history. According to this concept, democratic institutions were virtually the exclusive product of "Teutonic peoples" who had originated in the "forests of Northern Europe" and then gone to America. At least one leading modern intellectual historian has gone so far as to identify Adams as the most influential proponent of the "germ theory."[5] Today the "germ theory" appears markedly ethnocentric, even racist by most current standards in the United States. Despite this drawback, it is necessary to look carefully at Shinn's work in this regard. True, such phrases as these present a serious problem in the modern context:

> [The English and American settlers in 1837 California] held on with the tenacity of men in whose veins the blood of many generations of Aryan pioneers was flowing.
>
> Wherever men of our Germanic race found minerals, they developed a satisfactory system of local government... their judgements grew swifter, and their justice surer. In the hands of the Germanic race alone, this fierce gold-hunger has been controlled, utilized, and made a force of primary importance in the shaping of a civilized society.[6]

The "mining court" of the camp, in its earliest form, was simply the assembly of the freemen in open council. It was the folk moot of our German Ancestors.[7]

Now, the study of the mining camps of the Far West reveals the presence of primitive Germanic ideas more clearly in their land laws than in any other department of their jurisprudence.[8]

Shinn also disparaged the Spanish/Mexican heritage in California mining as showing the bad characteristics with which he contrasted camps that reflected the "Germanic" character.[9]

Yet several other themes evident in this work do much to redeem it. First, Shinn openly acknowledged unfair treatment of several groups in the early camps. He spoke highly of the industry of the Chinese. And, regarding Anglo-Hispanic relations, he even went so far as to state:

> This tendency to despise, abuse, and override the Spanish American may well be one of the darkest threads in the fabric of Anglo-Saxon frontier government.[10]

Indeed, the above statement sounds almost like the antithesis of his other ideas about Teutonic governmental superiority.

Shinn mixed some far more original ideas among typical statements of adherence to the "germ theory." These sound as though they might have been written by adherents of a completely different academic school. At the very onset of his book Shinn stated:

> Today, over the western third of the United States, institutional life traces its beginnings to the mining camp: that is the original contribution of the American pioneer to the art of self-government.[11]

Another revealing example is:

> The mines put all men for once upon a level. Clothes, money, manners, family connections, letters of introduction, never before counted for so little.[12]

These statements might be easily mistaken for later writings of the frontier school historians; the first sounds much like Turner while the second is amazingly parallel to a lengthy essay Webb wrote in *The Great Frontier*. In fact, Turner himself left rural Wisconsin to attend Johns Hopkins in the later 1880s. By then Shinn was gone but Turner did attend the classes of the same Drs. Herbert Baxter Adams and Richard Ely.[13]

The only difference between these two sons of the frontier who went to Baltimore, Turner and Shinn, is that Turner abandoned the "germ theory" completely. Prior to his explosion on the academic scene with the frontier thesis in 1893, Turner showed much the same influence from mentors who espoused the "germ theory" as did Shinn. In 1889 he clearly credited racial/ethnic qualities with influencing social and governmental characteristics of his own Wisconsin. However, his return there may have sparked some of his early memories of the area when it was just out of the frontier experience. Turner may have adopted one of the most famous academic ideas to originate in the United States *in spite of* graduate school at Johns Hopkins rather than because of it. Universities can produce unexpected intellectual results.[14]

Shinn, who had memories of a California perhaps even closer to its frontier than was Turner's Wisconsin, cited this same force. True, he tempered the concept with ideas from the "germ theory" but his recognition of the importance of frontier conditions in a major piece of scholarship preceding Turner is a little-known accomplishment. There are many instances of independent scientific and technological discoveries by different individuals at much the same time. In similar fashion, it appears the frontier school was about to emerge as an academic force of the times. Had Shinn abandoned the "germ theory" statements in his book, but retained those suggestive of Turner and Webb, he might be credited with founding the frontier school. But he left that notoriety to Turner. From the modern perspective, Turner's work appears much superior since it attributes human behavior to environmental forces, not to racial characteristics. However, Shinn's points in that direction should not be forgotten, despite their admixture with other ideas of little current standing.

Some discussion of subsequent writings by Shinn is in order. After graduation from Johns Hopkins, he returned to California where he became a professional writer for a variety of publications. He had always had a deep interest in the outdoors, so it was no accident that he became what might be termed a conservationist. By the early twentieth century he was deeply involved in the movement, which was entering a most active cycle. He was particularly outspoken in support of forest conservation. In 1902 he became one of the first chief rangers at the newly created Sierra National Forest.

Yet Shinn never forgot his affinity for the Act of 1872 which, as we have seen, gave legal sanction to the local power of the mining camps. He even defended the practice of hydraulic mining, which had become extremely controversial by the later 1870s. Farmers attacked this practice on the grounds that sediment released into rivers was detrimental to their interests. In 1884 they took the case to the State Supreme Court, which ruled that mining practices could not take precedence in that particular instance. Even so, Shinn believed the Court was wrong and mining law should still take precedence because, from a practical standpoint, the sediment actually created new farmland. Though he obviously had a personal academic ax to grind, the fact that he could be a conservationist yet still favor the mining law in the early twentieth century should not be surprising. Many others, from all walks of life, took this position as well.[14]

John Muir was undoubtedly the best-known, most influential of many figures who espoused the conservationist cause in the early twentieth century. A colorful character originally from Scotland by way of the Midwest, Muir had lobbied for legal protection of areas and resources for many years. He traveled for both pleasure and scientific studies. His backpacking in California's High Sierra is best known. He also went to Alaska where he observed glaciers. There he determined that similar masses of ice had produced the spectacular valleys at Yosemite and elsewhere. While camping along the Alaska coast in 1880, he helped to start the rush to Juneau when he pointed out placer gold to the two prospectors usually credited with the discovery. Muir did not participate in the resultant rush (he had become quite prosperous from growing citrus fruit) but he shared the views of his friend, Charles Howard Shinn, toward the mining rushes and their participants.[15]

After visiting a worked-out area along the Mother Lode, Muir wrote:

> As the heavy, long-continued grinding of the glaciers brought out the features of the Sierra, so the intense experiences of the

gold period have brought out the features of these old miners, forming a richness and variety of character little known as yet... It is interesting to note the extremes possible in one and the same character: harshness and gentleness, manliness and childishness, apathy and fierce endeavor... Contact with Nature, and the habits of observation acquired in gold-seeking, had made them all, to some extent, collectors, and, like wood-rats, they had gathered all kinds of odd specimens into their cabins, and now required me to examine them. They were themselves the oddest and most interesting specimens.[16]

Muir was clearly a well-adjusted person who could appreciate unique human beauty as well as the natural beauty for which he is famous. These comments could just as easily have been from Charles Howard Shinn as from Muir.

Subsequently, Muir visited some of the Nevada lode mining areas. He believed that "Nevada mining excitements were far more intense and destructive in their action than those of California." He accounted for such a difference by observing that the '49ers were forced, by the severity of the journey, to be more patient and to forget some of the "rush fever." Even so, he commented that the prospectors in Nevada had been quite "brave," and only one out of a hundred had found anything. Muir went on to state unequivocally, "Surely it is a fine thing that so many are eager to find the gold and silver that lie hid in the veins of the mountains." Certainly favorable mining laws were a major part of this "fine thing."[17]

Muir added that the "destructive unrest" of an early rush contrasts with the "orderly deliberation into which miners settle in developing a truly valuable mine." He described in some detail the equipment and processes evident at Eureka, Nevada, at the time of his visit (one of his last trips, about 1912) and gave them a favorable rating. Perhaps one of his most profound observations was a comparison between the ruins of mining operations that were even then present in the West with the ruins of medieval structures in Europe. The picturesque appearance of both called forth romantic emotions associated with contemplation of different but colorful historical periods.[18]

Muir was a pragmatist. He saw that even conscientious mining required a discovery. He wrote:

But after all, effort, however misapplied, is better than stagnation. Better toil blindly, beating every stone in turn for grains of gold, whether they contain any or not, than lie down in apathetic decay.[19]

He saw his own movement for conservation as bearing some success as an integral part of the larger Progressive movement, though the passing of the frontier may also be linked to the following statement:

> The fever period is fortunately passing away. The prospector is no longer the raving, wandering ghoul of 10 years ago,... but cool and skillful... capitalists, too, and the public in general, have become wiser, and do not take fire so readily from mining sparks; while at the same time a vast amount of real work is being done, and the ratio between growth and decay is constantly becoming better.[20]

Muir and Shinn were not alone in their view that mining did not necessarily run counter to conservationism. Almost as famous as Muir as a promoter for the creation of new national parklands in the early twentieth century was Enos Mills of Colorado. Mills served on the board of Muir's Sierra Club and frequently quoted Muir in his own widely distributed books. He lobbied for creation of a major new national park in the Rocky Mountains, north of Denver, in a particularly spectacular region where he had spent many summers and taken many tourists on climbing expeditions. A bill to create Rocky Mountain National Park cleared Congress in a remarkably short time. The Park officially dates from 1915.

Enos Mills himself had spent a good portion of his life as a miner. During the 1880s and 1890s he worked winters at Butte, Montana, a mining town notorious for its air pollution from smelting of sulfide ores. Yet Mills liked Butte and the camaraderie of the other miners, a particularly independent lot. He earned enough at Butte during winters to spend the summers in his favorite area of Colorado, which became Rocky Mountain National Park. On many hikes through the Colorado wilderness, he often stayed with prospectors and miners and wrote in his books of personal sentiments about them similar to those expressed by Muir.[21]

All through the Progressive Era, Muir's chosen editors of the *Bulletin of the Sierra Club* made no mention of mining law at all, even though Congress and other officials were continually studying the issue. It was, however, featured in other publications. Even in 1914, when House Report 639 appeared, the *Bulletin of the Sierra Club* printed nothing. During the period it did promote creation of the Grand Canyon as a national park, endorsed the "Save the Redwoods League," and even took a position many years ahead of its time by endorsing "controlled fires" in climax growth forest lands. Yet the leading conservationists of the period had no comment on the Acts of 1870 or 1872, even though these hindered creation of national parks, the primary goal of the organizations at the time.[22]

The journals of the scientific mining industry were not nearly as reticent as the conservationist press. Several major journals continually aired different aspects of the issue for years. The *Mining and Scientific Press* printed several relevant items during 1914 after House Report 639 had revitalized interest in amending the Acts of 1870 and 1872. Some examples show the wide range of views the journal expressed in detail. In a "letter to the editor," H. C. Callahan called for adoption of Australian laws. In a short article, Grafton Mason called for clarification of the concepts of "mineral lands" as compared with "agricultural lands," especially since only a discovery could be cited to designate "mineral in character." Most commentators, though, wanted the basic system of claims upheld. T. A. Rickard, formerly one of the foremost mining engineers, and then editor of the journal, took this position. So did Frank Davis, in a major article, though he favored an end to the "apex rule."[23]

One other commentator on mining laws as they stood in the Progressive Era was particularly noteworthy both for his then current professional standing as well as his subsequent career. He was mining engineer Herbert Clark Hoover. In 1912 he and his wife, Lou Henry Hoover, translated a classic volume on German mining techniques of the 1500s into English. This translation of Georgius Agricola's *De Re Metallica* is still the best published source on the trade before the nineteenth century. In a lengthy footnote to the section on mining law of Agricola's time, Hoover suggested that modern mining law was the fulfillment of the historical trend toward individualism and away from the power of an aristocracy who used the state for their own ends.[24]

The political changes of the Progressive Era have worked to obscure to some extent the fact that many aspects of life in the West continued much the same as always. In fact, labor disputes tapered off for a number of years, before several final episodes of deportations of union members at the start of World War I in 1917. These deportations, the most notorious at Bisbee, Arizona, marked the final fall of radical unionism and the triumph of the owners. However, the return of prosperity to most mining areas is important background that should not be overlooked.

For the typical prospector and even many miners, the situation was just like old times when a new rush erupted to Tonopah/Goldfield, Nevada, in 1902. The allure of a brand-new camp but with a classic character was too much for Josie and Wyatt Earp to ignore, perhaps because they had seen Nome, Alaska, mature in just a few years. They went directly from Nome to Tonopah, where Wyatt successfully ran a store for some time. Yet the Earps still longed for a life-style of frontier adventure rather than town residence, even in a gold camp. So they began prospecting in adjacent regions of Nevada and, subsequently, Arizona and California. At one point Wyatt helped a young friend, with the unforgettable name Tasker Oddie, recover his mine from would-be claim jumpers. Oddie later used his unusual name to good advantage in politics, ultimately going to the U.S. Senate from Nevada.

Over the ensuing two decades, Josie and Wyatt lived in the deserts, but the quest finally paid off as early as 1905 when they found good ore in San Bernardino County. The "Happy Day Quartz Lode Claim" bears both of their names and provided good income for many years. They worked the vein themselves periodically, between prospecting trips that resulted in over one hundred other claims. The Earps remained in California for the rest of their lives.[26]

Wyatt Earp was a figure often called a "boomer," an individual who goes from place to place, never staying too long, and trying a variety of jobs. Earp was more prosperous than most boomers, and thus had a wider range of opportunities. He had been a marshal, but he had also been a saloon keeper, cigar salesman, and a freight-

Josie and Wyatt Earp prospecting in the California Desert at about the time they discovered the Happy Day mine.
(Courtesy Arizona Historical Society)

er. Yet the trade or occupation that he maintained longer and more diligently than any other was certainly "prospector/miner."

Tonopah attracted another younger boomer who has left us an excellent personal diary that reveals much about mining and prospecting of the period. Very few materials of this type have come down to modern times. Frank Crampton was from a wealthy, influential New York City family, but was, by his own admission, the "black sheep of his family." He spent his adolescence at a military school dreaming of ingenious pranks. After finding that Columbia University was not to his liking, he "hopped a freight" to Chicago rather than face his family. He ended up at Cripple Creek, almost by accident, where he learned underground mining. Like many others, he went on to Tonopah/Goldfield when that area emerged, just as Cripple Creek was passing its peak. He was a personal example of the mining frontier working as a "safety valve"

Notice of Location for the Happy Day Mining Claim signed by both Josie and Wyatt Earp.

(Courtesy San Bernardino County, California Recorder)

even into the twentieth century. Unlike farming, the mines attracted newcomers with urban backgrounds.[27]

At Tonopah/Goldfield, Crampton admitted learning how to "high grade" ores. He found himself part of the community of the "Cousin Jacks" and, like the Cornishmen, regularly attended the Methodist Church. The mine owners had appealed to the minister for help against "high grading," and he obliged with a sermon on the subject "thou shall not steal," but he retained his congregation with a final observation, "Gold belongs to him wot finds it!"[28]

Crampton also observed the masses of prospectors in the area and learned that trade as well as enough "assaying and surveying" to make a profitable business. As a prospector, he staked his own claims, as well as finding some unusual cinnabar (mercury) ores on a long trek across the California deserts for a British firm that had hired him. Next he took a particularly dangerous underground job at Bingham Canyon, Utah, so he soon jumped at a chance to do surveying instead. Here he and his partner discovered "an orphaned fraction," an area of ten acres between a mass of claims of several major corporations, which no one had claimed. Even though he had "high graded" ore as an ordinary miner, Crampton let this opportunity, perfectly legal, go by. He did discreetly note it on the final maps that he sent to his employer. A comparison with the actions of Mark Twain and Augustus Heinze when confronted with similar situations is natural. Somehow Crampton, the "working stiff," comes across better than the more illustrious characters.[29]

Crampton had many other interesting experiences, including discovery of the remains of a family massacred some thirty years earlier, and his survival of chemical accidents and a cave-in. He was emphatically pro-labor but against the WFM. He even more vehemently opposed the International Workers of the World (IWW), a yet more radical labor group that was operating by World War I. He ultimately favored the Bisbee deportation. This was a 1917 event in which local authorities at Bisbee, Arizona, used the war effort to justify removal of 1,200 miners from the community. Sheriff's deputies herded all suspected IWW members onto waiting trains. The Arizona governor saw fit to consult with Crampton, a "working stiff," on the best courses of action in the aftermath of this delicate matter. Crampton's account is unique, especially since it covers a later period than most similar accounts. Good field studies by mining engineers are available, but few ordinary prospectors and miners left memoirs, aside from some '49ers and discoverers of the best-known bonanzas. If Crampton's observations are typical of most multifaceted Westerners, and there is reason to believe they are, the Acts of 1870 and 1872 were fully ingrained into the way of life by the early twentieth century.[30]

Yet another interesting figure who benefited from the Act of 1872 even into the 1900s was Junius R. Lewis. Originally a slave from Mississippi, Lewis became an orderly for Confederate General E. E. Johnson during the Civil War. In this capacity, he participated in many of the most famous battles of that epic conflict. After the war, he taught school in Texas, then drifted on to Denver where he managed the office building of a railroad in the 1890s. He acquired several mining claims in Boulder County, Colorado, most notably the Golden Chest Lode. He entered into a partnership with several other black entrepreneurs and raised capital to develop claims. As was so common in mining, he encountered legal actions, which he fought successfully. He applied for patent on the Golden Chest Claims on September 12, 1906, and successfully worked them into the 1930s. Lewis proved to be the most successful black mine owner in the West.[31]

The new century also saw important developments for one venture discussed earlier, which was not based on metals but on marble. The Colorado Yule Marble Company constructed a railroad spur in 1906, and an electric tram from the mines to a huge mill in 1910. Inside the mill, skilled stonecutters fashioned many large pieces of marble into the necessary forms. Generally stone for building comes from areas near local markets. For example, the brownstone buildings of New York City are from a sandstone quarry in Connecticut. Yule marble was remarkable enough that its fame spread throughout the country, even though other good marbles are quarried in Vermont and other Appalachian areas closer to major urban markets.[32]

In 1914 the company secured a contract to supply the marble for a major project undertaken by the federal government. This was a special memorial to Abraham Lincoln. The structure proved to be one of the most successful architectural entities, from an aesthetic standpoint, of any of the vast number in the nation's capital city.

Scholars and Reformers Study the Mining Law 149

Yet the materials that make it such a success came from a patented mining claim under the frontier Mining Act of 1872. It is fitting that the greatest American of genuine frontier background be commemorated by such materials.[33]

In 1929 the Vermont Marble Company bought the facilities at the appropriately named village of Marble, Colorado. The very next year the new owners secured another government contract almost as memorable as the one of 1914. Now the Yule marble would provide the material for a special tomb of an unknown American soldier from World War I, as well as for other construction in Arlington National Cemetery. Hence the town and the operation survived the Depression. A severe flood destroyed the mill in 1941, just as another war was about to start. The facility would provide no future memorials since it proved uneconomical to rebuild. Yule marble can still be purchased from stockpiles. Certainly its use for two of the most cherished monuments in the national capital is symbolic of the influence of the frontier on Eastern settled areas, as Turner and Webb suggested.[34]

The slab of marble destined for the Tomb of the Unknown Soldier leaves the plant. Materials for the Lincoln Memorial also came from Marble, Colorado. It is symbolic that the great national treasures in the East originated from mining claims in the West.

(Courtesy Colorado Historical Society)

CHAPTER NINE

Case Law for Mines: Straightforward Despite the "Apex"

After the government had finally written basic laws on both placer and lode claims, many points needed clarification. The mass of prospectors as well as small and large operations on government domain naturally generated various conflicts that required clarification and adjudication. The process required fully half a century to build up a major body of case law, just in time for the first legislative amendment to mining laws.

Cases have generally been of two very broad types. First, cases between rival claimants have started in state and territorial courts, as the Acts themselves provide. If appealed, such cases enter the federal court system, even though the government itself is not a party. Some important contests between claimants have gone all the way to the United States Supreme Court.

The government naturally has an interest in its own lands and the interpretation of its laws; hence the second broad type of cases. When problems arose over various provisions of the Acts of 1870 and 1872 that directly affected the government and allowance of the holding of particular mining claims, official decisions were forthcoming from several sources. In the early days, the commissioner of the General Land Office made many rulings. His decisions could be appealed to the Secretary of the Interior. If a party wished to contest the secretary's decision, the federal court system provided the means. In later years the Department has created a quasi-judicial system of administrative law courts that can meet in the locale of the case. If a decision of an administrative law court is adverse to the claimant (thus favors the government), an automatic process takes the case to the Interior Board of Land Appeals in Washington, where a panel reviews the case. Further appeals are available to the secretary or through the federal court system but are not automatic.

As early as 1874, the commissioner of the General Land Office and the secretary alone had issued enough decisions to fill 237 printed pages and had given circular instructions for a number of other contingencies. Many of these decisions were on routine points of clarification. Some, however, involved what would become major points as later upheld all the way to the Supreme Court. The following are a few of the most important points and are listed because they would later become major court cases.

1. In an 1870 case from Sacramento, the secretary allowed the "apex rule" to stand. Further guidance on this complex issue would involve private parties.[1]
2. Several cases upheld state and mining district laws, even those adopted after the date of the federal legislation. The net effect of such state and local laws is most commonly to designate smaller claim sizes than the maximum allowed under the Acts of 1870 and 1872. Such cases also validate whatever requirements may be designated by state and local authorities regarding "monumenting," nature of forms, and places of filing.[2]
3. After entry, the burden of proof of a discovery lay with the party alleging the mineral nature of the land. The government itself had a right to satisfaction on this point.[3]
4. Mining claims may be patented even within town sites.[4]
5. The Act of 1872 set no limit on the number of claims any party could hold but local restrictions still applied.[5]
6. The Sutro Tunnel took precedence over other claims.[6]

As the years passed these points arose again and again. Though the original cases that went to the commissioner and the secretary were rarely appealed, later cases that encountered the same problems eventually entered the court system. Most of the major early mining cases that went to the Supreme Court involved the refinements of the "apex rule." A federal commission that studied all the land laws as early as 1879 recommended that the government abandon recognition of state and local mining laws as well as the

Case Law for Mines: Straightforward Despite the "Apex" 153

"apex rule." The first point was already virtually moot, as discussed earlier. Further, organized mining districts gradually ceased to function and state legislatures generally modified their laws to fit federal statutes on claim sizes. The "apex rule" would be a major bone of contention and repeal might have proved advantageous. However, claims filed prior to a modification of the "apex" would have still fallen under that set of rules, so the situation might have been even more complicated (if that can be imagined at all). The validity of claims under the laws in effect at time of filing is a major consideration. In large part, the prospect of multiple sets of rules regarding claims has been a major reason for the lack of much subsequent action. The few amendments that have taken effect have created this very problem. These are discussed in sequence.[7]

The Mining Law of 1872 provided, in somewhat ambiguous phraseology, that disputes among rival mining claimants be decided by the state or territorial courts that had local jurisdiction. In 1900 the Supreme Court upheld this practice in *Blackburn vs. Portland Gold Mining Co.*[8]

In the 1879 case of *Stevens vs. Williams*,[9] a federal court defined the "apex" or the "top" as that part of a vein which comes nearest to the surface even though such "apex" may be below the surface. A valid claim of this part of the vein had certain "extralateral rights" beyond the surficial geographic limits of the claim boundaries. Subsequent decisions of the Supreme Court spun off this impoirtant decision.

In a very early decision, *Flagstaff Silver Mining Co. vs. Tarbet*[10] (1878) the Supreme Court decided that the strike and dip of the vein as shown by the surface outcrop determine the legal location lines and extralateral rights of the vein. This point holds even if the vein is substantially different under the surface.

Well-established precedents from mining districts had considerable influence before the Supreme Court. A particularly interesting case, heard by the Supreme Court in 1887, involved two claims that met at the middle along the surface strike of a vein. In *Argentine Mining Co. vs. Terrible Mining Co.*[11] the Court ruled that the entire vein went to the senior locator in accordance with the custom that it was an indivisible unit and separation was impractical. This case originated in the California Mining District in Lake County, Colorado, near Leadville. The justice who wrote the

Court's opinion was none other than Stephen J. Field, who had been influential in California.

The ground location of a mining claim takes precedence over written courthouse descriptions of a claim or even a survey plat of a patent. Hence the monuments themselves are much more than a formality; they can be crucial. So the Supreme Court ruled in *Consolidated Wyoming Gold Mining Co. vs. Champion Mining Co.* (1894).[12]

The Supreme Court addressed a number of cases that involved the limits of claims in regard to the ends of veins along the respective strikes. Problems of this nature could become extremely complex in cases of secondary veins relating to the primary one. Obviously, expert opinions would be called at the trial court level to establish which was a primary and which was a secondary vein. Even with such points recognized, the legal treatment of such matters required further clarification. No extralateral rights at all extend along the strike of a vein, only the dip. Additional claims are thus required to control the entire vein. Further, the width of the deposit underground can be no greater than the width of the surface claim. In *Tyler Mining Co. vs. Last Chance Mining Co.* (1894)[13] Justice David Brewer of the Supreme Court again relied on long-standing precedents of cases from mining districts.

The Supreme Court determined in *Iron Silver Mining Co. vs. Elgin Mining Co.* (1896)[14] that a claim had to have parallel end lines to qualify for any extralateral rights at all. This requirement accounts for the geometric parallelogram shape of many claims. The claim is divided into end lines and side lines with extralateral rights following the side lines but not the end lines. A claim of a different shape has only the rights directly under its boundaries. This decision by Justice Field was most unusual in that Justices Morrison Waite and Joseph P. Bradley filed a dissenting opinion. No other "apex" cases drew a single dissent.

If secondary veins "apex" within the location lines of a claim for the primary vein, the claimant will have some rights to the secondary vein under *Del Monte Mining and Milling Co. vs. Last Chance Mining and Milling Co.* (1898)[15] as expanded in *Cosmopolitan Mining Co. vs. Foote* (1900).[16] In the *Del Monte* decision, Justice Brewer cited the history of British and Spanish mining law, then stated that it was irrelevant anyway since Congress had

A veteran of California Mining camps was Stephen J. Field who went on to become a Justice of the U.S. Supreme Court where he was the "resident expert" on the mass of mining cases of the later 1800s. Despite his positions on other cases, Field favored the "little man" in almost all mining disputes. (Courtesy U.S. Supreme Court Historical Society)

full authority to write what it wanted and had done so in the 1866 Act. Here is full legal verification of a point this writer has made, in contrast to others who have attempted to identify European precedents in mining law.

However, the end lines are legally fixed for extralateral extension of both primary and secondary veins. A case from Nevada County, California, *Walrath vs. Champion Mining Co.* (1898),[17] resulted in this precedent. The claim in this case dated from 1857 under mining district law. The Court also decided that the Land Office could grant a patent under the Act of 1866 but not 1872.

Lower federal courts also issued some important precedents that have stood, since there were no contemporary appeals. In two related cases in 1900, U.S. District Courts made decisions that have become as frequently cited as many Supreme Court cases. In a situation where the surface strike of a vein made an arc, the most senior of the claimants took precedence on the rights extended underground, as held in *Bunker Hill and S. Mining and Concentrating Co. vs. Empire State Idaho Mining and Developing Co.*[18] Similarly, in a situation where an "apex" ran diagonally across two claims, the senior had some advantage in extralateral rights, though the junior retained rights to a smaller portion of the vein, according to *St. Louis Mining Co. vs. Montana Mining Co.*[19]

The situation that had almost made Mark Twain an early millionaire, a blind lead (or blind vein), reached the Supreme Court in 1901 in the case of *Calhoun Gold Mining Co. vs. Ajax Gold Mining Co.*[20] This case finally provided a definitive decision that was long overdue because of a number of divergent opinions from state courts. The unexposed vein belongs to the claimant owning the land under which the vein reaches its highest point. An entry tunnel location that discovers the blind lead has no rights unless there is no other claim at the surface above the highest point of the vein. The unanimous opinion adequately resolved the matter.

Related to the *Calhoun vs. Ajax* decision was the case of *Creede and Cripple Creek Mining and Milling Co. vs. Uinta Tunnel Mining and Transportation Co.* (1905).[21] The Supreme Court ruled that a tunnel claim is not a mining claim but only an exploration device to locate a potential discovery that could then be used to file a valid claim.

Many of the "apex" decisions were from lower courts, but the

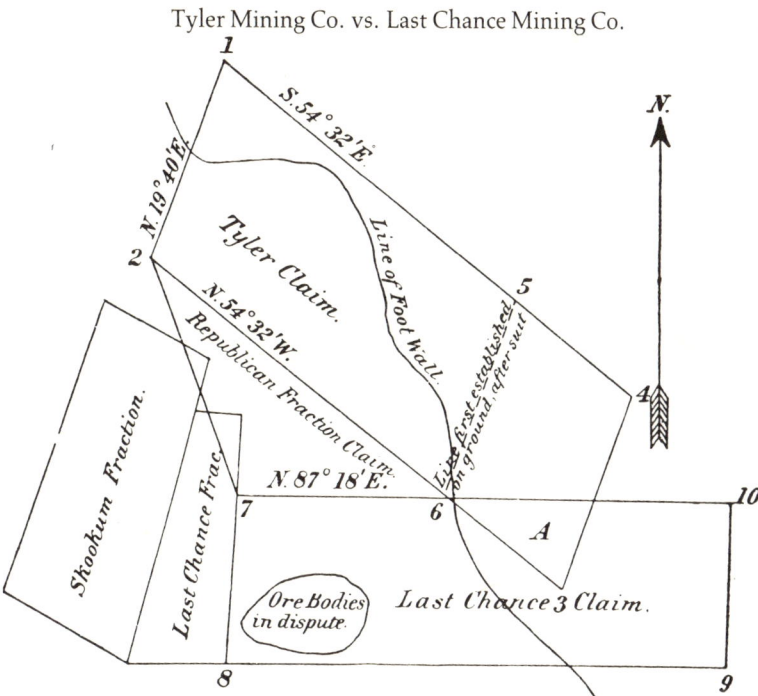

The U.S. Supreme Court found it necessary to place maps of complex mining cases (usually "Apex" rulings) in its published decisions. (From the case of Tyler Mining Co. vs. Last Chance Mining Co. as noted in vol. 157 of the United States Reports, 1894.)

Supreme Court finally upheld most of the basic principles in the 1909 case of *Mammoth Mining Co. vs. Grand Central Mining Co.*[22] The decision in this case, which had gone all they way through the state court system in Utah, was the work of Justice Oliver Wendell Holmes, Jr. Holmes is often known as a "great dissenter" from a number of other well-known cases. In the mining case, though, Holmes spoke for a unanimous court.

In a geological sense, veins fit in the category of epithermal deposits, and are more commonly near the surface and recognizable. They were also mined out rather early. Mesothermal deposits are more commonly found at some depth. They either lack vein structure or fit the general description of being a mass of overlapping veins. As mining matured, it was inevitable that veins would be worked first but that larger mesothermal deposits would come into play with appropriate techniques and discoveries. In essence, the courts had to adjust the inference of the law itself to acknowledge geological and technical differences in mining vein or epithermal deposits as contrasted with mesothermal deposits.

The first major locale to present cases that required this distinction was Leadville, Colorado, when that district erupted in the latter 1870s. Leadville was the first genuine rival of the Comstock and many claimants believed the precedent afforded by the one vein that ran under Gold Hill and Virginia City should also apply at Leadville. After many expensive lawsuits, though, the general character of Leadville was determined to be a mass of localized veins. Local cases in Idaho's Coeur d'Alene region were similar.[23]

So how can a vein be recognized? And when should a claim have extralateral rights, or simply extend downward from its surface boundaries? A District Court ruled that fifteen feet of offset in a vein from faulting was not enough to declare that two separate veins existed in the case of *Original Sixteen to One Mine vs. Twenty-One Mining Co.* (1918).[24]

After years of litigation in areas like Leadville and the Coeur d'Alene, the Supreme Court finally settled the matter in *Colorado Central Mining Co. vs. Turck* (1892).[25] Ironically, this case came from the Argentine District in Clear Creek County, Colorado, where most mines were on well-defined veins. However, the geologic situation did need some legal resolution. The case negotiated an absolute legal maze before the Supreme Court finally upheld the Circuit Court. In this case a claimant was working a vein under another claim presuming that the "apex rule" applied. The particular vein was not discrete but merged into a larger lode that unitized at depth below the surface of both claims. The court held that the "apex rule" did not apply in such a case but would for clearly unrelated veins. Here was a clear attempt to draw a legal designation from problems arising out of the complex geology of epithermal deposits above mesothermal.

By 1900 most of the types of cases that could be encountered regarding the "apex rule" had made their way up the court system. Consequently only two major "apex" decisions date from the twentieth century. Both involved unusual situations that had not previously been tested in court. In *Jim Butler Tonopah Mining Co. vs. West End Consolidated Mining Co.* (1918),[26] the Supreme

Case Law for Mines: Straightforward Despite the "Apex"

Court ruled in a Nevada case that the "apex" of a vein which was actually the crest of a geologic fold or anticline had clear extralateral rights in the subsurface from the claim in both directions. The Supreme Court also addressed an unusual underground configuration in *Tom Reed Gold Mines Co. vs. United Eastern Milling Co.* (1922).[27] In this case a vein dipped underground for a distance, then became horizontal. The extralateral rights extended as far as the dip but terminated at the point where the vein became horizontal. The Court thus strengthened the principle, long recognized by many mining districts, that horizontal veins had no extralateral rights.

The "apex" cases clearly upheld the priority of senior locators. After all, that was the intent of mining laws and the Acts of 1866, 1870, and 1872. The same principle held in *Jones vs. Wild Goose Mining Co.* (1910).[28] This matter originated in Nome, Alaska, but was not an "apex" case. Nevertheless, the Court applied the same favoritism to a senior locator used in "apex" cases to a situation involving placer claims. According to the Court, even if a senior locator has staked more than the legal maximum acreage for a claim, such claim is not immediately void. The senior locator may select the ground he wishes to retain within the legal maximum for claim size before junior locators may take possession of the remainder. (It was a good thing the owners of the Smuggler mine near Telluride, Colorado, had received their patents and bought out the competition before this decision was reached, because it would have negated at least a part of the celebrated 1,054 feet of that rich vein.)

Though the "apex rule" is today generally regarded as a legal anachronism because epithermal deposits are mostly depleted, some caution is advised in this regard. In one classic locale, Creede, Colorado, most of the original rush came from a single massive vein named the Amethyst. In the 1970s the discovery of the Bulldog, a blind lead parallel to the original and equal to it in value, brought something of a new rush. Hence the "apex rule" can arise again unexpectedly.[29]

The "apex rule" should also be noted as a career builder and source of early professional practice. In the mass of early cases between rival claimants, the mining engineer proved a crucial figure to give expert testimony, and present diagrams and maps essential to locating veins. The mining engineer also presented evidence regarding the value of materials as might be needed in contests among private parties as well as with the government. Naturally the mining engineer had many other duties in prospecting as well as management of producing mines, but expert testimony was often the highlight of such a career. Excellent accounts of some of the most notable mining engineers are available elsewhere. Indeed, it was one of the most respected, romantic professions into the present century. The most famous practitioners were John Hays Hammond, T. A. Rickard, and Herbert Clark Hoover.[30]

Court cases naturally required attorneys, and the "apex rule" provided more legal material for the legal profession than other aspects of early mining law. As discussed earlier, "apex cases" had built William Stewart's career in Nevada and were a key part of the background that sent him to Washington to help with the 1866 federal statute. It is quite ironic that he tried to amend the "apex" when he returned to Congress in the 1890s, but never succeeded. William Horace Clagett's career was similar. Stewart, Clagett, and a few others were just the elite of a specialized legal fraternity. Virtually every attorney and politician in the West had considerable practice in this area, simply as a matter of course. And most of the cases prior to 1900 involved contests with other claimants, most of them citing the "apex." Even though that legal bonanza gradually played out, new sources for cases arose which were quite important in several areas of the law.[31]

A major purpose of the mining laws had been clarification of possible conflicts with homestead and other land entry methods. The Acts themselves had included marked distinctions between agricultural and mineral lands. Obviously, other distinctions could be made. It was only natural that conflicts would occur between different types of claimants as well as between claimants for the same grounds which had any type of value. Such conflicts were a standing part of Western life.

Some problems did arise between agricultural and mining interests. However, it was not often that one party might stake a claim under the mining laws while another would claim the same lands under agricultural homesteads. The most serious problems emerged in the 1870s in California where many placer miners were using powerful pumps to dislodge huge masses of sand and gravel.

Case Law for Mines: Straightforward Despite the "Apex"   161

Debris then moved downstream, damaging agricultural lands. The resulting court cases, and eventual protective legislation, centered at the state level. This consideration became a major issue in state politics. It did not, however, involve federal mining laws.[32]

Instead of conflicts between mining claims and farming, the cases that created some of the most severe land-title problems involved holders of mining claims and those who staked claims for townsites under other federal laws. In some ways this should have been better anticipated. If a mine had genuine value, it would naturally demand workers. Hence a town would develop nearby. Yet such sites were in a mineralized zone, so mining claims usually covered the area as well.

A classic example of just about every problem imaginable as related to such a conflict developed at Tombstone, Arizona. A townsite company filed for patent in early 1879 under the federal townsite land laws. The group began selling city lots in what soon became the main portion of the booming mining town. As early as July 1880, some $125,455 worth of construction was present on the lots. However, the townsite overlay portions of five mining claims. The most important of these claims was almost entirely within the townsite, while smaller portions of the others overlapped. The claim in greatest conflict actually bore the name the *Gilded Age* claim, though most observers saw its opponents, the townsite promoters, as the characters portrayed in Mark Twain's novel. In fact, the *Gilded Age* included a working mine that employed a number of the town's residents. So which took legal priority, mining claims or townsites?[33]

Secretary of the Interior Carl Schurtz stated that the patent grant to the townsite had been premature but legal determination of this case, like disputes between mining claimants, had to go through territorial courts. The editor of one of the local newspapers, John Clum of the *Tombstone Epitaph*, attacked the townsite promoters. The possibility of violence over the matter was ominously real.[34]

The Cochise County district court upheld the mining claims but the promoters appealed. The Territorial Supreme Court unanimously decided for the mining claimants in April, 1881, in *E. Field et al. vs. M. Gray et al.*[35] Edward Field, the owner of the mining claims, then sought ejection of those on the claim, but this was a slow process. In the meantime, the promoters appealed to the U.S. Supreme Court. The entire issue provided a backdrop for election of a new slate of city officials in the fall of 1881. Further, the issue may have provided some of the backdrop of tension that resulted in the most famous gunfight in the West, between the Earp brothers and Doc Holliday against the Clanton gang in October, 1881. There were further violent incidents for the ensuing year or more.[36]

The promoters undoubtedly had caused a serious problem, and Edward Field had the law on his side regarding the claim, but what about the innocent third parties who had purchased town lots? The U.S. Supreme Court upheld the Territorial Supreme Court, but only on a filing technicality. After that, the situation resolved itself as might be possible only in a mining town. Within a few years a fire removed many of the structures that were in trespass. The mines cut back to the point that only 400 workers, about half the 1881 figure, were mining by 1887. As a result, lot prices had fallen so drastically that the issue was not as pressing. In a second related case, the Arizona Supreme Court struck down one of the claims, the *Mountain Maid*, because evidence showed it post-dated the townsite. This action gave the lot owners some leeway but even today, buyers are warned of possible title problems to properties in Tombstone. The second case also went to the Supreme Court, which avoided writing a genuine solution on the immediate case.[37]

Criticism of the U.S. Supreme Court for leaving Tombstone "hanging" is not really justified. The Court had already heard the issue and given some guidance in an 1885 ruling and would provide further guidance in 1891 to essentially cover the Tombstone situation. Ironically, the first case involved another of the West's most notorious mining and gunfight towns: Deadwood, Dakota Territory. Though "Wild Bill" Hickok had already met his demise when the case developed, the land conflicts were part of the background of local tension that marked Deadwood, just as with Tombstone and other mining towns.

At Deadwood, many parties attempted to jump mining claims by filing papers for preemption purchases, homesteads, or townsites. Under the law of the miner's district a mass of cases had gone to a court that simply did not have the expertise to sort out the legal tangle. The matter reached the U.S. Supreme Court in

1885 in the case of *Deffenback vs. Hawke*.[38] In a unanimous decision, the Court's resident expert on mining cases, Justice Stephen Field, wrote that Congress had recognized the possibility of mining claims within a townsite, but that prior filed claims took precedence. Mineral lands simply were not available through any other method, be it preemption, homestead, or townsite. Further, there could be no requirements added to the issuance of a patent other than those perscribed in the law.

In 1891 the issue arose again in the case of *Davis vs. Wiebbold* from Montana.[39] Field again wrote for a unanimous court, closely following the ruling in *Deffenback vs. Hawke*. In fact, the Court heard the case only because Montana's Supreme Court had defied *Deffenback*, so the U.S. Supreme Court felt compelled to make its earlier decision stick. The case did give Field an opportunity to clarify the distinction by stating," . . . if the land is worth more for agriculture than mining, it is not mineral land though it may contain some measure of gold or silver." Subsequent cases would define further the requirements for a designation as valid mineral land.

The government could protect itself against parties who misused land-entry methods, especially for an ulterior purpose, at least on lands of mineral character. In a significant 1914 case from Wyoming, *Diamond Coal and Coke Co. vs. U.S.*,[40] the Supreme Court noted that homesteaders had entered coal lands, received patents, and then sold the lands to the company. Since there was indisputable evidence of prior knowledge of the coal, the patents were void and the lands reverted to the United States.

The distinction between mineral lands and other lands proved a major protection for miners, large and small. It seems obvious that concentration of mineral holdings in the hands of bigger corporations was easiest where there was no such distinction. The iron ores of Minnesota, Michigan, and Wisconsin, which were specifically removed from the mining laws, are a classic case of that situation. As discussed earlier, the large operators were able to misuse other land laws to acquire those valuable lands.[41] Similarly, other misuses of land laws allowed timber companies to take valuable holdings under homesteads and preemption, since there was no clear distinction given forest lands. Mining lands, by contrast, had such legal distinction.

Several cases reveal the impact of the legal distinction of mineral land from other lands. Even a state could not violate the distinction, as Justice Miller ruled in 1880 in *Ivanhoe Mining Co. vs. Consolidated Mining Co.*[42] As written in the law regarding state selection of lands, Sections 16 and 36 were reserved *unless* they included mineral lands. If mineral lands were involved, the lands reverted to the U.S. and the state could select alternate lands. Though Justice Field might have been expected to issue the ruling on this case, he noted potential conflicts of interest since the matter came from California, and withdrew himself. The judgment shows that his ideas, as expressed in other opinions, were widely shared by his fellow justices.

If a state could not take the mineral lands, even on those sections specifically reserved to it by other federal law, what about other parties that had land grants? What about the huge acreages Congress had allocated to railroads? Here, too, the legislative intent was quite clear. The matter finally went to the Supreme Court in a case from Montana, *Barden vs. Northern Pacific R.R.* (1894).[43] Justice Field wrote the opinion in which he pointedly quoted the Act of Congress as stating: "railroad land grants for every alternate section of public land, not mineral." Field, so often cited as the extreme tool of big business, in fact opened masses of lands supposedly reserved for major railroad concerns to the "little man," the ordinary prospector. In farming country, many families believed they were homesteading on federal lands, only to find they were on railroad lands. Often they had spent years on the land and made considerable improvements. Under Field's decisions, the prospector could do the opposite! He or she could go onto railroad lands. If such prospector made a valid discovery he or she could stake a claim, in which case the mineral lands reverted to the United States. Then a full mineral patent application was in order. Interestingly, even the phraseology that Field quoted from the Act was not enough to dissuade Justices Brewer, Gray, and Shiras from filing a dissent. They felt the railroad was entitled to the minerals anyway.

The prospector could go onto railroad land grants and patent a claim, but what could he claim? In a sequel case, *Northern Pacific Railroad vs. Soderberg* (1903),[44] the same company that had tried to stop prospectors found that a wide variety of "little men" could enter what it had thought were its land grants. Justice Brown wrote a decision that upheld a granite quarry as a sufficient enough discovery to invoke the mining laws. The case applied both to the railroad's lands as well as to the government's own lands. The Court was willing to credit just about anything as "mineral" that could be removed from the ground at a profit. Ultimately such decisions would result in amendments to the mining laws, as described in the next chapter. Justices Brewer and Peckham dissented, probably carrying some sentiments forward from the earlier case. This time the dissenters did not even write out their objections, so motives are conjectural.

Ultimately the United States employed this same principle against none other than *The Octopus* as Frank Norris had called it, the most hated railroad in the West. The case was *U.S. vs. Southern Pacific R.R.* (1919)[45] in which oil lands at Elk Hills, California, had been patented in 1904. The Court overturned a Circuit Court decision and revoked the patents, following earlier railroad cases as well as the *Diamond Coke and Coal* case. By this time Justice Van Devanter could write for a unanimous court and give the government a valuable reserve of its own, since Congress removed oil from the minerals subject to mining claims immediately after the decision. In fact, this case was an important prelude to the Mineral Leasing Act of 1920.

In some instances the government identified reasons to contest the legitimacy of any claim at all within certain locales. The government based some of its denials of the legitimacy of such claims on the phrase in the Act of 1872 which states that "all valuable mineral deposits... be free and open to exploration and purchase." The Department of the Interior faced the question of defining a "valuable mineral deposit." In 1894 while sitting in a quasi-judicial capacity, the Secretary of the Interior rendered a decision in *Castle vs. Womble* that addressed this issue:[46]

> ...where minerals have been found and the evidence is of such a character that a person of ordinary prudence would be justified in the further expenditure of his labor and means, with a reasonable prospect of success, in developing a valuable mine, the requirements of the statutes have been met.

Note that the secretary's statement specified a person of ordinary prudence. He was not sexist, even in 1894. The average miner may have been; the common phraseology of the concept has become the "prudent man rule." Of course, women claimants were invariably granted equal rights in contests even in the 1800s.

The United States Supreme Court considered the prudent person rule in the case of *Chrisman vs. Miller* (1905)[47] and upheld the concept. In fact, Justice Brewer quoted the earlier decision by the Secretary of the Interior for a unanimous court. The primary point is that simple indications of the presence of valuable minerals were insufficient grounds for designation of a mining claim. A valuable deposit had to be clearly present. Hence the market price of a particular mineral became the key factor that the Department of the Interior considered in determining the validity of a claim. At low prices a particular deposit could be worthless, but at higher prices the same ore could justify a valid claim.

In the case of *Union Oil Co. of California vs. Smith* (1919),[48] the Supreme Court expanded certain points of the "prudent person rule." Though a prospecting or exploring party could not legally file a claim before making a discovery, the physical presence of such a party justified their exclusive right to the area if they were legitimately prospecting. Justice Mahlon Pitney, writing for a unanimous court, followed the defendant's logic in his opinion, which adopted what is known as the doctrine of *pedis possessio* to mining claims. In more recent times the simple presence of a prospecting party has meant the difference of millions of dollars.

The Act of 1872 includes the requirement for $100 worth of work on a claim every year to maintain the claim. This requirement is usually called the annual assessment work. During the period 1900–1920, a number of court cases involved questions as to which kinds of costs qualified for annual assessment work. Also, costs that met the required fees for approval of patent came under scrutiny.

These cases are all rather technical and none established a major precedent along the lines of *Castle vs. Womble*. They did cost some claimants their claims, though. And they gave jobs to attorneys, both for the government and the parties.[49]

As time passed, federal courts rendered a series of decisions that generally placed ownership of mining claims on the same legal level as ownership of any private property. In 1889 Justice Field wrote a decision holding that corporations were allowed to hold claims in the case of *McKinley vs. Wheeler*.[50] Many other business-related decisions of the period followed the same principle, so this decision must be regarded in its context. Field had endorsed the concept of the corporation as an "artificial person" in a dissenting opinion in the so-called "Slaughter House cases" in 1873.[51] Within a few years he saw the idea win approval by a majority of the Court and was ultimately able to write his own unanimous opinion in extending corporate rights to mining claims. This decision was in keeping with his better-known reputation.

Several decisions related much more to the small claimant than to the mining corporation. The property status of claims began to take on clear focus with these interrelated decisions. A U.S. Circuit Court of Appeals ruled that a mining claim follows inheritance laws in the owner's state of residence in the case of *O'Connell vs. Pinnacle Gold Mines Co.* (1905).[52] In the case of *Bradford vs. Morrison* (1905),[53] the Supreme Court ruled that a mining claim is real property and as such is subject to liens. The phraseology of the original mining law is straightforward, according to Justice Peckam, in affirming the Supreme Court of the Arizona Territory.

As early as 1885 in *Deffenback vs. Hawke*, the case from Deadwood, Dakota Territory, the Court had ruled that the government could not place restrictions on a patent other than those allowed by law. In 1900 the Court expanded the implications of *Deffenback* in *Roberts vs. United States*.[54] The owner of a valid claim has the *right to a patent*. Over the years the government thus found it necessary to use its own experts to examine claims and issue reports as to their validity.

Another important case involved the power to withdraw lands from application of the various land distribution laws. In 1915 Justice L.Q.C. Lamar, writing for a unanimous Supreme Court, had held that the president had the power to issue such withdrawals in the case of *United States vs. Midwest Oil Company*.[55] The opinion noted that as far back as 1881 Colorado Senator Henry Teller, owner of numerous claims himself, had cited the executive withdrawal power. However, such withdrawals were subject to any prior valid rights. Claims filed before the date of the action could continue, though no new claims were allowed.

Given these earlier decisions, the Supreme Court's judgement in the most crucial case of *United States vs. North American Trans-*

portation and Trading Co. (1920)[56] followed the general thrust of the relevant precedents. The U.S. Army had confiscated a placer claim at Nome, Alaska, in 1900, as part of the corrupt Spoiler gang's actions described earlier. The U.S. Court of Claims had awarded $23,800 to the company, but an appeal went forward anyway. The time lag until a final Supreme Court judgment meant the claimant won $100,000 plus $7,500 interest per year since 1900. Justice Louis Brandeis wrote a unanimous opinion that stated the government had violated the constitutional doctrine of *eminent domain* by such confiscation, at least in a case of a valid claim. An additional effect of this decision was to greatly strengthen the concept of "grandfathered" status of mining claims under laws in force at the time of legal filing.

The year 1920 saw a second crucial decision. In *Cameron vs. United States*, a case went to the Supreme Court regarding claims in the Grand Canyon.[57] Justice Van Devanter dismissed out of hand the argument that President Roosevelt's withdrawal of the lands as an area of "scientific interest" had been illegal. The claims were actually at the trail head near the railroad station and had no value other than as a nuisance. The test of the "prudent man rule" as required by *Chrisman vs. Miller* was unmet. The land was clearly "non-mineral" as the Secretary of the Interior had ruled. Even so, the Court required "due process" of law for the government to strike down any claims, even those obviously of nothing more than nuisance value. As a result, the traditional informal hearings before officials of the Department of the Interior became a judicial type of proceeding before special administrative law judges. Further processes also became standard with appeals to the Interior Board of Land Appeals. (Ironically, other claims with valid discoveries within the boundaries of the Grand Canyon did qualify for patent and operated into the 1980s, much to the disgust of environmentalists.)

Finally, the Supreme Court in essence summarized all the property aspects of mining claims in *Wilbur vs. U.S. ex. rel. Krushnic* (1930).[58] In yet another unanimous decision, Justice Sutherland noted the right of sale, mortgage, transfer, and inheritance of mining claims, even prior to patent. Indeed, the claimant is under no obligation to proceed to the full patent. (This point had been questioned during the debates of the mining laws.) Also, the Court

Case Law for Mines: Straightforward Despite the "Apex"   169

strongly endorsed "grandfathered rights" since this case involved oil shale claims from Garfield County, Colorado. Congress had amended the mining laws in 1920 regarding oil. The claims, however, predated that legislation and still fell under the original laws. This case conclusively eliminates any question that the government offers free use of its resources.

The historical implication of these cases is that Congress effectively transferred its decision-making authority to the courts upon enactment of the mining laws. Of course, this is true in most realms of law making, but the creation of a form of property strengthened the situation even more than in most areas of legislation. The principles of eminent domain now came into play, with the result that repeal or amendment to the law applied only to claims filed after the time of legal change. The "sacred cow" primarily results from the concept of a mining claim as property with a further right to a full patent.

The resistance to amendment of the Act of 1872, even on the troublesome "apex rule," stemmed from the mass of case law that had developed from the courts. The "grandfathered" status of claims filed prior to other major governmental actions undoubtedly came into play. Congress realized that even if it amended the Acts of 1870 and 1872, claims filed prior to the date of amendment would still fall under the "apex rule." Claims filed subsequent to that date would fall under the amended rules. If the "apex" alone was confusing, that result could have been worse. Though the highly trained mining engineers favored such an amendment, there was massive sentiment to keep an already complex situation from going berserk. The most powerful influence on Congress's typical inaction was the Supreme Court.

The reverse was true in other aspects of application of the law. In fact, the Acts of 1870 and 1872 were so clear-cut that the courts long reflected the same attitude of the Congresses that had passed the Acts. The unquestioned goal was simply to encourage mining claims whenever possible as part of the overall settlement of the country. Few stronger testaments to the validity of the Turner/Webb thesis can be found as follow-up to the original land distributions. It was not until the Progressive Era that some changes in this position were evident in a few court decisions. A U.S. District Court in Idaho declared in the case of *United States vs. Riz-*

zinelli (1910)[59] that the government has (in land under mining claims) a valuable estate that it is entitled to protect against waste and unlawful use. Despite this early decision, effective management regulations of Forest Service lands did not appear until 1974. Those for the Bureau of Land Management did not appear until 1980.

An important case that aided the conservationist movement came from the 8th Circuit in 1901. This case was *Teller vs. United States*.[60] The Court ruled that an unpatented mining claim could not be used for commercial lumber production, though timber on the claim could be used within a mine owned by the claimant. This decision was quite important in the enforcement powers of the new Forest Service and possibly accounts for that agency's lag in adopting complete mining claim regulations, a surprising situation, considering the Service's Progressive origins.

Even as early as the 1920s most important matters were well precedented and few landmark cases appeared during ensuing decades. With development of environmentalist sentiment in the 1970s, some important new cases and other new departmental policies finally emerged. The trend of mining cases was rather clear after the first two decades of the twentieth century. Prior to 1900 most cases were between rival claimants and involved the "apex," though some cases involved conflicts between mineral usage of lands and alternate usages. From approximately 1900 to 1920 most cases involved contests of claims by the government but generally resulted in upholding claims as a form of private property. These cases did establish guidelines as to requirements for contests and criteria to be followed. The Progressive Era contributed the most enduring part of the "sacred cow," through the Supreme Court, even with a changing membership. The only exceptions were two conservationist decisions.

Supreme Court Justice Stephen Field, a veteran of early California, wrote several significant decisions. He undoubtedly contributed to others behind the scenes. However, in mining cases the court was almost always unanimous, with decisions from a number of justices. Field is well-known for his overall pro-corporation stance. The entire court eventually adopted that position regarding the mining laws. The decision to uphold corporate ownership of claims was unanimous. Yet on another crucial mining decision, Field wrote an opinion that clearly placed mineral lands, with access by anyone, in a legal status paramount to a major railroad land grant. Other justices felt the land grant should have been superior; Field can thus be considered as more realistic on the issue than some historians have been willing to credit. With the exception of the railroad case, most of the decisions relating to property rights of mining claims came after Field had left the bench in 1897. He may only be regarded as having been more influential in applying California mining law to the "apex" and to other contests between rival claimants.

A somethat larger method of placer mining employs use of a sluice box, still well within the capability of the miner with little capital for equipment. Placer mining of very fine materials requires heavier equipment, including pumps and even dredges.

(Photo courtesy Arizona Historical Society)

Chapter Ten

The Progressive Era Finally Forces Changes

One can discern a clear transformation of most of the Populist movement's ideals of the 1890s into the widespread Progressive Era of the early twentieth century. There is little doubt that the entire mood of the country changed within just a few years as a severe economic slump ended and considerable social change ensued. Even the mining law would reflect some of the changes, though not until 1920.[1]

In the meantime, other governmental actions did affect administration of the laws. The General Land Office still existed and still had as its primary duty the disposal of as much land as possible. However, many lands within the public domain went to other agencies in the early twentieth century. The central goal of these agencies was not to dispose of the lands to private parties, but to maintain them for a variety of purposes. The president began to designate areas of other value as no longer open to mining claims. The fact that some areas were withdrawn from application of the Acts of 1870 and 1872 undoubtedly satisfied the conservationist lobby enough so they did not attack the laws on principle alone. As noted in an earlier chapter, leading conservationists endorsed mining if it had no serious conflicts with other values.

In addition to Enos Mills's Rocky Mountain National Park, Congress created several other famous national parks in the Progressive Era. They are Glacier National Park, Montana; Lassen Volcanic National Park, California; Wind Cave National Park, South Dakota; and Grand Canyon National Park, Arizona. The Acts creating these areas ended the possibility of filing new mining claims in those particular parks. However, a number of existing mining claims had "grandfathered" rights and mining operations continued on these claims. Ultimately such claims could be patented, as usual. As abandoned claims could not be restaked, there was a gradual attrition of claims in parks. (The most famous park of all, Yellowstone, as well as Sequoia and Yosemite, had been protected early enough that mining claims had never been a factor.)[2]

Presidents of the United States created other preserved areas by proclamation; these became national monuments. Here again, new mining claims were prohibited after the date of establishment of the monument but existing claims were "grandfathered." In some cases the government purchased claims in both parks and monuments but others were simply too expensive and remain to the present.[3]

Another agency that clearly reflected Progressive Era values was the Forest Service. Previously, the Timber Cultures Act had allowed private parties eventually to gain title to such lands by planting and cultivating trees; it was simply the Homestead Act adjusted to the forest. However, major logging operations so blatantly abused the Timber Cultures Act that Congress authorized presidential withdrawals in 1891 and attempted to adjust the policy in 1897. The United States Geological Survey of the Department of the Interior conducted surveys of the newly designated National Forests. Actual management of forest lands remained the responsibility of the General Land Office. The Mining Law of 1872 was not suspended by the new designation. A special commission established in 1896 to investigate the abuse of forests recognized the problems created by lumber companies. The commission, however, explicitly favored continued use of forest lands for mining purposes. It even recognized the common necessity for removal of trees for use as mine timbers.[4]

Gifford Pinchot, one of the best known conservationists of the times, had been chief of a minor office in the Department of Agriculture. With the backing of President Roosevelt, Pinchot lobbied for transfer of federal forest holdings from the jurisdiction of the General Land Office to his Department. In conducting his effort, Pinchot proved a most astute politician. He sat on a new land law review commission that met in 1903-1904 and recommended transfer of forest lands to the Department of Agriculture as well as a number of other measures.

Significantly, the commission's final report noted that changes in the mining laws were overdue but made no specific recommendations in that area. Possibly the commission placed its priorities on the raw numbers of acres distributed under the various land laws. By June 30, 1904, some 96.5 million acres had gone to patent under the Homestead Act alone, while 61.3 million acres had gone to patent through 718,348 cash sales, bringing the government $121,745,346. In 1903 alone there had been 12,449 entries under the Timber and Stone Act, totalling 1,765,222 acres. Virtually all of this was for lumbering. By June 30, 1904, the grand total of lands distributed under the Mining Laws of 1866, 1870, and 1872 stood at just over one million acres, with an additional quarter million acres pending. The commission did recommend repeal of the Timber and Stone Act of 1878.[5]

Pinchot enlisted the support of major lumber industries for the transfer. He organized a celebrated American Forest Congress in early 1905 that received massive publicity. Influential businessmen who attended represented railroads, mines, livestock, and irrigation, as well as lumbering. Pinchot unabashedly approached numerous members of both houses of Congress in their own districts. He succeeded marvelously. The Forest Service has remained in the Department of Agriculture despite numerous attempts to return it to the Interior Department.[6]

Obviously, this jurisdictional change within the executive branch of the government represented the ascendancy of the Progressive Era ideology over the older ideology. The new Forest Service, however, did not have complete control over its lands. The position of the 1896 commission of encouraging mining on forest lands carried over into the new agency's authority as designated by the Act of Congress of February 1, 1905. Mining claims remained legal on Forest Service lands. Mining claimants could still apply for patents of such claims. The General Land Office still decided on approval.[7]

While conservationism had become a main theme of the Progressive Era, the free silver movement had been an important precursor of the era. The mining law, closely associated with free silver, was the sole survivor of the old liberal land distribution policies in the area that fell under the new Forest Service. The point of the creation of the agency had been the end of abuses of homestead and timber cultures patent methods by major lumber companies. Yet mining claims and patents still stood on Forest Service Lands. This is another clear-cut instance of the survival of the General Mining Laws even in the era of reform legislation as part of their incredible status as the proverbial "sacred cow in the American West." The law would ultimately survive through yet another era of intense social reform because of its association with the Populist free silver movement. The survival is directly associated with the psychology of the frontier as explained by the Turner/Webb school. Further, the law would survive still later reform eras for a variety of reasons.

By the early twentieth century the economic development of the mining industry in the American West was maturing. One noted economic historian, Walt W. Rostow, stated that the economy of the United States reached a point that he considered mature in 1910, exactly the mid-point of the period of study.[8] It is quite true that "rush" stages were still ongoing in Alaska and at Tonopah/Goldfield, Nevada, in the early years of the century. However, the great majority of mining concerns removed relatively low grade ore from districts where the rush was long gone. In many locales silver ores in epithermal veins sat atop mesothermal deposits of industrial ores of lead, zinc, and (especially) copper. Though silver was gone, mining at the site could continue. The famous "copper war" of Montana in the 1890s marked the early stage of the metal's importance. In the twentieth century, copper continued to rise with the burgeoning automobile industry. Toward the end of the Progressive Era, the increased demands of World War I made copper a new bonanza. The vast bulk of total production came from the West in this period, but some important mines in the upper Great Lakes region still made substantial contributions.

In addition to Anaconda, the central participant in Montana's "war," other giant firms came to dominate other regions. Kennecott became the leader in Utah, including the largest single mine of all at Bingham Canyon. Kennecott was also influential in New Mexico, with the major Santa Rosa mine near Silver City. Phelps Dodge, and American Smelting and Refining (ASARCO), came to dominate Arizona. Phelps Dodge began operations as a small firm

The Progressive Era Finally Forces Changes   177

in the 1880s when it sent Dr. James Douglas, a physician turned geologist, to study low-grade ores. Ultimately, he consolidated holdings at both Jerome and Bisbee and developed more adequate milling techniques. Yet another mining town ultimately acquired his name. By 1909 some 34,121 miners were employed in copper operations in the states of Arizona, California, Utah, and Montana. Their total value of ore produced was $104.5 million, which represented nearly one half million short tons. During World War I, production doubled again, though it fell back by the early 1920s. Prices ranged from 12 cents per pound in peacetime to nearly 30 cents during the war.[9]

The "average" copper miner had little choice in employers beyond the major corporations; in 1919 the majority of Arizona's 16,831 mine employees worked in the nine facilities employing over 500 workers. Some smaller mines operated in the state, but many of these produced gold and silver instead of copper. The total number of producing operations in Arizona was 172.[10] At that time copper mines were underground facilities. Open pits did not appear until the 1930s, with the single early exception of Bingham Canyon.

Obviously, no single firm held a monopoly on copper in the national and international market. A number of companies, however, dominated different local areas in the West and Great Lakes region. They were able to institute company towns, including company stores, much like the coal mining towns of the Appalachian region.

Though copper had rather recently acquired the starring role among mineral products of the West, the precious metals still had important supporting roles. Many silver mines again showed handsome returns throughout the period. Gold mines were important in the last of the rush locales, noted above, but the bulk of gold production appeared as a by-product of mines that primarily produced other metals. Gold had a fixed price of $20.67 per fine ounce. Silver generally brought from 50 to 60 cents per ounce, but during World War I it increased to over $1.00.[11]

Precious metal mining had entered a stage of dominance by medium-sized business operations. Outside of Alaska, the placer deposits that had enriched men with sluice boxes were gone. However, the days of the Comstock Lode and such giants as George

Hearst were gone as well. A United States mint had first struck coins at Carson City in 1870, but the last coin bearing "C C" mint mark came from that facility in 1893. By 1900 there were only 2,636 miners counted in the Census throughout the entire state of Nevada, though this figure rose considerably after the 1902 Tonopah/Goldfield strike. While initial development of underground precious metal mines did require substantial capital, depleted mines could be purchased by smaller interests. The remaining low-grade ores often proved valuable when prices rose. In addition, there was always the chance of finding a new vein.[12]

The state of Colorado was the epitome of a local mining-based economy, dominated by medium-sized businesses. In 1909 some 1,177 different "hardrock" mines were operating in the state, owned by 453 different companies. Some 439 of these companies mined primarily gold and silver. The fact that 56.4% of the 8,689 employees worked for firms with fewer than 100 employees is particularly revealing and a marked contrast with Arizona or other mining regions dominated by copper. Colorado essentially maintained much of the flavor of mining in the previous century.[13]

Another interesting point about Colorado in this period is the proportion of foreign-born and first-generation miners. Some 50% were foreign-born and 25% more were of foreign parentage. Though the first generation of skilled hard rock miners in the West had been Englishmen from Cornwall and Devon, the typical miner by this time was more likely to be Irish, Italian, Scandinavian, Austro-Hungarian, or Mexican.[14] The days of the individualist miner/prospector were waning, yet Colorado certainly was not simply an extension of multinational trusts. Instead, it was a ground for the assimilation of immigrants into the mainstream of American life, a role usually associated with the major cities of the East. Labor problems certainly reflected the demographic changes superimposed on a region emerging from a frontier into an industrial economy.

The early 1900s, the age of Pierre and Marie Curie, saw early uses of radium in medicine and research. A few uranium mines began operation in this era, and virtually all of these mines also produced vanadium, a metal geologically associated with uranium, which is used in manufacture of hard steel alloys. In fact, vanadium is usually the primary product. Deposits of uranium and vanadium occur in sedimentary rock on the Colorado Plateau, primarily in the states of Utah, Colorado, and New Mexico, a region where there had been little earlier mining. By 1919 perhaps 1,000 people were engaged in mining these materials in twenty-five mines. The tiny uranium/vanadium mines were little more than a footnote to the overall industry of the times, but a later era would see them in entirely different focus.[15]

The maturing economy of the West is perhaps best revealed by the fact that coal miners substantially outnumbered "hardrock" miners. In Colorado, for example, 15,461 miners worked on coal in the year 1909, nearly twice as many as those in "hardrock."[16]

There is simply no way to overestimate the overall importance of mining, both "hardrock" and coal, on the economy of the West. Five states, Montana, Colorado, Idaho, Nevada, and Arizona, had over 10 percent of their labor force engaged in mining in 1900. Four others, New Mexico, Utah, Wyoming, and Washington, had over 5 percent in mining. Outside the West only two states, Pennsylvania and West Virginia, had over 5 percent. Minnesota and Michigan each had less than 2 percent, despite their iron and copper.[17] The nature of the work and tools of the underground miner in the early 1900s differed little from that of his counterpart two decades earlier. However, carbide lamps had replaced candles, improving working conditions.[18]

Even with the maturing nature of the economy, mining in the West was less dominated by major business concerns than mining in the rest of the country at this time. Both small and large concerns mined coal in the Appalachians. Iron in the upper Great Lakes region was almost entirely the preserve of the emerging giants in the steel industry. Lead and zinc in the Missouri Valley were becoming more dominated by larger concerns as mining went deeper, requiring more capital. The fact that Eastern mining was completely restricted to private lands is a most significant fact.[19]

One aspect of mining in the West must be emphasized. All manner of businesses, both large and small, could and did successfully engage in mining. The situation was not unlike the case of cotton in the South. Though the great plantation in *Gone with the Wind* was the stereotypical cotton producer, the reality was that virtually all small farms grew the crop as well, both before and after the Civil War. In fact, everyone depended on cotton in the South well into the 1930s, either directly or indirectly.[20] Western mining was a surprisingly similar economic force in that region, even in the earlier twentieth century.

Despite the survival of the General Mining Laws on National Forest lands, in the early Progressive Era, Congress ultimately did make some major amendments to the entire system in 1920. The time lag for the movement to bear fruit is the most remarkable aspect of the situation. The primary catalyst was the development of an entire new mineral industry that was not envisioned by the authors of the mining laws but which fell under the Placer Act of 1870 virtually by default. The new industry was petroleum. The wording of the Act of 1870 stated that "all forms of deposit" except veins of quartz or other rock in place could be removed from the public domain by those with mining claims. The Secretary of the Interior wrote a series of administrative decisions that interpreted this phraseology as applying to oil in the 1880s and early 1890s.[21] However, the Department completely reversed all of the earlier decisions in the *Union Oil Co.* case of 1896.[22] The resultant political storm over the issue soon brought yet another about-face by a new acting Secretary of the Interior who took office with the McKinley administration the next year. However, the issue was powerful enough that it reached the Congress. The brief Act of 1897 unequivocally placed petroleum under the Placer Mining Act of 1870.[23]

A more considered method of disposition of petroleum from federal lands would undoubtedly have prevented many ensuing problems and returned some money to the Treasury. In 1897, though, only a subtle suggestion was given of the importance petroleum would assume within a few years. Even the great Texas discovery at Spindletop did not occur until 1901. There was even less indication that federal lands would be substantially involved. Through the 1880s, developers often recovered petroleum by literally mining oil-laden rock or sands. In other cases they dug wells to the very shallow oil-bearing strata by hand rather than by drilling. There had been sporadic oil mining on public lands in California as early as the 1870s but discovery of the first major fields awaited the 1890s. Significant production did not occur until a massive demand for automobiles in the next decade. Thus the stage was set for a chaotic situation in which oil companies vied with each other and

The Progressive Era Finally Forces Changes 181

the government over rights on federal lands in California. An inadequate set of laws and regulations caused much of this chaos.[24] Three individuals, Thomas R. Bard, Wallace Hardison, and Lyman Stewart controlled California's oil industry in the 1890s. They merged operations to form Union Oil Co., the same firm that figured in some major court cases. By the early 1900s two other major firms from other regions, Shell Oil Co. and John D. Rockefeller's Standard Oil Co., were giving Union serious competition in the California market. These three companies rather evenly divided about 70% of the business, with a number of minor firms splitting the rest: Rockefeller's firm dominated the oil industry in the East and ultimately faced antitrust action in the Northern Securities Case. However, the California market was a competitive situation almost from the onset of oil production.[25]

By the early 1900s, a pattern of conflict arose between oil developers using the Placer Act of 1870, and parties who entered under other land distribution laws. The companies competed among themselves for mining claims, much as the 49ers had in an earlier era in the same state. The rivals of the oil men were generally attempting to tie up the land first in anticipation of an oil discovery; these parties were rarely genuine entrants under homestead or other agricultural entry laws. Beginning in 1904 the Department of the Interior ordered that certain lands be withdrawn from agricultural entry, resulting in protection of the oil interests on those particular lands. The orders, however, did not constitute a permanent "tie up." The Secretary of the Interior usually lifted the withdrawal orders after a relatively brief period.[26]

By 1909, some question began to arise concerning the government's own requirements for oil reserves. The director of the U. S. Geological Survey suggested that the government withdraw some lands for preservation of oil reserves while they were still available. On September 27, President William Howard Taft issued an order that closed three million acres from all forms of entry, including mining claims. Taft seriously questioned the constitutionality of his own order. Perhaps this action, more than any other, shows why he personally viewed his subsequent position as Chief Justice of the United States Supreme Court as greater even than the presidency. Taft requested sanction from Congress. The legislative process moved in a devious route but ultimately produced the Pickett Act of June 25, 1910. This law was not exactly what Taft had requested, and it was far from the demands of many conservationists of the times. Nevertheless, it was an important piece of legislation. The Pickett Act first drew a distinction between a group of non-metal minerals, namely oil, gas, coal, sodium, and potash, and all other types of ores. Under the Pickett Act, a withdrawal could be made for these materials, but not for any other.[27]

Taft immediately reissued his original withdrawal under the authority of the Pickett Act. After detailed scientific studies, he went on to issue permanent withdrawals of relatively small acreages that contained positively identified oil reserves. The withdrawals Taft designated for the navy in 1912 were at Elk Hills and Buena Vista Hills, California. Taft's successor, Woodrow Wilson, issued a similar withdrawal for naval oil at Teapot Dome, Wyoming, in 1915, and for oil shale in a large region of Colorado and Utah in 1916. The Harding Administration withdrew further oil lands in Alaska in 1923, just as Secretary of the Interior Albert Fall was exposed in the infamous scandal involving the Teapot Dome reserves,[28] only one of several problems that involved federal policies on oil and gas.

By 1919, following World War I, the movement was gaining strength in Congress to address at least some of the problems caused by the new petroleum industry that relied heavily on removing resources from federal lands. The problems were compounded by the fact that huge acreages were still withdrawn from entry.

The legislative history of the Act that ultimately became law on February 25, 1920, reveals the changed outlook of Congress. A bill calling for a mineral leasing system on federal lands originated in the Senate Committee on Public Lands, though similar proposals had been made in several earlier Congresses. The chairman, Republican Reed Smoot of Utah, personally introduced the bill in the first session of the Sixty-sixth Congress, then guided it all the way through the legislative process. Smoot had long opposed a leasing system and had acted against such proposals in previous years. By 1919, though, he faced the harsh reality of widespread sentiment to open the large tracts still under various withdrawal orders. Only a leasing system that would allow several usages of the land at once could end the dilemma. (Thus began the doctrine of "multiple use" that has since become a cardinal guiding point of federal land management agencies.)[29]

The twenty-two members from eleven western states were aligned by party: thirteen Democrats and nine Republicans. On this matter they all followed Smoot, even though his was the minority party in the region. The debates on the leasing proposal proved to be a remarkable touchstone for sentiment toward the General Mining Law. The Acts of 1866, 1870, and 1872 were the work of Radical Republican Congresses of the Reconstruction period. It is thus most ironic that the Democrats of 1919 regarded these Acts as unalterable. For example, Senator Henry F. Ashurst of the mining town of Prescott, Arizona, stated that the 1872 Act alone had allowed settlement of several entire Western states. Ashurst dwelt on the equality of opportunity the Mining Law of 1872 provided to all comers in staking claims and noted that no governmental entity had ever mined gold or silver. Rather, individual miners had performed the task. Nevertheless, Ashurst conceded that a problem existed with oil and gas and commented, "I may hold my nose and vote for it."[30]

Another Democratic senator, Charles S. Thomas of Colorado, supported Ashurst, noting that the Act of 1872 was "the basis of our development in the West."[31] Senator William H. King, Democrat of Utah, observed that the start up costs of a major copper mine were at least a million dollars and conceivably as much as fifteen million. The mining law was a definite aid to any firm attempting development of a new mine in light of these huge requirements for capital outlay.[32]

Perhaps the strongest remarks were those of Marcus A. Smith, Arizona's other Democratic senator. Smith noted that one group of miners on Mt. Graham, near his own hometown of Tucson, had been illegally evicted from the dwelling they maintained on their mining claim by the U.S. Forest Service. Though he had personally intervened on their behalf, with an amiable solution, he still had bitter feelings about any form of tinkering with existing Mining Laws. Smith proceeded to say, unequivocally, "If it had not been for the law of 1872, I am satisfied that the Great American Desert, as it was called in the geographies when I was a boy, would be a desert still." He added his belief that modern conservation, if adopted in the 1870s, would have thwarted Western development.

Smith went on to credit the law with the discoveries of oil in California that had created the current controversy, and reaffirmed his belief in free enterprise.[33]

Western senators did realize they faced a problem that needed attention. Smoot observed that the country had a shortage of five million barrels in annual production that could be resolved by leasing.[34] Albert Fall, Republican from New Mexico, cited figures showing some five million acres in his state were under placer claims that had been staked for oil.[35] James D. Phelan, a California Democrat, expressed concern about alien ownership of leases.[36] However, the only critics of the basic idea of a leasing system for oil and gas, somewhat surprisingly, were from outside the West.

Senator Thomas Sterling of South Dakota expressed extreme displeasure that the oil leasing matter was taking far too much debate time. He wanted to proceed to the question of prohibition.[37]

Senator William Kirby, Democrat from Arkansas, offered an amendment that would have allowed the president to order mining of coal, oil, or gas, in a national emergency. He based his proposal on some well-recognized problems the nation had faced a few years earlier in mobilization for World War I. Kirby knew that his measure had no chance; he may have offered it simply to see the reaction of the Western senators. Even in perpetrating a legislative joke, Kirby did not dare include "hardrock" minerals in his list. Kirby's amendment failed without a recorded vote.[38]

Republican Senator Robert M. LaFollette of Wisconsin offered a somewhat more seriously considered amendment that would have allowed the government to set the retail price of oil removed from federal lands under leases. This proposition, however, would have been difficult to enforce. LaFollette's personal prestige probably accounts for the ten votes the proposal garnered.[39]

The Senate ultimately cast a voice vote on a measure that was little different from Smoot's original bill.[40] The House retained the basic format of the Senate bill but revised several provisions. Again, members of both parties from the Western states dominated the proceedings. Much of the impetus to take some sort of action came after Representative John E. Raker, a Democrat from California, quoted a report of the U.S. Bureau of Mines that flatly stated the country had an oil reserve of only ten years. Raker also

The Progressive Era Finally Forces Changes 185

sponsored a workable solution to the problem of alien ownership of leases.[41]

Representative John A. Elston from Berkeley, California, one of the best-known progressive Republicans, believed that the government stood to profit from the measure and that it might even help control Standard Oil.[42] Representative Edward T. Taylor, a Colorado Democrat, made similar statements and noted the profits that might ultimately accrue to the government from leases on oil shale, a material widespread in his district.[43] Representative Benigno Cardenas Hernandez, a New Mexico Republican, paid careful attention to fine shades of meaning in the wording of the bill, suggesting changes to avoid future problems in administration.[44]

Representative Frank W. Mondell, the Wyoming Republican who had been a critical figure in the 1905 placement of the Forest Service in the Department of Agriculture, again played the most critical legislative role. Mondell reached a workable compromise for allocation of the money that would be made through leasing.[45] After considerable debate, a tally of votes on a motion to recommit the bill showed 201 members against recommittal, with only 44 in favor (6 voted "present" and 181 did not vote).[46] This tally was tantamount to final passage. In conference, the Senate rehashed the measure for a matter of months but finally agreed to the House changes.[47]

The overall debates in both houses included several statements that the Mining Law of 1872 was the third great charter of democracy and American heritage, after the Constitution and the Declaration of Independence themselves. Such a claim is most indicative of the overall views of the region. The assertion of any item to be the "third charter of democracy" is rare enough to attract considerable attention when it does occur. The Midwestern states that originated from the Northwest Ordinance of 1787 have sometimes proposed that law as the "third charter." Black Americans have proposed Lincoln's Emancipation Proclamation or the Civil Rights Act of 1964. The mining West thus showed its system of values as they stood in 1920 by advancing this position. However, the region did allow amendment for other materials.

The terms of the Act's thirty-six pages require some discussion. The reader will recall that the Pickett Act had created a list of materials to be protected by land withdrawals. The materials on the list were: oil, gas, oil shale, potassium, and sodium. The Mineral Leasing Act of 1920 removed these same materials from the provisions of the Mining Law of 1872 and made them subject to the newly created leasing system. The Act of 1920 also applied to coal. The Act of 1920 gave some protection to the holders of valid mining claims for oil (dating from before the Taft withdrawals of 1910) by allowing them to exchange the claims for 20 year leases with a minimum royalty of 12.5 percent.

The Act created an administrative unit called the "known geologic structure." This term designated an area not to exceed 3,200 acres that had known commercial quality oil and/or gas deposits. No more than one half of any known geologic structure could be leased to any one party. New leases were granted in two ways. In a known geologic structure, competitive bidding initiated a lease for a block of no more than 640 acres over twenty years at 12.5 percent royalty. The Secretary of the Interior could allow a renewal. For lands outside a known geologic structure, the Secretary first issued a two year prospecting permit covering as much as 2,560 acres.

If a discovery did occur, the permittee could obtain a lease of 640 acres for twenty years at 5 percent royalty with a renewal right. The permittee could also lease the remainder of his prospecting permit area at a royalty of 12.5 percent to 25 percent, at the discretion of the secretary. Alien ownership of oil leases was allowed, provided the alien owners were nationals of countries that granted equal rights to U.S. citizens. The distribution of royalties was, quite naturally, a matter of considerable debate. The ultimate result was a share of 52.5 percent to the reclamation fund, 37.5 percent to the state in which the well was located for education and roads, and 10 percent to the U.S. Treasury.[48]

The Mineral Leasing Act of 1920 represented a consensus among oil operators, large and small, among Westerners of all walks of life, among the administrations of Theodore Roosevelt, William Howard Taft, and Woodrow Wilson, and among the members of Congress of both parties. There can be no doubt that the conditions which formed such a consensus were a "crisis," not only for the oil industry, but for usage of federal lands. The crisis had to have been severe for Westerners in Congress to change the Mining Law of 1872 in any way at all.

The leasing system should be evaluated in terms of resolving the crisis that spawned it. In view of the policies toward immigration the United States was taking in the 1920s, the alien ownership provision was strikingly liberal. The collection of royalties has been generally good but occasionally some problems have arisen. Even in the worst cases, however, there has never been an abdication of enforcement as marked Army administration of the early lead mines. The Teapot Dome scandals of Albert Fall and Harry F. Doheny did not involve leases but the naval oil withdrawals, noted earlier. Congress and the Department of the Interior have refined the leasing system over the years, though a lottery system in use in recent years for award of leases has been abused.[49]

Congress passed an act in 1953 that extended the basic principles of the leasing system to include oil and gas from offshore wells in American territorial waters.[50] In fact, this aspect of mineral leasing has become much more important as a revenue producing measure for the federal government than have the oil and gas leases on federal lands. Senator Reed Smoot should be well remembered for the leasing system, not the Smoot/Hawley tariff that has carried his name into textbooks.

Prior to 1920 a wide range of parties could remove any "valuable" mineral deposit from a large portion of public lands. The government had made some exceptions on the basis of unusual areas with other values, but the Mineral Leasing Act was the first to set forth different laws for different types of mineral materials to be removed. The materials that fall under the Mineral Leasing Act of 1920 are simply known as "leasable" minerals. Materials that could still be removed under the authority of the Acts of 1870 and 1872 (presumably under a mining claim) have become known as "locatable" materials. Federal officials, as well as those involved in mining, generally designate the materials by these terms.

The minerals enumerated in the Mineral Leasing Act of 1920 are no longer a part of the story since they had been removed from the provisions of the Act of 1872. The materials that remained under the 1872 Act were still of considerable economic importance in 1920. The Mineral Leasing Act represents Progressivism, but in the economic sense rather than the conservationist, since it still encouraged development so long as the government received royalties.

Congress has made only relatively minor changes in the Act of 1872 since 1920. It has created a third legal category of materials to be discussed in sequence. The senators and representatives of 1919-1920 would not be the last legislators to view the Act of 1872 as a "Sacred Cow in the American West."

The Mineral Leasing Act of 1920 marked a belated end to the period that might be called the frontier stage of American mining law. The United States was not the only country to undergo a frontier experience in the nineteenth century, nor was it the only one in which mining was a major part of that experience. Several striking parallels between mining laws of the United States and other frontier nations can be drawn. There are some important differences as well, so a brief discussion is valuable.

By the early nineteenth century, the major European nations had a long-established body of legal precedents and government enforcement practices regarding mining. In the cases of European colonies, the mining laws of the mother country theoretically applied to the new lands. The gold rush condition, though, often forced abandonment of these long-standing legal systems. Just as California miners themselves devised codes for their own use, similar legal systems arose in South Africa's first diamond rush of the late 1860s, in Australia's gold rush of the 1850s, and in Canada's rushes from 1880 into the early 1900s.[51] Early Australian rushes brought parallels with California, as described in an earlier chapter, despite attempts by British authorities to dictate a different approach.

After the rush stage had passed and larger operations were needed to recover low grade, deeper ores, new mining laws appeared in all the frontier areas. In Australia a "ten foot regulation" permitted the small miner to dig as far as that depth but required leases for anything deeper. The result was domination of mining by major concerns. By 1897 large companies were demanding an end even to the minor surface claims. The small miners conducted a violent confrontation when the head of the federal government, Sir John Forrest, visited Western Australia. The system was not changed, despite the fact that deposits at less than ten feet did not last much longer.[52]

In South Africa a "ten foot regulation" would have done no good, considering the depth of the gold in the area around Johannesburg, and its presence in extremely hard quartz veins with virtually no placer deposits. By 1886 the Colonial government was requiring official permission for mining. A few large firms soon dominated the industry. By the mid-1890s, Cecil Rhodes had succeeded in merging most of these into a single giant operation. English domination of mining was clearly an element in the conflict that developed between that group and the Boers, the farming people of Dutch descent, in the late 1890s. The mines caused a massive demand for labor that brought an influx of black workers from far beyond the country.[53]

One nation with a magnificent mining heritage under Spanish legal precedents was Mexico. This nation was different from the others discussed above in that the mines at cities like Guanajuato, Zacatecas, and San Luis Potosí were old by the later nineteenth century. Much good ore remained in the remarkable mines there, but the political chaos of the new republic proved a severe hindrance to continued production. Under dictator Porfirio Diaz, Mexico abandoned her entire mining law in 1884 and established a new code specifically favorable to major corporations from the United States and Europe. These firms, led by the Guggenheim interests, renovated many older gold and silver mines but also discovered new deposits of copper and other industrial metals in Mexico's northern states. One gold rush to Sierra Mojada in western Coahuila in 1878 was much like rushes in the United States. Mexico's experience combined elements of the frontier with a more general need to attract capital for any economic development at all.[54]

The Mexican Revolution of 1911-1920 resulted, in part, from resentment at foreign domination of the country's economy, as well as resentment against Diaz himself. Mining temporarily suffered from the violent phase of the Revolution but the Constitution of 1917, a direct legal product of the Revolution, initiated an even more enduring cycle of change. Article 27 of the Constitution gave the government power to expropriate all subsurface materials. Though some foreign businesses returned in the 1920s, the government successfully used Article 27 to regulate them, in marked contrast to the Diaz years. By 1938 the government completely expropriated foreign-owned oil interests under authority of Article 27. However it has allowed some foreign investment in "hardrock" mining up to the present.[55]

Canada's frontier mining laws were more fragmented than those of the United States. In areas still in a territorial stage, Dominion law applied. When a territory became a province, however, the laws of that particular jurisdiction applied. These laws varied widely; in some provinces mining claims were allowed while others used a leasing system. Some provinces allowed claimants eventually to acquire a patent, just as on federal lands in the United States, while others had no such provision. On Dominion lands mining claims were used at first. By the 1920s, though, the Dominion used a leasing system. Claims still provided a means for establishing rights prior to development. During the Klondike rush of 1898-1899, Canada attempted to collect royalties on placer and was partially successful. Nevertheless, many escaped payment. Further, the tax undoubtedly caused many miners to abandon the Territory for neighboring Alaska and new rushes to Nome and Fairbanks.[56]

Given mining conditions in a wide range of countries during the nineteenth and early twentieth centuries, the Western United States stands out as favoring the "little man." Only Canada could compare to the United States in giving equal rights to all in securing mining claims on lands still publicly owned. In South Africa, Australia, and Mexico, major corporations dominated the industry to a far greater extent than in the United States. Any form of government control over access to mining lands in any country simply led to corporate dominance in the late nineteenth century. The United States saw a similar situation in the Great Lakes iron mines where the Mining Law of 1872 had no force, but the Western part of the country, the region where the law specifically applied, was virtually unique in the world. This difference in access to mineral resources contributed to other massive social upheavals in several other countries, though mining law was only one cause of large-scale violence in those countries. Both South Africa and Mexico suffered full scale wars with mining and access to mining wealth as a major theme. Compared to these countries, the United States' labor problems of the early 1900's paled. Australia's situation was not nearly as severe as Mexico's or South Africa's, but was sufficient to show how its mining laws differed from those in the United States. The arrogant attitude of the major concerns regarding the "ten foot regulation" is without parallel in the United States. Leasing there guaranteed dominance by major firms.

It is no wonder that Western senators spoke so highly of the Mining law of 1872, or that they expressed reluctance to change it at all despite changing circumstances. Yet oil and gas did require separate consideration. The Mining Law of 1872 had been a direct product of the times but now a more mature economic stage presented problems that writers of the law had never foreseen. Considering the use of leasing systems in other countries, and considering the United States lead mining lease system of the earlier nineteenth century, the Leasing Act of 1920 has proved a success.

While the 19th century prospectors had usually been unmarried adventurers, the Great Depression of the 1930s saw many families move to traditional placer areas in an attempt to find some useful means of livelihood. (Courtesy Arizona Historical Society)

Chapter Eleven

Western Mining, the Great Depression, and the New Deal

Western mining in the 1920s was virtually a continuation of that of the Progressive Era as industrial metals replaced gold and silver as primary products. Official reports at the end of the decade show nearly 50,000 employees of mines of ores "predominantly lead and copper" in the West. Placer gold was employing only 686 miners. Mines "dominantly lode gold" had some 5,887, and mines, "lode silver," had 2,838. The 1920s did differ from the earlier twentieth century in the West in that there was no parallel to the severe labor strife.[1]

The onset of the Great Depression brought collapses in the prices of copper and other industrial metals and even in the price of silver, though gold stayed at a fixed price of $20.67 per ounce. Copper fell from over 18 cents per pound in 1929 to only 5.67 cents by 1932. Production fell from almost exactly one million short tons to less than one quarter million. Silver fell from 53 cents per ounce to 27.9 cents over the same time, with production falling from 61 million ounces to 23 million.[2]

As with businesses everywhere, numerous mining concerns, large and small, cut back or closed completely in the early 1930s. Newspapers in mining states displayed a continuous procession of bad news for miners, administrators, and stockholders alike. The term, Depression, even in the historical sense applying to the entire world, must always be understood first as a psychological description of the populace of the times. The economic problems, with no prospect of substantial recovery, spawned serious problems in mental outlook for millions of victims of the economy. The "depressed" status of the average citizen's income spawned a yet more "depressed" condition as the word is used by modern clinical psychologists. It was the second type of "depressed" quality that led to non-functional lives that sometimes ended in suicide.

It is no wonder that the new presidential administration of Franklin D. Roosevelt meant so much to the American people in 1933. Roosevelt's appearance and style of public speaking proved a great benefit to the populace in overcoming psychological depression, which was probably the most debilitating of the interrelated problems. Roosevelt addressed this common mental condition with such statements as the resounding "We have nothing to fear but fear itself. . . ."[3] Such statements, however, even when often repeated in "Fireside Chats" on the radio, would have been of little value without a definite program of tangible actions to fight the economic side of the Great Depression. Although the bulk of Roosevelt's famous New Deal program is beyond our scope, several of the new Administration's policies did relate to mining both directly and indirectly.

Roosevelt, by Executive Orders, abandoned the gold standard for domestic matters on April 5, 1933, and for foreign matters on April 20.[4] The President had already begun purchases of large amounts of gold and issuance of additional currency backed by it. Congress saw the need for a new definition of the "Uniform Value of Coins and Currencies," as part of the end of the gold standard. The debates on the issue are quite revealing of other complex problems of the times. One opponent of the bill, Representative Louis T. McFadden of Pennsylvania, though a Democrat, linked it to an "international conspiracy of Jewish bankers." Various members from across the political spectrum rebuffed him for "making the first racial attack from the floor of the House in history," and for "Hitlerism."[5] Unfortunately, other influential figures outside Congress would make similar attacks on the gold/silver issue. In Congress the sentiment was different, to the body's credit.

Representative Martin F. Smith, Democrat from Washington, emphasized this point by stating, "The enactment of this law is another emancipation proclamation, declaring liberty for 120 million Americans from the thralldom and cruel yoke of gold which has enslaved the human race."[6] Somehow, Bryan himself had said it better, possibly because he was able to contrast silver with gold. Now the government was just basically making a technical adjustment. Even on such a "narrow gauge" measure, the emotional level is clearly discernible from the transcripts of the debates. The bill passed the House by 283 to 57 with 1 present but not voting and 90 not attending, on May 29. The Senate rehashed the House arguments, then voted 48-20 for the bill, with 28 not voting, on June 3.[7] This action shows the strength of the new Democratic majority in Congress that accomplished so much during the "Hundred Days" of the New Deal.

The principles of the Act remained in the more considered Gold Reserve Act of 1934. Though both houses debated the bill at length, the final tally of 360 to 40 (with 32 not voting) by which the House approved, and the Senate count of 66 to 23 (7 not voting) showed the strong sentiments in its favor. Representative Martin Dies of Texas was not alone when he expressed regret that the law did not go further.[8]

This Act allowed the President to fix the weight of the gold dollar at a lower figure. On January 31, one day after signing the bill, Roosevelt designated the weight to be 15 and $5/21$ grains, a reduction of 41%. The price of gold rose by a corresponding proportion from $20.67 per oz. to $35.00 per oz. With the price fixed at this higher level, it is no wonder gold production skyrocketed until World War II, even though the government itself soon stopped gold purchases. Despite the fact that the estimated 1933 production level had remained in the same range as in the preceding decade, at 2,292,000 ounces, the 1934 estimated figure reached 2,779,000 ounces. Even this 21% increase proved to be only a "warm up." By 1937 the estimated total reached 4,117,000 ounces and by 1941 it peaked at 4,751,000 ounces, a volume of gold equalled on a yearly basis only in the early twentieth century.[9]

The Acts of Congress relating to gold had carried much of the sentiment of Bryan and Populism. A true fulfillment of that sentiment had to involve silver. Certainly there was no lack of proponents of a silver purchase plan with the ostensible purpose of inflation; almost all senators and representatives from the West favored such legislation, as did many from the South and Great Plains, the areas that had supported Bryan in earlier years. Leading the "silver faction" were Senators Burton Wheeler of Montana and Key Pittman of Nevada. Even during the "Hundred Days," Wheeler could be counted on to make a speech for silver or insert some newspaper editorial or petition from a mining community into the *Congressional Record*.

Wheeler's position is a major strike against any claim that mining laws simply represented major corporations. His overall political philosophy is best demonstrated by his nomination as the Progressive Party's vice presidential candidate in 1924. Robert LaFollette had headed the ticket that year in one of the more respectable third party showings in United States' history. Wheeler's progressivism went back many years in Montana. He had strongly opposed the Wilson Administration's notorious violations of basic civil rights during World War I. Most relevant to mining, he had long opposed the economic and political influence in Montana of the giant Anaconda Corporation. But Anaconda was not the only mining firm in the state. Wheeler, with his impressive Progressive background, saw no incongruity in supporting the Mining Law of 1872, as well as federal silver purchases, while opposing Anaconda.[10]

Despite the prestige of some sponsors, proposed changes in silver policy failed in the First Session of the 73rd Congress because the president dominated the agenda. The "silver faction" skillfully consolidated its support in the Second Session. Wheeler and Senator William H. King of Utah proposed a silver purchase amendment to the Gold Reserve Act of 1934, mentioned above, which failed by only two votes in the Senate.[11]

The Administration split over monetary policy at the same time; gold purchases had caused dissension in the ranks of the advisors. In fact, the government stopped gold purchases in early 1934 but only after the dollar was remonetized and gold revalued. Roosevelt himself realized that the "silver faction" was growing and came to oppose it. He sent top advisor, Dr. Raymond Moley, to attempt to talk Wheeler out of the proposal, but to no avail.[12]

The "silver faction" first succeeded in attaching the measure to a farm bill but removed it when Roosevelt threatened a veto. Undeterred, Westerners in the House offered it again as a new bill, without trying the rider route. They were candid enough to give the proposal the informal title of "The Pittman Bill." Its primary provision was government purchases of silver until the government's supply of the metal reached one quarter the total market value of the gold stock.[13]

The House considered and approved the bill (designated H.R. 9745) in near record time. Representative Clement C. Dickinson of Missouri set the tone of the debates by recalling his own attendance at a Free Silver Convention in 1895 that had been a part of the development of the issue brought forth in the Democratic Convention the next year. Dickinson recalled that Bryan himself had been the key speaker at the preliminary convention as well as the more famous party convention. The House approved the measure by an overwhelming 272-37 on June 6, 1934; obviously the issue had a level of emotional appeal that went far beyond the mining states.[14]

In the Senate, Elmer Thomas of Oklahoma proposed a realistic amendment to remonetize the currency with new certificates redeemable in silver or gold, thus establishing true bimetallism. Thomas noted that, without his amendment, the proposed bill could cause a price rise to $1.29 per ounce that would prove most costly to the government. Though Thomas eventually voted for the bill as proposed, he quoted many objections to the projected costs, including those by columnist Walter Lippmann.[15]

At the same time, Father Charles Coughlin, a noted radio commentator with a large political following, latched onto the issue because of its Populist heritage. In remarks that forecast his later extreme views, Father Coughlin even advocated silver as the "gentile metal" to Secretary of the Treasury Henry Morgenthau, who was Jewish. The House of Representatives, which had attacked similar talk on its floor the year before, could not control Coughlin, who would become thoroughly radicalized in another few years. Coughlin's group invested heavily in silver.[16]

Though Senator Thomas ultimately lost his Amendment by 65 to 17 (14 not voting), he succeeded in attracting the interest of some of the best known figures in the history of Congress. Senator William Borah of Idaho noted that both Hamilton and Jefferson had wanted both metals to be full legal tender. But on this issue, no figure out of the past could entice the emotional appeal evoked by the mere mention of Bryan. George Norris, representing Nebraska more than Republicanism, endorsed the proposal as fitting the spirit of his state's best known statesman. The Senator most adept at invoking the name of Bryan was unquestionably Huey P. Long of Louisiana, possibly the most flamboyant character in all the history of American politics. Long made a speech on June 9 that portrayed Bryan as the "true Democrat," and even castigated long dead Grover Cleveland as a traitor for having been a "gold Democrat," hence really a Republican. Though Thomas's amendment had already failed, Long proposed two amendments that would have specifically reestablished silver as the standard for the value of the dollar. These amendments failed 59 to 18, with 19 abstentions. Perhaps the extreme position of Long's amendments eased the way for the bill itself. The Senate voted positively 55 to 25 (16 not voting) after defeating the Long amendments.[17]

Historians have followed a curious pattern in studies of the silver measure in the years following its passage. Despite the massive contemporary media coverage given the issue, the first two decades of studies of the New Deal, by "insiders" and scholars alike, omitted discussion of silver. Finally, in his 1957 book, *The Coming of the New Deal*, noted historian Arthur M. Schlesinger, Jr., made some important observations that are worth reanalysis.[18] Other well-known New Deal historians, including William Leuchtenburg, have essentially echoed Schlesinger.[19]

First, Schlesinger notes Roosevelt's original opposition to the silver bill but glosses over the point that the President did in fact sign the bill and even gave Secretary Morgenthau instructions to be "enthusiastic" in enforcing the new law.[20] There is little doubt that a Roosevelt veto would have been overridden by the House but probably not the Senate.

Secondly, Schlesinger notes the cost of $1.5 billion over the subsequent fifteen years, a sum far more than farm price supports, but for only 5,000 people in the silver industry. However, this point overlooks the fact that the Roosevelt Administration committed itself to the "enthusiastic" administration of the law. As the *Arizona Republic* noted at the time of the bill's passage, the law did provide for a goal of one quarter of the total precious metal reserve, but it did not place any limits on the time by which the amount of silver had to rise to that level.[21] Consequently the executive branch could have administratively minimized the cost of the Act, but chose not to do so.

Regarding the figure of $1.5 billion, the government would un-

Western Mining, the Great Depression, and the New Deal 199

doubtedly have purchased some precious metals for currency backing anyway, so this sum is too high. The figure of 5,000 people who benefited refers only to those in mines that were primarily silver producers. Within just two weeks of the bill's passage, Phelps Dodge Corporation and Miami Copper Corporation, two major Arizona firms, announced that they would reemploy a total of 1,000 miners. The companies specifically gave the silver bill the credit because silver is an important by-product of many copper ores.[22] The experience throughout the West over the ensuing years was obviously much greater, and the aid to copper had a most important implication, as discussed later in this chapter.

Finally, Schlesinger notes that the bill gave little impetus to inflation despite the introduction of new silver certificates into the money supply. This point is true, but again the administration could have decided to issue more certificates in larger denominations. Such action would have eventually increased the money supply and caused some price rises.

Schlesinger's overall evaluation is clearly exaggerated, though there is a strong element of truth to it. The cost of the silver bill was exorbitant but not as much as stated. Roosevelt could have controlled it even more. Nevertheless, Schlesinger's final statement on the matter is quite valid. He said that the silver policy was the "most remarkable — as well as least remarked — special interest triumph of the period."[23] The silver policy had a major additional cost that has not previously been identified, but which will be discussed below.

To understand the mining situation, and the nature of mining law, it is first necessary to consider the problem of soil erosion, one of the most significant fundamental conditions of the natural environment of the 1930s. In the West the condition proved nothing short of ludicrous because the great bulk of lands with severe erosion problems were owned by the government. On vast expanses of the public domain, many individuals still freely grazed various types of livestock on open ranges. Government regulations, much less controls, were simply nonexistent. Hence many years of overgrazing severely damaged range plants throughout the region. The loss of much of the ground cover had brought severe soil erosion, just as bad as that in the infamous "dust bowl" of the Great Plains of the period.[24]

Even before the New Deal began, Republican Representative Don Byron Colton of Utah had proposed comprehensive legislation to control grazing on government-owned land. Ironically, the Democratic sweep of the 1932 elections probably delayed passage of such a measure, because Colton fell before the electoral onslaught. After the New Deal was well established, Representative Edward T. Taylor of Colorado proposed a measure very similar to the earlier Colton bill. Hence the final Grazing Act of June 29, 1934 (passed just a few days after the Silver Purchase Act) became commonly known as the Taylor Grazing Act. The Taylor Act set up a system of allocating portions of the range for grazing, with fees going to the federal government. An administrative agency, the Grazing Service, issued allotments, collected fees, and patrolled for trespassers. (The Grazing Service merged into the Bureau of Land Management after World War II.)

Most significant to the land policy of the government, the Taylor Act effectively ended homesteading and most other forms of land entry initiated for the purpose of ultimately acquiring a patent. Although the Taylor Act did not contain a formal repeal of homesteading or other land entry procedures, the Act did forbid these practices in newly established grazing districts, except where individuals in the process of establishing such patents had "grand-gathered" rights. The Taylor Act, however, explicitly allowed continuation of mineral entries. The same principle that followed forest lands when they went to the Department of Agriculture in 1905 still applied when another new land management agency began operations in 1934. To this day, sections 5 and 6 of the Taylor Act allow mineral rights, including full patents, under the Mining Law of 1872, on lands which were then closed to entry under all the other land acquisition methods. The final Act closely followed the initial proposal Taylor had submitted. He knew that support from his fellow Westerners in the "silver faction" was critical to passage of any act at all, so he included protection of mining claims in the original bill. Also, the fact that Taylor's own Colorado district included many mining communities undoubtedly precluded any other action on his part if he wished to survive politically.[25]

The House Committee on the Interior considered virtually all aspects of the Taylor bill before enacting it in a series of hearings and other investigations that dragged on for nearly a year. However, the very first day of testimony, June 7, 1933, revealed the status the Mining Law of 1872 had attained. Present on that date at the same time before the committee were the Secretaries of Interior and Agriculture, Harold Ickes and Henry A. Wallace. Both men were among the leaders in Franklin Roosevelt's cabinet. Wallace would ultimately become Roosevelt's second vice president and would himself become a candidate on an ultra-liberal fourth party ticket in 1948. Both Secretaries made preliminary statements supporting the Taylor bill as written, including preservation of the mining laws, then faced members of the committee.

Representative Harry Englebright, Republican of California, was particularly interested in protecting the mining law. He phrased questions to suggest that the Taylor bill might contain "loopholes in this regard." Finally he asked point-blank, "But there is no regulation that could prevent a prospector from taking up a mineral claim at the present time, under the lode law?" To this Secretary Ickes replied, "It is not the purpose to do anything that would interfere with the right-of-way laws or the mining laws." Yet even this did not fully satisfy Englebright, for he was concerned with the right of mining claimants to secure timber for use in mining. That aspect was also part of the Act of 1872, so Secretary Ickes pointed out that Section 6 of the bill also protected timber removal for mining purposes and reiterated, "The mining laws remain in full force and effect." Even this statement was not enough. Another committee member, Representative James W. Robinson, Democrat from Utah, asked once again, "Is there any purpose to change the mining laws by this bill?" And Ickes responded, "No; not in any way. Mr. Englebright, I want to be clear as to verbiage."[26]

A Republican representative clearly had misgivings about the Roosevelt Administration, but on mining law, at least, there was no disagreement. The above exchange is perhaps the most convincing to date of the "sacred cow" status that the General Mining Law had attained by the 1930s.

The skepticism that Englebright showed in the committee hearings ultimately produced a beneficial result. When the bill reached the floor of the House he shrewdly asked why the proposal excluded the Forest Service from administering the policies. The Forest Service, a division of the Department of Agriculture, did have considerable experience in management of grazing on federal lands, but had estimated its costs for the additional territory at $2 million per year. Secretary of the Interior Harold Ickes declared that his department could do the job for $150,000. Though Representative Vincent Carter, Republican from Wyoming, challenged Ickes's estimate, Congress ultimately placed the new agency, the Grazing Service, under the Department of the Interior.

The provision protecting mining laws was never questioned on the floor of either house. Administration of mining laws remained the responsibility of the General Land Office, while the new Grazing Service had jurisdiction over the surface of the land and plants and animals on it. The House passed the bill 265-92, while the Senate, with almost no floor debate, passed it by a voice vote. This lack of debate probably reflects the fact that the "silver faction" had demonstrated its strength on its pet issue just a few days earlier.[27] However, the Taylor Act would probably have continued the Mining Law of 1872 even without the example of the "silver faction." The "automobile gold rush" of the Depression, described later in this chapter, also contributed to the political desirability of continuing the law.

If the Depression had negatively affected all forms of mining, the Taylor Act might well have included an end to new mineral entries along with homesteading and other land entries. The renewed interest in conservation could well have brought that result. As it was, though, industrial metals were the victims of the early years of the Depression while precious metals were its beneficiaries. Precious metals had always been the primary interest of proponents of the mining laws, so they naturally continued.

Later critics of the mining law, who have pointed with scorn to the fact that legislation signed by Ulysses Grant is still on the books, have overlooked a crucial point. The same Congress that passed the famous New Deal legislation also passed a law that effectively repealed the best-known of all government land distribution measures which ostensibly helped the "little man," the homestead laws. That repeal was timely, however, for homestead had outlived its usefulness. The same Congress in the same Act explicitly endorsed and continued the mining laws with the obvious belief that they were still quite useful and relevant to the national crisis of the Great Depression. The legislation took effect with the signature of Franklin D. Roosevelt. Here is one more powerful testament to the status of the mining law as a "sacred cow." The highest government officials saw it as an important factor in ending yet another national crisis.

With the rise in both gold and silver prices, mining activity for these metals increased dramatically, while the entire economy improved only modestly during the mid 1930s. Estimates for total U.S. gold and silver production immediately before and after the price increases are shown in Table 1. Such marked price increases clearly stimulated a wide range of renewed mining activities. Those who benefited included owners and workers in mills, transportation, assay offices, and equipment supply firms, as well as the mines. In fact, the Rocky Mountain states were perhaps the least affected by the Depression after 1934.

Production would never again reach these marked levels even with much higher prices after World War II. The rise in prices of both metals during and after 1934 brought a considerable increase in investment activity, even for properties that had no current production. As one typical example, the Bullard mine in central Arizona sold, just as the Silver Purchase Act of 1934 passed Con-

Table 1 (a)
Gold and Silver Output (millions oz.) and Silver Price (cents/oz.)

year	gold	silver	silver price (gold fixed $35/oz.)
1933	2.3	23.1	34.7
1934	2.8	32.8	47.9
1935	3.2	48.5	64.3
1936	3.8	61.2	45.1
1937	4.1	71.4	44.9
1938	4.3	61.7	43.2
1939	4.7	64.4	39.1
1940	4.9	70.4	34.8
1941	4.8	67.0	34.8
1942	3.5	54.1	38.4
1943	1.4	41.5	44.8
1944	1.0	34.5	44.8

(a) U. S. Department of Commerce, Bureau of the Census, Historical Statistics of the United States, Colonial Times to 1970 (Washington: Government Printing Office, 1975), p. 606.

gress, for an "undisclosed but substantial sum." The Bullard mine had seen no activity for over half a century.[28] Similar transactions occurred frequently throughout the West until World War II severely curtailed gold and silver mining.

In the earlier discussion of the interpretation of historian Arthur M. Schlesinger, the effect of price rises on copper production was briefly noted. Data presented below reveal the sustained effect over the years. Table 2 shows figures for copper alone because estimates for lead and zinc include massive amounts from outside the West. These metals generally followed the same pattern as copper over the years.

The rise in prices from 1934 through 1936 simply was not enough to generate the corresponding production rises; only the demand for gold and silver by-products can account for these production increases. The 1937 production figure is due primarily to a significant rise in the copper price alone. The impact of wartime demands is also evident, even with the fixed price.

For 1939 a detailed statistical comparison can be made with corresponding figures in 1929, the year prior to the Depression. United States Censuses of 1930 and 1940 included major surveys of the industry. In addition, a Works Progress Administration (WPA) study also covered mining for 1939. Table 3 shows the relevant values for copper, lead, and zinc. A scattering of uranium/

Table 2
Copper Production, 1933-1944 (same source as Table 1)

Year	Production (short tons)	Price (cents/lb.)
1933	190,643	7.15
1934	237,401	8.53
1935	386,491	8.76
1936	614,516	9.58
1937	841,998	13.27
1938	557,763	10.10
1939	728,320	11.07
1940	878,086	11.40
1941	958,159	"
1942	1,080,061	"
1943	1,090,818	"

vanadium mines still produced on the Colorado Plateau but these were comparatively minor. A comparison of the figures for 1929 and 1939 shows a substantial drop in the numbers of mines and miners, as might be expected. The total value of the materials produced also fell along with price. It should be noted, however, that the total weight of production, most notably of copper, was not much less in 1939 than 1929. The fact that only 42 mines with 23,000 employees produced almost three-fourths as much ore as had 162 mines with 39,000 employees ten years earlier is significant.

The increased efficiency of the industry, as noted above, can be attributed to technology. During the 1930s both large and small operators gained access to more and better equipment. Even the most modest placer operation could mail order suction dredges that

Table 3 (a)
Copper, lead, and zinc mines in the West

		1929	1939
Copper:	Price per lb.	18 cents	11 cents
	Production (millions $)	253.8	130.0
	Production (thous. sh. tons)	997.5	728.3
	Number mines	162	42
	Employment	39,368	23,100
Lead:	Price per lb.	6.8 cents	5.0 cents
	Production (millions $)	41.1	19.6
	Production (thous. sh. tons)	648.0	414.0
	Number mines	141	67
	Employment	10,132	5,339
Zinc:	Price per lb.	6.8 cents	5.5 cents
	Production (millions $)	17.0	10.1
	Production (thous. sh. tons)	724.5	583.8
	Number mines	40	30
	Employment	2,000 (b)	1,600 (b)

(a) U. S. Department of Commerce, Bureau of the Census, Census of Mines, 1939 (Washington: Government Printing Office), pp. 381-419. (b) Approximations made by excluding figures for mines in states outside the West, specifically Michigan, Minnesota, and Wisconsin.

could be used to gather gold from loose gravel in shallow streams. The suction dredge, in essence nothing more than a giant vacuum cleaner, became readily available during the 1930s. Mass-produced equipment of more traditional designs replaced "homemade" equipment. The Denver Gold Saver, basically a mechanized sluice box, became widely available. Undoubtedly the increased price of gold encouraged the industries that produced these items.[29]

For the larger operator, much more equipment was available for underground mining than had been even in the 1920s. Battery-powered electric lamps had replaced carbide lamps by 1939. Even one of the toughest jobs, "mucking," the gathering of pieces of ore from the mine's floor after dynamite had dislodged them, became mechanized. New equipment could pick up the pieces and dump them into ore cars.[30]

By the late 1930s the largest copper operations had adopted a new approach to mining that gave even greater efficiency. The leading companies developed the first open pit mines at Bingham Canyon, Utah, and at several sites in Arizona. Kennecott was the first firm to attempt this procedure but other companies followed by the end of the decade. With open pit mining the largest power shovels, trucks, and full-sized railroad cars could be used to remove ore. More lower grade material could be developed by this method than by expensive and relatively small scale underground mining. Open pit mining was still a comparatively minor undertaking compared to what it would become. Even in Arizona, over twice as many copper miners worked in underground mines as in open pit mines in 1939. No open pit mines then existed in Montana. Nevertheless, the industry had made an important start.[31]

The "bottom line" analysis of the improvement in mining productivity is quite dramatic. In 1939 the average copper miner removed 1.3 tons of ore per working hour compared to 0.7 in 1929. The average miner was recovering 34.9 pounds of copper in that mass of ore, an increase of 70 percent over the 1929 figure of 20.5 pounds.[32]

Efficiency improved for gold and silver mines as well, but not as dramatically as for copper. Undoubtedly the price situation drew many small operators into the precious metal business, while small operators fled the copper industry. Improved efficiency in the mining industry paralleled other industries in the 1930s. The Depression forced management to modernize and make improvements to stay in business at all. As just one other example, railroads developed more powerful steam locomotives that could run much farther. Freight car capacity increased substantially. Even a few of the first Diesel locomotives were running by the end of the decade.[33] The analogy between mining and railroading is striking.

One common theme of the 1930s, often shown in old newsreels made into teaching films for public schools, is the "down and out" lifestyle. Scenes of bread lines, of makeshift shanty towns called "Hoovervilles," of "Okies" moving in broken-down trucks, symbolize the era. Surprisingly, many individuals who might have otherwise been in similar circumstances found a nominal job and a place to live through mining (almost always placer). Because the Act of 1872 allowed residence on a mining claim, even a poor bit of river gravel could marginally support a family. These very small operations accounted for less than 3 percent of total gold production, and were not even listed by the Census as mining firms. Nevertheless, they certainly enhanced the psychological state of their owners who could feel that they were more productive than many other victims of the Depression.

The fact that a particular family had previously worked a mining claim and had built a cabin at a given place often led to a deep-seated sense of ownership even without a patent. The sons of "oldtimers" often returned to such locations. But many others who had no background in mining also participated. First, local newspapers reported "automobile gold rushes." Soon national publications picked up the story. The *Saturday Evening Post* ran three separate articles on Colorado, California, and Nevada.

In the original areas of California the scene almost replicated 1849, but with whole families involved. An estimate for 1932 indicated some 25,000 were actually mining. Most of these were just panning and did not have claims. In Nevada the situation was much more traditional, as might be expected for lode country. Prospectors did differ from those of earlier days by generally using automobiles. One discovery by the owner of a small hotel at Winnemucca brought an offer of over $1 million, but he kept the mine. Colorado's situation was somewhere between those of California and Nevada. A tent city existed near Fairplay in a long-worked placer area. Yet there was considerable restoration of older mines that had been abandoned even before the advent of cynadization, an improved milling process that had appeared in the 1890s. Such restoration cost at least $50,000, obviously a major sum in the Depression. The Denver mint lowered the minimum gold purchase from 5 ounces to 2 ounces to aid the small miner.[34]

The federal government's own relief agencies did not overlook mining as a possible source of employment. The WPA created literally millions of jobs of every type imaginable. In Denver and other cities near mining locales, the agency conducted training programs in the form of mining that was easiest to learn and cheapest to begin: placering. One "oldtimer" would demonstrate panning to over a hundred adult students at a time. Unfortunately, there is no way of knowing if many of the students actually became the marginal placer miners noted above; most such cases appear to have been of people with some mining background. However, WPA work of any description was rarely preparatory to future careers. At least the gold prices created by the government gave this project a little more psychological validity than many other WPA projects. Without the General Mining Law, the WPA mining projects would have had no such validity at all.[35]

Depression era mining saw several significant developments. When World War II began, the industry was able to meet the emergency despite the serious lack of manpower. Obviously, the copper industry was more than critical to the war effort. The fact that copper had recovered from its lowest levels around 1932-1934 because of gold and especially silver cannot be overlooked. Neither can the fact that copper mines soon employed experienced men and even used some equipment that had worked in the gold and silver mines at their peak. A thorough housecleaning of inefficient methods could not have occurred if the industry had remained in the doldrums. Undoubtedly, even dormant mines would have revived in the crisis. After all, American ingenuity responded to the war with whole new industries like synthetic rubber. The costs and time lag of reviving a fully dormant hardrock mining industry, however, would have placed additional strains on an already overextended system. The 1930s provided a streamlining and preservation effect that served the country well.

The Mining Law of 1872 undoubtedly aided the industry in the 1930s but any numerical estimate simply cannot be made. The free access to the mineral deposits that the law provided helped to keep some businesses in operation that would have closed if another system had been in use. However, a modified law that allowed existing claims but prohibited new ones would have been just as effective. Though the "Okie" style placer miners of the 1930s might be more romantic as beneficiaries of the Mining Law of 1872, the larger operations with their trained underground crews also benefited. It was the latter group that would prove critical in the war.

Charlie Steen, the best-known "rags to riches to rags again" mining magnate of the uranium rush. (Courtesy Museum of town of Helper, Utah)

CHAPTER TWELVE

Wars, New Agencies, and a New Type of Rush

The early stages of World War II from the United States' viewpoint were rather inauspicious for the mining laws. The official position was to discourage precious metal production, because it distracted from industrial metals. At the same time, deposits of copper, lead, and zinc were well enough known that new discoveries were a very low priority in the war effort. Officially, the government viewed the manpower then engaged in gold mining as having much greater utility in other wartime applications, either in or out of uniform. Hence in 1942 a special order on business in the war, L 208, effectively closed gold and silver mines. This action brought criticism since only a few genuine gold camps remained in existence and the total manpower released for other uses ran only in the hundreds. Precious metals had come full circle within just a few years, from highly prized, subsidized commodities in the 1930s to trivial items in a World War. Ironically, gold and silver production continued since they are by-products of ores of industrial metals.[1]

During the war the world's greatest open pit copper mine at Bingham Canyon, Utah, was particularly active. The owner and operator, Kennecott Copper Corporation, applied for and received patents on several claims allowing expansion of the pit. The General Land Office did assign a Mineral Examiner, Walter Koch, to write a report to justify the validity of the claims. The Examiner's final reports, three pages for each claim, included the results of some token samples he took. In short, the government was becoming a bit more scientific in looking at patent applications, but in the face of a location on the world's largest mine, and forms signed by D. C. Jackling, one of the best-known mining engineers, there was no real doubt as to validity. Even so, the increased interest in taking some samples even on claims of major firms was a harbinger of future practices.[2]

As a further wartime adjustment, Congress exempted all claim holders from the requirement of annual assessment work, the $100 worth of "development" the Act of 1872 required to legally hold a claim. There was no need to penalize claimants who might be in war zones or factories across the country and simply could not perform the required tasks. The requirement took effect again after the war was over. In another, more important aspect, mining had yet another unexpected leading role in the war, a role that extended into the postwar era.[3]

The conflict ended in 1945 with the start of the new Atomic Age. This event has become such a historical cliché that many of its secondary effects have been overlooked. The development and production of the first nuclear bombs in the famous Manhattan Project required outright construction of whole towns, as well as the laboratories and industrial facilities for production of the necessary fissionable materials. As noted earlier, a scattering of remote mines on the Colorado Plateau had produced some uranium for medical purposes since early in the century. The bulk of uranium in that region naturally occurs in conjunction with vanadium, itself useful in manufacture of some metal alloys. Hence the military was able to quietly purchase from these mines materials necessary for the first nuclear bombs over several years, ostensibly for other uses. In addition, some lands, withdrawn from mining for other military uses, also contained uranium.[4]

The production of the first atomic bombs, then, depended on military activity as supplemented at first by major universities and subsequently by civilian businesses under contract to the military. This project was very much a part of the same overall policy whereby the government undertook the war effort. Air bases, shipyards, and other facilities required construction of whole new towns. Contracts with private companies were the key to production of war equipment.

The Manhattan Project had been a secret from the American

public (but not from the Soviet Union) until the use of atomic weapons at Hiroshima and Nagasaki in August 1945. This secrecy shows that high officials anticipated the volatility of the political and legal implications of uranium. That fact should not be surprising since the end of World War II was politically volatile in all aspects. Uranium had so dramatically emerged in the headlines, that the United States government initially gave it a legal status different from any other mineral, no matter how crucial, in history. At first, President Harry S Truman was almost exclusively responsible for this approach.

Japan was in the process of officially surrendering, and the world was still trying to comprehend the immense implications of atomic weapons, when Truman issued Executive Order 9613 on September 13, 1945.[5] By this Order, he withdrew uranium-bearing federal lands from entry with mining claims under the Act of 1872, except for those already under standing claims. Prospectors could still claim all other locatable minerals on public lands, but if they found uranium they could not legally claim it. In issuing the Executive Order, Truman responded to the obvious need for some policy on uranium now that its value was no longer a secret. As a senator, Truman had held a key role in overseeing efficiency of the war effort. As president, he chose a similar course as he saw it regarding uranium. As of the date that Truman issued the order, the United States was still officially at war, certainly a major consideration in the policy. (A subsequent Executive Order, No. 9701, of March 3, 1946,[6] further tightened the policy by requiring that all mineral leases under the Leasing Act of 1920 contain a clause exempting uranium from removal under any such lease.)

The first Executive Order was obviously a stopgap measure. The importance of atomic energy and the establishment of future policies is revealed by the fact that Truman issued a major statement on the matter on October 3, 1945, just a few days after Japan officially surrendered. Truman's phraseology is most revealing:

> The first and most urgent step is the determination of our domestic policy for the control, use and development of atomic energy within the United States.
> We cannot postpone decisions in this field. The enormous investment which we made to produce the bomb has given us the two

vast industrial plants in Washington and Tennessee, and the many associated works throughout the country. It has brought together a vast organization of scientists, executives, industrial engineers and skilled workers — a national asset of inestimable value.

The powers which Congress wisely gave to the Government to wage war were adequate to permit the creation of this enterprise as a war project...Prompt action to establish national policy will go a long way towards keeping a strong organization intact.[7]

To fulfill these ends, Truman proposed comprehensive legislation on atomic energy, which would include creation of a special Atomic Energy Commission (AEC) of five members appointed by the president with confirmation by the senate. The basic structure as proposed was similar to several other regulatory bodies that had enforcement bureaucracies. Nevertheless, Truman believed the AEC "should interfere as little as possible with private research and private enterprise," though it would have some aspects of real power. He flatly suggested:

All land and mineral deposits owned by the United States which constitute sources of atomic energy, and all stock piles of materials from which such energy may be derived, and all plants or other property of the United States connected with its development and use should be transferred to the supervision and control of the Commission. The Commission should be authorized to acquire at a fair price, by purchase or condemnation, any minerals or other materials from which the sources of atomic energy are derived, and also any land containing such minerals or materials, which are not already owned by the United States....

Under appropriate safeguards, the Commission should also be permitted to license any property available to the Commission for research, development, and exploitation in the field of atomic energy. Among other things such licensing should be conditioned of course upon a policy of widespread distribution of peacetime products on equitable terms which will prevent monopoly....

The measures which I have suggested may seem drastic and far-reaching. But the discovery with which we are dealing involves forces of nature too dangerous to fit into any of our usual concepts.[8]

Whether it was from the recent war experience, or his own personality, Truman believed in forceful actions. His atomic energy proposals were characteristic. The very next day after the proposal, October 4, 1945, he ordered the Navy to take over some twenty-six oil refineries that would have been shut down by a strike. In 1946, he took control of the entire railroad industry for the same reason, and in 1952 the steel industry. The last action finally brought a Supreme Court ruling that such orders were unconstitutional. Compared to the outright seizures, Truman's policies on uranium appear rather mild. He did turn the matter over to Congress, which unquestionably had authority, even if some Executive Orders were legally suspect.[9]

Congress enacted a comprehensive Atomic Energy Act on August 1, 1946, which created the regulatory commission, and carried out much of the intent of Truman's recommendations. This measure, which began as S.B. 1717, proved to be one of the most technical measures ever committed to legislation. Various aspects included national security, future research and development, industrial processes, peacetime applications, rights of inventors (for *that* kind of patent), as well as mining. Senator Brian McMahon, Democrat of Connecticut, chaired the new Committee on Atomic Energy and conducted months of hearings on numerous aspects of the legislation, including very technical points. The "big name" scientists who had participated in the Manhattan Project appeared as witnesses, including Robert Oppenheimer, Harold C. Urey, and Edward Teller. Hence it was some time before the subject of mining even appeared in the transcripts. The matter could not be ignored forever, though.[10]

Secretary of the Interior Harold Ickes first broached the issue, and supported Truman's ideas, by stating that the Government reserve for itself all fissionable materials so that it would not have to buy them back. It should be recalled that Secretary Ickes had appeared as a witness on the repeal of homesteads through the Taylor Grazing Act of 1934, but had then favored the Mining Law. Now he took the opposite position. Yet the draft legislation already under scrutiny favored repeal of the Executive Orders and reopening uranium to mining claims under the Act of 1872.[11]

Much of the uranium that the military had purchased was from the Vanadium Corporation of Colorado. Two of the firm's top officials, Edwin Bransome and Fredrick F. Kett, appeared to address the production of ores, since they were among the few to have practical experience. The officials noted the need for massive production and the fact that deposits are generally small and widely scattered. The chemistry of uranium, which is usually a secondary material found in conjunction with vanadium, was a crucial scientific point that could not be overlooked. Hence they strongly endorsed use of the Act of 1872, including the mineral patent procedure, even for uranium.[12]

Following the opening statement, Chairman McMahon pointedly asked, "What specifically do you suggest should be incorporated in S. 1717 to accomplish that objective?" Kett responded:

> Taking the bill itself... I will read that sentence incorporating our suggestions:
>
> The term "source materials" shall include any ore *after but not before mining, extraction, and removal from its place of origin* containing uranium, thorium, or berrylium....
>
> That would cure the whole business. That would simply mean that anything still in the ground is not to be controlled. In other words, no Government department can take 3,000,000 acres from circulation and say, "You cannot locate claims here or patent claims, or have anything to do with it."[13]

Senator Bourke Hickenlooper, Republican of Iowa, then asked the crucial question, "You would still retain the independent property rights and location?" Kett responded unequivocally:

> I mean that the mining law should not be changed at all. Anybody should be allowed to stake a claim, work it, and patent the claim, after which they own it in fee simple, with no restrictions on the prospecting, location, and development of claims containing vanadium and uranium, which it always contains out there.[14]

Hickenlooper followed up by asking, "Just watch them after they get the ore out of the ground?"

Kett responded favorably, "The minute the stuff is mined, OK, all the control you want on it; but don't stop free prospecting for the materials."[15]

The chairman then tipped his hand by quietly stating, "That

would seem to me to be rather sensible." Shortly he became more explicit:

> ...Of course everybody should be permitted to mine the material... It is the intent to make the manufacture of fissionable materials a Government monopoly in the field. It is not the intent of the bill to make a Government monopoly of the mining of the source materials.[16]

This support from the Chairman, though from the opposite party, led Senator Eugene Milliken, Republican of Colorado, to make what was unquestionably the most impassioned impromptu speech in all the months of hearings on the Atomic Energy Bill:

> I would say for the record, for I don't know whether it is understood in the East and in other parts of the country, the prospector for ore is the greatest and perhaps the last remaining individualist in the United States. He operates on the same incentives that the inventor operates on. The next shot is going to make him rich and he won't let anybody tell him where to put in that next shot... He has his complete independence, and you couldn't get him to forsake it. You couldn't hire him by a corporation and tell him to go out and prospect a particular area. He wouldn't be interested in working for a private corporation.
>
> He wants to find this mine and make its development, and get his place in mining history, and make a fortune, just as an inventor operates under the same kind of stimulus.
>
> You cannot regiment prospectors. You cannot give a prospector orders as to where he is going to look and what he is going to do...
>
> He is a class of person all to himself, and he is the fellow that has developed the mining industry of this country.[17]

Milliken then excused himself for becoming emotional. His ideas were well received and became part of the committee's reported legislation. The frontier thesis of Turner and Webb can find no greater testament to its validity than these remarks and the fact that they were shared by the entire committee. The faith in the West in possessing the wherewithal to solve even the latest, most complex problems of the technological atomic age is obvious.

In a few brief concluding remarks, Vanadium Corporation's Kett stated that his firm was a relatively small producer, compared to Union Carbide, the uranium giant. He disparaged Interior Secretary Ickes's temporary withdrawal of 3,000,000 acres from the mining law, even though all but 220,000 were restored. Chairman McMahon said he would look into the matter.[18]

Kett even requested that all future withdrawals of federal lands from the mining laws be ended. This suggestion was unrealistic. Overall, though, these hearings are one of the most remarkable testaments to the "sacred cow" status of the Act of 1872, especially occurring as late as 1946. Milliken's final remarks in disparagement of leasing markedly reinforce the theme.

The bill reached the Senate floor on June 1, 1946, amid several other pressing legislative matters, so debate lasted only that single day. Despite the wide range of items the bill addressed, the only point that aroused any controversy was on the mining provisions. Chairman McMahon clearly set the tone at the start of the debates by firmly saying:

> The bill makes provision for free mining... We believed that it was necessary to see to it that the independent mining system which now exists in the United States should not be disturbed any more than was absolutely necessary for the security of our country...
>
> I learned... many lessons on mining law from the Senators from Colorado who are on the Committee, and I learned much about the way independent prospectors carry on their operations. So we weighed this problem from every angle and decided it was better to encourage the independent prospector to find and discover other deposits and to see to it that when they were discovered the Commission would be the only buyer of them at a price fixed by the Commission.[19]

Senator Carl A. Hatch of New Mexico, though a Democrat, roundly disparaged Truman's withdrawal as having stopped much prospecting. Milliken drew the support of several Westerners when he stated that the committee had debated but rejected all proposals which would have involved future withdrawals. He summed up the entire policy:

We decided that since we want fissionable material we should encourage the production of such materials. That is one of the reasons why we were so careful to exempt the rights of a man who has a valid location.[20]

One Western senator, however, actually felt that the proposal did not go far enough to protect the independent prospector. Joseph C. O'Mahoney, Democrat of Wyoming, asked if those major producers who had prior knowledge of ore deposits from the Manhattan Project would be excluded from use of such knowledge in locating claims. When he found that the bill had no such restriction, he offered it from the floor because he did not want use of "inside information." Even Colorado's senators saw no need for this, but backed down and let the amendment go into the final Act because of time constraints. A voice vote was all that was needed for the Senate to pass the Atomic Energy Act of 1946. It is significant that the only change in the complex bill resulting from the final debate had involved mining claims.[21]

In the House of Representatives, the matter of mining did not arise at all in final debate. Some industrial aspects of the bill drew Republican opposition, though, and the total vote recorded was 256 to 78. Aside from the legislative end of his own Executive Order on mining claims, Truman got everything he had requested in his proposal, so he signed the Atomic Energy Act.[22]

Congress could have endorsed Truman's proposed policy and provided direct government mining of uranium, either by the military or by the new civilian Atomic Energy Commission. Or Congress could have provided a contract system with industry to mine uranium, or even a lease system, since that method had been used successfully for oil and gas since 1920. Instead, Congress specifically restored uranium to the applicability of the Act of 1872, reversing the Executive Orders. Such a reversal is all the more remarkable since a strongly Democratic Congress united with the Republicans against a Democratic President and Secretary of the Interior on this sole aspect of the Act of 1946. It is interesting that Robert Swenson, who wrote one government-sponsored study of land laws, speculated that a leasing system might have been feasible in place of the first federal Act of 1866. That point is questionable, but it is certain that any of a number of alternate systems using leasing or royalties would have been logistically feasible by 1946.

The stated policy of encouraging as much uranium production as quickly as possible clearly supports the Turner/Webb thesis in explaining the psychological state of the lawmakers. The legal position of the country in the Atomic Age was the same as it had been for settlement of the West generations earlier. Like President Polk, who aided in starting the gold rush for other reasons of national sovereignty, Congress had several motives in the Atomic Energy Act of 1946. In part, the goal of settling a remote region still drew support. It was only by chance that the primary ores were on the Colorado Plateau, the most remote, sparsely settled region in the country outside of Alaska. Other ores subsequently came from a remote region of Wyoming, which clearly reflected the same considerations. Once again, free lands and the resources they contained would be the government's tool in promoting settlement. Preservation of the Act of 1872 extended the "little man" appeal even into the Atomic Age, certainly an integral part of the frontier thesis at a surprisingly late date. As might be expected for legislation that unanimously passed the Senate, no opposition to the Atomic Energy Act of any note was voiced among the public. The *Bulletin of the Sierra Club* made no mention of the legislation at all. The frontier thesis can account for this fact too, especially when linked to national security.

Just as assay offices and mints had long purchased gold and silver for the Government, the Atomic Age saw depositories for uranium purchases on the Colorado Plateau. Indeed, the Government established at the onset the policy that silver miners had fought for over many years: guaranteed purchases at prices determined by a standard formula of amount and quality of ores presented. True, the Atomic Energy Act of 1946 contains an "escape clause," a concession to wartime necessities, that allows the government to remove uranium even from patented mines if necessary. It has never chosen to do so. After the Atomic Energy Act, uranium joined gold, silver, and copper as a primary ore produced on federal lands under the "sacred cow," the Act of 1872.[23]

The debates show that Congress had a clear and definite intent to promote yet another mining rush. Once it began operations, the

Atomic Energy Commission took definite actions to further this end. Such a policy was almost certain to succeed but took some years. Undoubtedly, the eventual rise of the Cold War with the Communist bloc aided in creating yet more interest in uranium and in a form of "national service" in prospecting. Winston Churchill remarked on the "fall of an iron curtain" as early as 1946. Subsequent events that contributed to the "Cold War" psychology, both among officials and the general public in the United States, included the blockade of Berlin, the Soviets' own nuclear explosion, and the conflict in Korea. In light of such events, the emergence of a new spirit of patriotism which included support for an arms race is understandable.

The Atomic Energy Commission was not the only new federal agency to appear in the years immediately following World War II. This period saw massive government reorganizations, including a new armed service, the Air Force. The year 1946 also saw the creation of another agency that had direct bearing on the newly important uranium mining industry. At the very end of 1945 Congress had passed a Reorganization Act that gave the President virtually a free hand in creating, abolishing, or merging agencies within several of the major departments, including the Department of the Interior.[24]

Truman made the most of the Reorganization Act. The new President saw the need to manage more closely the Western lands with the certainty of the Atomic Energy Act and the uranium rush it would create. Hence he inaugurated a new agency on July 16, 1946, just two weeks before Congress approved creation of the Atomic Energy Commission. The new agency, the Bureau of Land Management (BLM), assumed the functions of the venerable General Land Office, which ceased to exist. The BLM also assumed the functions of the relatively young Grazing Service, which Congress had created to administer the Taylor Grazing Act of 1934.[25]

There is a story so timeworn that it must be true: the first director of the BLM simply requested "forty good cowboys" to administer the new agency, and got them. In fact, the great majority of the professional positions in the early BLM were livestock related. However, the agency could, and did, approve or disapprove mineral patent applications. It also found occasional need to contest the validity of claims before the patent process. The old General Land Office had performed these functions for all federal lands, even those under the management of other agencies. The BLM thus found itself examining claims on Forest Service and Bureau of Reclamation lands as well as its own. Also, it had to enforce the Leasing Act of 1920. Obviously, the agency assumed an important role in the concerning mineral matters from the time of its creation.[26]

The leading role in the immediate postwar period though, was that of the Atomic Energy Commission, a glamour agency through the 1950s in a way similar to the National Aeronautics and Space Administration (NASA) in the 1960s. In 1948 the AEC fixed uranium purchase policies, including a minimum price of $3.50 per pound of material of 87 percent purity. By 1950 the AEC even went so far as to offer a $10,000 bonus for certain major discoveries. The agency also printed booklets that showed "how to" prospect for uranium. The rush was beginning, but was more gradual in gaining momentum than the classic placer rushes of the last century. It would prove more enduring.[27]

In 1951 the agency was true to the amendment that Senator O'Mahoney had forced in the Act of 1946 when it opened to mining claims nearly 12,000 acres that had previously been withdrawn because of known reserves. It was a latter day version of the Oklahoma land rushes of the 1890s. In the area near Grants, New Mexico, some 4,000 prospectors staked 6,000 claims within days of formal opening of the area. Grants and the area around Uravan (named from uranium and vanadium), Colorado, were the early centers of activity but even larger districts awaited discovery.[28]

Instead of a burro, the prospector used an army surplus jeep or, if he could afford it, an airplane. Geiger counters and other equipment could detect radioactive materials. Hence many participants had little or no prior experience.[29]

Colorado Plateau ores are entirely different from most other highly valuable materials since they are in sedimentary rock formations spread widely over the region. This diffusion prevented uranium prospectors from focusing on any particular sites. In exploring for traditional hardrock minerals, the presence of epithermal and even many mesothermal deposits is obvious. Any such recognition aids the prospector in further focusing a search on locales where the materials might be economically concentrated.

Subsequently, researchers have found that natural factors have concentrated uranium in certain locales within sedimentary rocks. However, much less indication of these locales is given than in traditional ores. In the late 1940s and early 1950s, searchers had very little to guide them for they did not yet know many of the tricks of the trade.

Prospectors first combed the Colorado Plateau for outcrops of the Triassic-aged Chinlee Formation and the Jurassic-aged Morrison Formation. Both of these consist of spectacular multicolored strata. The Chinlee forms the Painted Desert in Arizona. However, both the Chinlee and the Morrison cover literally thousands of square miles, exposed in some places but well below the surface on most of the Plateau. It is no wonder the rush took some years to develop momentum. Subsequent discoveries have shown some ore in the Cutler Formation, just below the Chinlee. The ores are dispersed between the grains of sandstones in these strata.[30]

The most important discoveries did prove to be on BLM-administered lands, but some uranium in commercial quantities was on Indian reservations, primarily the Navajo. Such discoveries did not fall under the Act of 1872, but provided a royalty to the tribe. These mines are proof that uranium deposits, if rich enough, could operate at a profit even if a royalty was required. Several classic nineteenth century mining rushes had resulted in forced removal of Indians. Now a tribe was running its own mines, though legitimate questions, beyond our scope here, have been posed as to the long-term benefits.[31]

Many earlier rushes began rather modestly until a spectacular claim or "grubstake" made a legendary overnight fortune. Somehow the personification of any rush resulted in a redoubling of efforts and many newcomers. Examples discussed earlier include Tombstone's Ed Schieffelin, Telluride's J. B. Ingram, Leadville's H. A. W. Tabor, and Cripple Creek's Winfield Scott Stratton. The uranium rush would parallel this portion of the nineteenth century experience.

In 1948 a young geologist, not yet out of his twenties, decided the oil industry in his native Texas was too crowded. So he took his family to the expanses of the Colorado Plateau. His name was Charles Augustus Steen, just "Charlie" to 'most anyone he met. Steen looked carefully at outcrops of the Chinlee, though his fam-

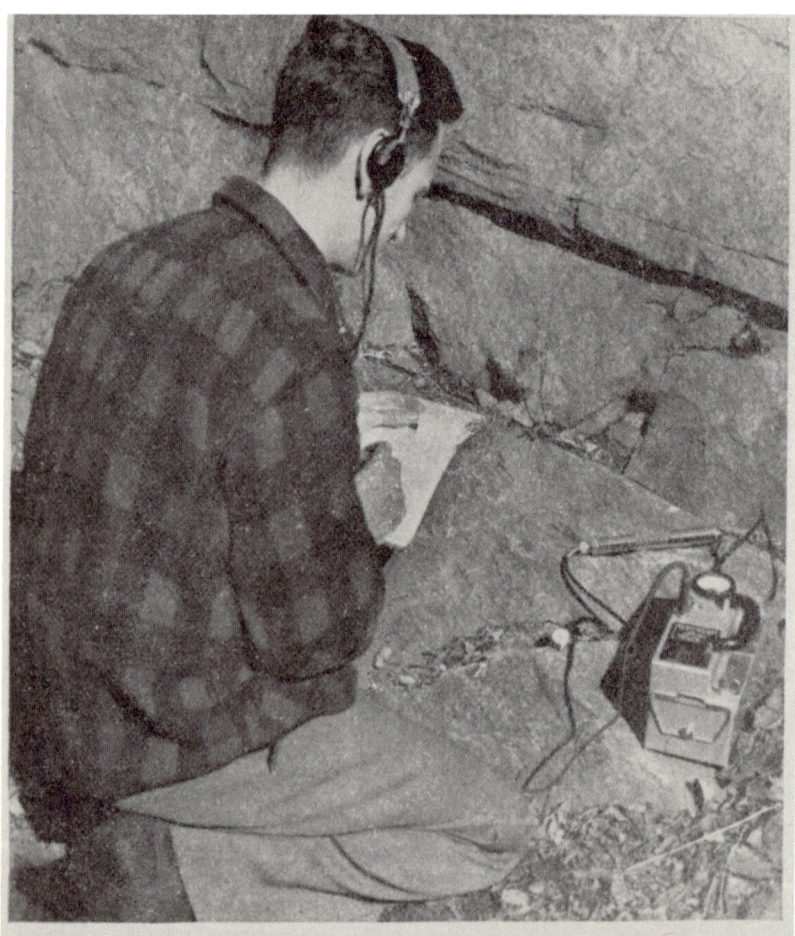

A prospector uses his Geiger counter to determine the radioactivity of a specific point in a generally radioactive area. A background count was taken before this specific reading was made.

The U.S. Atomic Energy Commission published materials to promote a major uranium rush in the late 1940s.
(From a 1949 booklet, *Prospecting for Uranium*.)

ily practically starved. By 1952 he thought he had something, but the AEC had already decided the locale was "barren." Steen did not give up. He filed the *Mi Vida* ("my life" in Spanish) claims in the Big Indian Valley of San Juan County, Utah. Finally he raised enough money to demonstrate a genuine discovery and disprove rumors of "salting." The claims began a new life not only for Steen and his major mine, they began development of the Big Indian District and then the adjacent Lisbon Valley District, which became the most productive on the Plateau. Steen had recognized, when no one else had, the type of geology in a faulted anticline that might contain ore.[32]

Steen's story made the news magazines. Other aspects of uranium provided pictorial stories in *Life*. By 1953, even early television was contributing to the rush to the Colorado Plateau. That same year Steen secured funding for a refining mill in the Big Indian District and thus became the best-known individual in the history of the uranium rush. Ironically, he would lose his entire fortune, just as H. A. W. Tabor had, but that would be from bad stock investments in the late 1960s.[33]

Another figure repeated Steen's experience on a smaller scale. Fred Schwartzwalder, a native of Germany who immigrated after World War I, was a high school janitor in Denver. He found rich uranium in epithermal veins in nearby Jefferson County, Colorado, in 1953. This type of ore, pitchblende, is rare in the United States. Coincidentally, the site, which eventually became the Schwartzwalder mine, is just a few miles from the famous Colorado School of Mines at Golden, also in Jefferson County. Yet the experts there denied that uranium as pure as the samples produced by Schwartzwalder could be from the area at all; they suspected salting with material from the Belgian Congo or Canada. Eventually, the part-time prospector proved them wrong, just as Steen silenced the critics. He sold his claims for $300,000, a figure far below ultimate production, and eventually lost what he did make to bad investments, just as did Charlie Steen.[34]

The stories of Steen and Schwartzwalder captured publicity, but few other figures from the rush left enduring stories. Several other millionaires, however, were more successful at maintaining their fortunes. One prospector, with the appropriate name of Vernon Pick, repeated Steen's experience and found himself worth

$10,000,000 by early 1956, yet never entered the folklore of mining. Somehow the overall event of the uranium rush has escaped the attention of historians as well as ordinary storytellers. Much more has been written on many relatively small nineteenth century rushes. Yet the uranium rush was more remarkable in many aspects than any of the earlier rushes.[35]

Uranium peaked in 1954–1956, forcing local services in existing communities to the limit. In addition to Grants, New Mexico, and Uravan, Colorado, the towns of Moab, Monticello, and Blanding, in southeastern Utah, became major centers of distribution, milling, and residences near the Big Indian Valley and other deposits in both the Chinlee and Morrison formations that cover the region. All the county seats saw considerable activity in recording claims and annual assessment work. Grand Junction, Colorado, became the regional federal administrative center. "Penny stocks" in various ventures traded at Salt Lake City. Uranium provided the basis of much of the regional economy. The rush did not end with a crash, but tapered off into the early 1960s leaving behind a more mature uranium industry.[36]

During the peak of the rush, conditions in the field often replicated the old days. There were many cases of claim jumping, both intentional and accidental. At least one murder near Moab was attributed to this long-time source of Western conflict. A newer situation involved the corporations. Senator Milliken's comments about prospectors and their lack of willingness to work for others were simply erroneous. In fact, the romanticized prospector that he portrayed had been rare, even in the previous century. The majority of the Colorado Plateau prospectors were independent, but in the uranium rush, unlike other rushes, major companies sent their own employees into the field with much more equipment and backing than most individuals could muster. Naturally the situation promoted bitterness, yet the thrust of the Atomic Energy Act, including the last-minute amendment by Senator O'Mahoney, did give at least some chance to the "little man," just as had been intended. Charlie Steen himself, a "little man" made big, drew headlines and a slander lawsuit by denouncing certain major firms and individuals by name. He even went so far as to take control of a small bank at Dove Creek, Colorado, to provide "grubstakes" for marginal prospectors.[37]

Much of the problem of "big versus little" related to the technical problems of prospecting in sedimentary rock. There was only so much ground that individuals could reach from the surface, even with geiger counters. Soon it was evident that a mass of sample drill holes were the only adequate method of covering the vast expanses of potentially ore bearing formations that were at depth. Such equipment and methods obviously required capital. It was no wonder that major companies undertook their own prospecting.[38]

The question still remains whether the government was better off having sponsored a rush under the Act of 1872, as compared to other possible methods. Probably the most extreme action was the repeal of the withdrawal of known deposits at Grants, New Mexico. There is no way of telling how much direct government mining would have cost, while the actual expenditures for fissionable materials were intentionally hidden in the budget process of the Cold War era. A contract system with one or more major mining concerns might have been feasible financially, but, as we have seen, was not feasible politically. A leasing program for a situation in which the government was the sole buyer did not make much sense, as Senator Milliken had observed. Ultimately, though, there was a free market even in uranium. Enough "peacetime uses" emerged with enough licensed buyers to hold up a price well above the AEC's minimum. So even leasing might have been of some value in the longer term. As it is, though, uranium is still subject to claims under the Act of 1872.

After its creation, the BLM gradually acquired sufficient experience in its relatively new missions to provide leadership in promoting some policy changes. The General Land Office had simply distributed lands. Though the BLM did grant mineral patents, and some other land transfers, it had a different mission as encompassed in its very name: Land Management. Now the government was to hold the lands but see that they were used effectively and productively. The key philosophical tenet of the agency became "multiple use." Many lands in the West could be used for several different functions at the same time. These points of basic land use philosophy guided the young agency not only in its own policies, but in requesting departmental policies from the Secretary of the Interior, and legislation from Congress.[39]

Once again the question arose as to what constituted "valuable" deposits. Could parties legally use mining claims to develop such materials as common stone, sand, clays, and gravel? True, unique materials such as the Yule marble described earlier had long been patentable. Yet many other deposits of less spectacular materials were still of local use for road and construction materials.[40]

In a brief Act of 1947, Congress quickly created a new legal classification of mineral deposits. The matter was straightforward and required no committee hearings. The BLM and other agencies of the Department of the Interior were allowed to sell the materials at a locally appraised value. Some vegetative materials also fell under the provisions of this Act. Quite logically, these types of materials now fall into a category commonly called "salable" minerals. In some cases, as with state and local governments and some charitable institutions, such as summer camp groups needing a road, free use permits are allowed. If a sale were proposed for more than $1,000, competitive bidding would be required.[41]

In 1955, while the uranium rush was in high gear, Congress passed three important pieces of legislation relating to mining claims and usage of federal lands within a period of seventeen days. Two of these directly reflected the uranium rush. Long-standing withdrawals prevented the filing of claims on large areas of coal lands. Other withdrawals, dating from the dam building projects of the 1930s, covered some seven million acres for future power site development. Congress reopened all these areas to mining claims in two of the 1955 measures.[42]

The third of the 1955 Acts, though, went in the opposite direction. This measure, generally designated simply as P.L. 167, amended the 1947 legislation designating that third category of "salable" minerals. P.L. 167 added such "common varieties" of materials as pumice, pumicite, and cinders to the list no longer subject to new mining claims. Existing claims for such materials, however, could stand. In addition, Congress gave the BLM a legal mandate for its philosophy of "multiple use." Several distinct activities can reasonably transpire on the same tract of land. The BLM was to see that no party unreasonably attempted to monopolize the uses of lands. This philosophy naturally extended to lands that had such diverse uses as grazing, timber, and mineral development under any of the three categories. Specifically, mining claimants were now under greater legal obligation to protect vegetation on claims. The BLM also had more legal grounds and defined procedures for contesting claims, including hearings before the Department of the Interior. BLM soon undertook examinations to clear a number of nuisance claims.[43]

Congress passed P.L. 167 just as quietly as it had the Act of 1947, which had created the class of salable materials. There were no hearings and only a very brief committee report. Yet the measure drew a surprising degree of praise from the Sierra Club. This organization had long supported conservationist measures but had not editorialized in its publications on the various mining laws, even when controversial measures came up in Congress, as with the Atomic Energy Act. The Club's notice of P.L. 167, then, indicates a changing focus of the organization.

Dr. Edgar Wayburn, the Club's conservation chairman, and M. M. Barnum, a regional forester of the U.S. Forest Service, wrote an editorial that fully recognized that the mining laws had originally been "enacted for the purpose of encouraging exploration and development of the mineral wealth of the West." At the time the "single-purpose" of the laws was understandable but in later years such laws were "neither protecting the real prospector on the one hand nor serving the general public on the other." The authors even noted that much of the mining industry itself favored some changes and that "valid claims lose no rights under prior law." The club was lobbying for designation of Wilderness areas and the authors saw that as a potential conflict with mining, but did not take an anti-mining position in the editorial. Instead, they praised P.L. 167 as "an outstanding conservation achievement of the 84th Congress."[44]

During the later 1950s the BLM found itself making a number of examinations of various mining claims. Even so, with total patents granted running only about 100 per year, the patent process had not returned to the status it had occupied half a century earlier, when over two thousand claims per year became private property. Other examinations were for elimination of "stale" and "nuisance" claims.[45]

Since uranium was often in extremely poor country, the value of the full patent was considerably less than in some other cases. Comparable non-mineral desert lands sold for perhaps ten dollars per acre in the 1950s. Further, once the lands became private property, they were subject to local taxes. For these reasons, Steen's Utex Corporation applied for patent on only one of over seventy claims in the immediate vicinity of the initial *Mi Vida* discovery. Utex sought the one patent because of the traditional reason of a rival claimant to that particular claim. The process dragged from 1955 to 1959 since the provisions for appearance of parties opposed to the government's action came into play. Ultimately the BLM overruled the rivals and granted a patent on the Ann Lode claim to Utex. Only one other mineral patent in the Big Indian Valley, the most productive area of the Colorado Plateau, dates from the 1950s. The paperwork the BLM officials used to complete the application still bore the letterhead of the General Land Office. Again, the agency made the token effort to present a formal statement on the validity of the claim, accepting the presence of the active mine on the *Mi Vida* claim nearby along with Utex's drill samples. The examiner saw no need for the government to take its own samples.[46]

Also in the 1950s, the state of Utah saw a much less known mineral development that resulted in the granting of some patents for iron ore. Since World War II, a major steel industry had developed near Salt Lake City, using nearby coal and iron ore deposits. Appropriately, several iron ore claims went to patent in Iron County in southwest Utah.[47]

In 1956, the BLM began clearing a large number of so-called "stale" claims at the request of the Forest Service, primarily in the Sequoia National Forest in California. Such a process required field examinations to see if the questioned claims met the "prudent man test." Wholesale inspection of areas would be a rare procedure for the land management agencies, though it certainly was well within their legitimate authority. Many other cases could have paralleled the Sequoia National Forest example. However, the manpower and expense of the process required a special congressional appropriation for Sequoia. Obviously, attacks on "stale claims" presented a logistical problem.[48]

* * *

A final brief observation regarding the uranium rush is in order. The immediate northern neighbor of the United States also had massive uranium deposits. In fact, Canada's uranium area near the Great Bear Lake, in the remote Northwest Territories, had extremely pure pitchblende deposits. Canada is a nation with a lengthy frontier background. Proponents of the Turner/Webb school have interpreted that nation's history as reflective of the frontier thesis in a way quite similar to the United States itself. Significantly, the Canadian government used the sudden demand for uranium to generate a rush of its own. If imitation is the highest compliment, U.S. policy regarding uranium must receive some credit after all.[49]

Lower grade ores, especially those of copper or iron, can be removed on a large scale to be economically feasible though considerable capital is necessary. Activity in the region started with underground mining but removal of the volume shown would be prohibitive with that method. Open pit mines are usually in geologically mesothermal deposits which originally formed at some depth and cooled more slowly than epithermal deposits. This is one of the earliest open pit mines at Sacramento Hill, Bisbee, Arizona. (Courtesy Arizona Historical Society)

CHAPTER THIRTEEN

Serious Movements for Reform

Though the uranium rush tapered off in the later 1950s and early 1960s as the government filled its stockpiles, the Cold War continued as a major fact of life in the national consciousness. American policy makers and much of the public embarked on a defense buildup further encouraged by rocket technology after the Soviet success with Sputnik in late 1957. The capture of Cuba in 1959 by a Communist government and its use in 1962 as a Soviet missile base is sometimes cited as the height of the Cold War from the U.S. perspective. Construction of a wall dividing the city of Berlin in 1961 added to this general sense of foreboding. These events encouraged continuing demand for uranium. Indirectly, the Cold War promoted a sense of the usefulness of the Act of 1872.

Even as the uranium rush was gaining steam, some movement for reforms did develop. In 1947 Congress called for a high-level commission to investigate the feasibility for a complete reorganization of the executive branch of the government. This commission included several prominent political figures, with former president Herbert Hoover at the top. In fact, the conclusions of the investigation are usually called the Report of the Hoover Commission. As noted earlier, Hoover himself had been a career mining engineer and had written on mining law in the early twentieth century. Given the background of the chairman, it was no wonder that the commission issued a statement specifically on the Act of 1872, while overlooking other matters.[1]

The commission observed the following "evidences of need for revision":

1. Decline in the number of claims patented from 2,500 in 1905 to 100 in recent years.
2. The inapplicability of the law to concealed deposits because of its requirement of exposure of valuable minerals in order to establish a valid claim.
3. Lack of provisions for adequate protection of the heavy investment required for subsurface exploration during a period of sufficient length to establish clear title.
4. The liberal provisions of the mineral laws which permit the acquisition of surface rights in addition to subsurface rights have opened the way to the filing of numerous claims to secure valuable surface rights under the guise of mineral claims.
5. The fact that the federal government itself had no records of the claims on its own land had made a most confusing situation for both patents and other mining operations.
6. Discovery requirements are impossible for some types of deposits.[2]

To resolve the problems it had identified, the Hoover Commission recommended a number of changes in the mining laws to "encourage exploration on the public domain." After all, the government's own sponsorship of a new uranium rush was quite current and simply could not be overlooked.

The Hoover Commission suggested opening as much of the public domain as possible to claims, with only national parks and monuments as obvious reservations. To adjust to changes in prospecting technology, it suggested recognizing the validity of claims without an exposed area of ore as traditionally understood to mark a "discovery." A variety of inferential techniques for estimating value, such as nearby deposits or theoretical projection of mineral zones, could be employed. As a similar adjustment, the commission recommended abandonment of such terminology as "vein, lode, and apex." Claims would follow the surficial boundaries of the lands, which would conform to the rectangular survey system. Obviously, the "apex rule" would be dead if the Hoover Commission had its way, at least for claims and patents filed after a given date. For such new claims, the parties would have no more than three years to obtain sufficient evidence for a patent, with some possibility of a time extension.

The commission recommended that the government keep its own records of claims rather than relying on the local recorder.

Owners of existing claims who legally surrendered rights under the old laws and adjusted to the new ones would no longer be required to perform the troublesome annual assessment work. The commission also suggested tighter regulations for protection of timber and other resources on the surface of mining claims. Finally, it recommended that the United States Geological Survey have the right to cancel claims at any time prior to patent. It could take such action only if the agency administering the subject lands made such a request and could cite strong evidence to cast serious doubt the plausibility of a profitable operation.[3]

It is curious that the commission made the last recommendation at all. The government already had the suggested power on the basis of long-standing court decisions. However, such a determination was the responsibility of the BLM rather than the Geological Survey.

The Hoover Commission Report included such a mass of proposals for changes in the entire executive branch that the final result was several shelf feet of softbound materials. Many of the proposals ultimately did become part of the executive branch reorganization, but many did not. In addition to its suggestions for the Act of 1872, the commission also wanted to merge the BLM with the Forest Service in the Department of Agriculture, a change never undertaken.[4]

Some of the commission's proposals regarding the Act of 1872 related to conservationism. Other proposals appealed more to industry, specifically the larger operators. As late as 1966, an industry conference endorsed much the same slate of principles, while textbooks on the topic that appeared the same year quoted the Hoover Commission as proposing the most appropriate reforms. The Hoover suggestions were on strong legal ground in recognizing valid existing rights, thus stating that the changes would apply only to new claims. The thrust of several court decisions discussed earlier strongly supported this approach. Even if the mining laws were completely repealed, many legal precedents would almost certainly protect *valid existing rights*. Both the Constitutional prohibition on *ex post facto* legislation and the requirement that the government pay a just price for properties would have been controlling considerations in court challenges that unquestionably would have resulted.

The prestige of the Hoover Commission motivated a special House Subcommittee on Public Lands to hold brief hearings. Some support for the Hoover Commission's recommendations came from larger industrial representatives. The subcommittee endorsed the proposed changes. However, the debates on the Atomic Energy Act of 1946 had recently aired the entire subject, with the results noted in the last chapter. The Hoover Commission would ultimately have some impact on mining laws, but not for many years after it issued formal conclusions in 1949.

There were other important mineral developments in the 1950s in addition to uranium. It was a period of economic expansion, both as part of continuing military construction and from a civilian economy making up for the forced limitations of World War II. The mining industry, however, had few high grade deposits and was forced to work with the available lower grade ores. Thus the natural movement of mineral development was toward even larger operations, requiring massive equipment and yet more capital. Industrial metals, especially copper but even some iron ores, were of growing importance in the West. There had been some open pit mining for years but now this method became the hallmark of the industry. Open pit mining was usually in an area that had long produced some minerals from smaller underground mines. When the equipment and profit margins were available, operators began to remove the lower grade ores that surrounded the older workings in higher grade materials. The copper states of Arizona, New Mexico, Utah, and Montana saw far more open pit development, but similar deposits were worked in the remote regions of Nevada for the first time. Open pits were usually on mining claims or outright patented lands that had long standing. There can be little question that this method is environmentally damaging, almost as much as strip mining coal. Even so, there was little chance that repeal of the Act of 1872 would have prevented many such operations, though other legislation could have done so at an earlier date.[5]

With the beginning of the Kennedy Administration in 1961, the Department of the Interior actively sought new roles in developing land policies. Kennedy's Secretary of the Interior, Stewart Udall of Arizona, had been closely associated with such organizations as the Sierra Club. Under the leadership of Dave Brower, this organization and others were developing yet more activist political roles. In fact, the term "environmentalism" generally replaced "conservationism" during subsequent years. Udall himself wrote a popular book, *The Quiet Crisis*, which espoused preservation of remaining wilderness areas, a policy certainly reflective of the interests of the Sierra Club and similar organizations.[6]

As with much of the legislative program proposed during the brief Kennedy Administration, the Wilderness Act did not appear on the statute books until after the tragic assassination of 1963. Udall was among the cabinet officials who stayed on and found the new president, Lyndon Johnson, had the political ability to get measures through Congress that Kennedy had only dreamed of accomplishing. Udall successfully promoted two new national parks, Canyonlands in Utah, in 1964, and North Cascades in Washington State in 1968. Both of these parks are among the least developed and most genuine wilderness in the system. North Cascades lacks any roads at all.[7]

Stewart Udall had other successes as well. Congress passed the full fledged Wilderness Act of 1964. This legislation required the various federal land management agencies to inventory those areas of 5,000 or more acres without roads for potential designation as permanent Wilderness. The interim status of Wilderness Study Areas required further investigation by the agencies before a final recommendation could be given. Congress made the final decision. The Wilderness Act allowed the filing of mining claims and their development until December 31, 1983. At that time, all valid existing rights were further preserved. However, claims filed between September 3, 1964, and December 31, 1983, cannot go on to patents for the surface, though patents for the mineral materials are allowed. Older claims can still go to full patent. Any actions to work or develop claims in a Wilderness Study Area require a formal notice to the government agency, including plans for a cleanup, and a time requirement for review of the proposed actions.[8]

Stewart Udall and the environmentalist organizations were somewhat disappointed that prospecting could continue for nearly twenty years in the Wilderness Study Areas. However, they did get passage of the measure and soon saw the designation of literally millions of acres as Wilderness on lands managed by the BLM, the Forest Service, and even the Park Service. Also in 1964, yet another commission met to study problems of federal land law. While this body, the Public Land Law Review Commission, was conducting its investigations, neither Udall nor the environmentalist leadership addressed the Act of 1872. This commission did not report until late 1971. Despite a growing environmentalist movement, it recommended keeping a claims system but with many of the changes suggested by the Hoover Commission twenty years earlier.[9]

Stuart Udall was no longer Secretary of the Interior when the Public Land Law Review Commission reported, since the 1968 election had ousted the Democrats. Yet he was still quite influential. Udall suggested full repeal of the mining claim system and replacement with a leasing system. Further, he suggested that a limit of three years to apply for patent be established for all current claims.[10]

The frontier was still a powerful concept in the mind of the American public. Many elected officials in the government reflected this concept. The survival of the Act of 1872 reveals the strength the frontier still had in the general psychology. Yet the nature of the country was clearly changing. Naturally the land itself had physically changed, with less suggestion of the frontier. Now some officials were willing to denounce the Act. That had been unthinkable as recently as the 1940s.

Even the return of the Republican party to the executive branch did not stem the rising environmental consciousness, despite the long association of the party with business. Within his first few months as president, Richard Nixon signed the National Environmental Policy Act (NEPA) of 1969. This measure requires government agencies to conduct an Environmental Analysis (EA) of projects and, if such study finds the project to be a "major federal action," to then write a lengthy Environmental Impact Statement (EIS). Mineral leases of various types fell under these rules.[11]

By the early 1970s many firms in mineral development were better known for oil and gas than hardrock ores. Hence they were quite familiar with the leasing system. Even concerns that still specialized in hardrock found it just as easy to deal with the government for exploration and expansion as with the mass of individuals who held speculative claims on almost every piece of prospective land. John McPhee, a well-known author on a variety of environmentalist issues, observed the Sierra Club's Dave Brower in heated discussions with a leading geologist associated with major mining firms. In his book, *Encounters with the Archdruid* (1971), McPhee quoted the geologist as *opposing* the Act of 1872, while calling for leasing. Such a position may not have been the public relations stand of the major companies, since they may have wanted to maintain good relations with smaller operators. Yet privately most certainly agreed with that position, in part because a leasing system would be too expensive for many smaller businesses. The same problem that Jefferson had forecast involving the competition of private lead lands with those requiring royalties obviously is a fundamental economic principle that will always have an impact.[12]

There was also ongoing sentiment for reform of the entire organization and purpose of the BLM in the early 1970s. However, a series of political and international crises, including the Watergate scandal and the initial energy shortage from an oil embargo by major producers of the Middle Eastern nations, delayed any real action until 1975–1976. Finally, Congress did write an important piece of legislation known as the Federal Land Policy and Management Act (FLPMA) of 1976, which primarily reorganized and expanded the BLM in both personnel and mission.

Both the Senate Committee on Energy and Natural Resources, chaired by Henry M. Jackson of Washington, and the House leadership supported the basic idea of FLPMA. So did top officials of the Department of the Interior under the administration of Gerald Ford. The final legislation ran to a total of fifty-two pages. The subject of mining claims emerged both in the Senate Committee and from the administration. The committee recommended limiting the filing of new claims to two more years with patent applications required for all claims within another five years. The Ford Administration recommended the same but with the respective time limits of only one and three years. Both agreed that the BLM should have its own record of mining claims and that the agency should be able to enforce more stringent surface protection measures. The committee reported S. 507 with a ten-year limit on claims before application for patent.[13]

On the Senate floor, this proved to be by far the most controversial part of the entire bill. Senator James McClure, Republican from Idaho, made several points that might have been taken right out of the Atomic Energy Act debates of three decades earlier, if not the debates of 1920 or even 1872. This time, though, he was in the minority rather than speaking for a unanimous Senate such as had passed the 1946 Act. McClure defended the Act for encouraging prospectors to find minerals even if large companies ultimately developed them. He noted that since the bill under consideration was for the BLM and its lands, Forest Service lands would still be subject to mining claims without limit. In addition, the measure might force some claimants to file for patent on claims they would abandon in a few years. Some revisions of the mining laws were needed but not a stringent limitation, a point which drew the support of Senator Lee Metcalf, Democrat from Montana. McClure concluded with the statement:

> The only thing that can be said for this provision... it will only happen for the next 10 years. But an awful lot of barns will be broken into and an awful lot of horses will be out of the barns within the next 10 years.[14]

Senator Floyd K. Haskell, Democrat from Colorado, countered by calling it a simple "housekeeping measure" and noted that the Administration wanted only a three-year limit for patent. Any claimant could apply for an extension beyond the ten years. The Senate floor vote was 78 to 11, with the ten-year rule still in place. The opponents were all from mining states in the West.[15]

The House version of the bill, H.R. 13777, made no limits on claims aside from the requirement for recording with BLM and surface protection measures. Even without the measure that had drawn controversy in the Senate, the House version slipped by on a vote of 169 to 155. As a result, the conference committee required between the two houses for such cases adopted the provisions exactly as approved by the lower house, thus killing any time requirements for patent applications on existing or new claims. Even so, the Act had made two of the major changes as suggested years before by the Hoover Commission: that the BLM keep its own records, and that surface protection measures be utilized.[16]

Of course, there was always a legal problem with the attempt to limit the time that a claim could be held prior to a patent applica-

Serious Movements for Reform 241

tion, at least for claims in existence before such an amendment. Had the House concurred with the Senate and the administration on this point, court challenges would have resulted. Based on several decisions described in Chapter 12, such challenges would almost certainly have been successful. It is true that the legal climate of the 1970s still could have yielded a new precedent, but that possibility was highly unlikely. The certainty of such court challenges probably was another reason the House chose not to add such a measure to its bill, despite the support of the Senate and the administration.

FLPMA contains yet another measure of large scale importance. In a number of previous instances, presidents and Secretaries of the Interior had ordered lands withdrawn from application of the mining laws. This power obviously had the potential of repealing the mining laws anyway. In 1976 Congress removed the power of withdrawal from the executive and kept it within the legislative function. This power coupled with possible expansion of the Wilderness system gives Congress a more streamlined means of limiting the areas subject to claims even if it maintains the Act of 1872 on the books.[17]

FLPMA was a success. Even so, sentiment to amend the Mining Laws remained, and carried over into the next session of Congress. In the Senate, the same Committee on Energy and Natural Resources under Henry M. Jackson that had succeeded with FLPMA issued a report that once again enumerated the reasons for repeal. This report, actually written by career BLM official Irving Senzel, clearly summarized the problems that had been discussed in many previous sources.[18]

First, Senzel noted "costs to the government" by maintaining the mining laws:

1. Land and Resource Damage, including the use of the laws to acquire title to other values.
2. Problems in Administration.
3. Problems in Rehabilitation.
4. Mining claims prevented other land uses.
5. Surveys of unusual shapes of claims do not fit into the rectangular system used for all other matters.
6. Mining claims prevented some law enforcement functions.

Next, Senzel noted "costs to the individual" presented by the maintenance of the mining laws:
1. Promoters of scams had use of the full extent of federal lands for various frauds.
2. Claims often simply worked as a nuisance to other parties' legitimate uses of lands.
3. Many hazards are left over from abandoned operations.
4. Claims give some parties private rights to lands otherwise open to the public.[19]

Senzel also reprinted the two criticisms lodged as far back as 1880 in the Public Land Commission Report at that time which focused on the problems of the "apex rule" and the use of local laws. He did note that patents for mining claims in genuine frontier environments were clearly part of the overall policy of land distributions.[20]

When the Senate committee issued the report and called for full repeal, President Jimmy Carter's administration endorsed this proposal as well. Hence the bill that was submitted became known as the Administration Mining Bill. Obviously, support could be expected in the Senate, since the upper house had passed a similar repeal as part of FLPMA the year before. The action, however, had stalled in the House in 1976. The next year, action also fell short in the lower house, but in such a way as to make a much more interesting political story; some might say a tragic story.

The undisputed leader for matters of land policy in the House in 1977 was Representative Morris Udall, Democrat of Arizona. "Mo" Udall, brother of former Secretary of the Interior Stewart Udall, chaired the House Interior Committee. Indeed, "Mo" Udall in 1977 held a position of high prestige throughout the political scene. He had been a candidate for the presidency the year before in the Democratic primaries. He did not fare well in the campaign, which eventually saw Jimmy Carter win both the nomination and the general election. However, he maintained excellent relations with the administration and served a vital function in securing passage of several major pieces of legislation, including a massive increase of the National Park System in 1980.[21]

"Mo" Udall represented a district in southern Arizona, including the city of Tucson and the University of Arizona, as well as a large mining region. Instead of simply endorsing the Administration

Mining Bill, he initiated his own proposal for full repeal of the mining laws. In fact, under Udall's proposal, the holders of existing claims would have had to file immediately for patent. And, of course, there would have been no new claims. Obviously, if enacted, his legislation would have drawn court challenges, but in the meantime he drew plenty of political challenges. He went to his constituency, including the miners, with the proposal in public meetings. Undoubtedly he did not expect the massive reaction.[22]

Udall appeared at a special forum on July 6, 1977, before the Arizona Small Miners' Association, an organization with total membership of 4,400. He summarized his position by stating:

> We need the minerals your industry produces but we can do it with a mining law that's fair to the people who live on the land. New mining laws are coming and miners can help mold them into regulations they can live with.

He added that the matter was so pressing it would continue even if he was recalled from Congress.[23]

A representative member of the association, independent miner William Saegart, retorted by stating the measure was an "overkill of federal regulation and would put small mine operators out of business." Then the organization firmly placed itself on record as not only opposed to the bill, but favoring a special recall election against Udall.[24]

Subsequently Grover Heinricks, president of the Mining Club of the Southwest, followed the Small Miner's Association. Heinricks stated that Udall's proposal would promote monopoly of public property by putting bonding requirements out of the "little guy's" reach and granting dictatorial powers to the Secretary of the Interior. He concluded, "we're already seeking a candidate to challenge him in 1978, and we'll find a good one."[25]

It is most interesting that the opposition to Udall came from small miners and their organizations. The larger firms, of which there were several in Udall's own Congressional district, issued no statements.

The firestorm Udall brought on himself is almost reminiscent of a localized version of Stephen A. Douglas's fiasco with the Kansas-Nebraska Act back in 1854. The fact that the issue of mining law was not simply of interest to one particular group is revealed by the stand taken by Pima County Board of Supervisors. Pima County, which includes the city of Tucson, had seen some recent conflicts between mineral development and residential considerations. Udall unquestionably expected the local conflicts to promote support for his measure among the urban populace and their political leadership. Here, too, he made a major miscalculation. The board of supervisors went so far as to pass a resolution condemning Udall's proposal. Even newly elected member David Yetman, well-known for support of environmentalist measures, opposed Udall, a most striking position for those familiar with local politics in Tucson.[26]

As traditional, Congress took an August recess, but when members returned, Udall had apparently had time to reconsider his position. His Washington office issued the statement, reported in Tucson papers on August 31, 1977, that he was dropping his own bill to repeal the Act of 1872. He justified his change of position by observing that the copper industry was becoming quite depressed. Indeed, total layoffs were reported at over 8,000, certainly a sizable segment of the labor force of southern Arizona. The next day Udall's office issued a follow-up statement in which he expressed opposition to the Administration bill as well. He refined his change by saying, "I'm caught in a position in which a major industry *psychologically* feels that this poses a threat to them...I refuse to be in a position where *psychologically* I tip the balance, even though advocating a law I've been involved in for about 10 years." He went on to claim he had not been fully aware of falling employment in the copper industry. Somewhat philosophically, he said, "We've lived with this mining law for 100 years and we can get along with it for a few more." Interestingly, at the same time he also reversed position on another proposal involving federal lands, a proposal that had drawn the opposition of cattle ranchers who had permits to graze herds in certain areas.[27]

Naturally Udall's reversal drew criticism. Many in the Small Miner's Association doubted his sincerity. Christina Collins, an editorialist for the *Tucson Citizen* was more charitable but emphasized that the political heat had influenced his own psychology to take such a drastic step. Ironically, Don Robinson of the *Arizona Daily Star*, a Pulitzer-affiliated paper generally more supportive of

Udall than the *Citizen*, noted that the congressman had last been on record as defending his own bill as late as August 24, but had reversed by August 30. Robinson attacked Udall for a "tendency to shift so easily with the wind," and even suggested that he be opposed in the next election by a candidate who would support such a change.[28]

Udall's shift saved his own political career, but effectively killed any chance for repeal of the Act of 1872 for well over a decade. Had he simply conducted hearings on the Administration bill when it came to his committee, he could have probably achieved some revisions, possibly including an end to new claims in exchange for recognition of those already in existence by a certain date. Such a system would have followed the precedent of the Wilderness Act of 1964. In hindsight, the whole matter was a colossal political blunder, all the more remarkable for a congressman as experienced as "Mo" Udall.

The discussion of mining claims under FLPMA as well as the aborted Udall proposal show that environmental considerations were becoming quite important by 1976. Certainly there was more serious thought of repeal than had ever previously emerged. Yet the basic principles of the Turner/Webb thesis still applied among enough of the public to force a leading politician to oppose his own bill. Udall himself openly stressed the *psychological* power of the issue, which was exacerbated by the traditional appeal of his Democratic Party for promoting jobs. Though he was a favorite of the Sierra Club and generally represented its specialized values, there were enough older values among his constituents to prevail. Glynn Burkhart, the president of the 4,400-member Small Miners' Association, had commented, "It is inconceivable that such a professed populist is so actively engaged in burying the little man." There, in a nutshell, was the crux of the issue.[29]

Despite the controversy, Udall was probably correct in stating that repeal of the Act of 1872 would have little effect on actual mineral production because the major firms would not have been affected. The large mines were already under patent or on claims that could have been patented immediately. The "little man," the ordinary prospector/miner and small businessman, was the primary opponent of Udall's proposal. Congress had initially directed the Mining Laws of 1866, 1870, and 1872, at this group. Over a century later considerable evidence exists that the "little man" who was supposed to benefit from the law was still doing so, at least *psychologically*.

Perhaps Udall was a little ahead of himself in another respect. The Federal Lands Policy Management Act of 1976 (FLPMA) had given the BLM more administrative power over mining claims and more personnel to enforce its regulations. The changes in the agency and its work were of considerable importance.

In the early 1970s BLM's total personnel, including Washington D.C. offices, numbered about 4,200. After FLPMA this figure jumped to nearly 10,000 by 1979 with most of the increase in professional field-related jobs. Some of this increase was clearly related to the need for environmental assessments under the National Environmental Protection Act of 1969. A marked rise in the Bureau's budget, however, is directly attributable to FLMPA. As a result, BLM became a much more influential entity within the Department of the Interior. The Department's total employment stayed at about 80,000, while other agencies were losing personnel.[30]

Training of the mass of new BLM professional specialists became an acutely serious problem, so the agency established a special Lands and Minerals School at Phoenix, Arizona. Newcomers to the organization attend intensive full-time classroom and field instruction at this facility for periods of as long as five months. Specialists in range conservation, surveying, administration, and wildlife as well as mining have separate training programs.[31]

In BLM training, the geologists went to the field, took actual samples, and wrote practice mineral reports on the validity of mining claims as required by the Act of 1872. These exercises prepared the individuals to conduct patent examinations OR to declare claims invalid and thus release the land for other purposes. The training included a moot court appearance before federal administrative law judges to realistically prepare for actual contest cases of claims declared invalid.[32]

The expansion of BLM was fortuitous in that the agency was more prepared for a new period of increased mineral development. The oil embargo of late 1973 had only been the initial stimulus of expanded development. Naturally oil companies sought more leases under the appropriate laws but alternate energy sources also drew attention. Generally, all mineral products increased in value through the decade of the 1970's despite the temporary downturn that "Mo" Udall cited in 1977. By 1979 the overall pattern had returned with a vengeance after a further disruption in foreign oil supplies. The ouster of the Shah of Iran by Ayatollah Khoumeni caused a second sharp increase in prices in energy minerals and, indirectly, caused a massive rise in prices of other "hardrock" materials as well. Electric power utilities began converting to nuclear power plants. Even though the government had uranium stockpiled, the open market for "yellowcake," a processed form of the material, rose to over $41.00 per pound from an average of little more than half that. Gold rose from less than $200.00 per ounce in 1978 to nearly $900.00 by late 1979. Silver rose from $6.00 to over $40.00 an ounce. Both a medium sized uranium rush and a medium sized precious metals rush developed along with more demand for industrial metals.[33]

With FLPMA, the BLM began to assemble its own records of mining claims. Though the Act dated from 1976, claimants did not have to provide the information until 1979. BLM demanded that copies of the courthouse records of all standing claims be provided by the claimants. The initial deadline for these filings saw such an avalanche of paperwork descend on the BLM that its employees thought they were working for the IRS on April 16. Further, as an ongoing measure, the agency requires copies of the annual assessment affidavit (or a notice of intent to hold the claim, good for only one year). Upon review of records, BLM found many defective and began to invalidate claims on this basis only. In some cases the claimants had filed at the local office while the proper recipient was specifically the state office of the BLM in each respective state. Other cases simply hinged on late dates of filing. Further, BLM conducted more contests for other purposes than it had before.[34]

Many of the contests of claims, even those based on improper filing of paperwork with the BLM, went on to Department of the Interior Administrative Law proceedings. In such contests a special judge hears arguments in a formal setting with attorneys for the claimants and the government. In the event of a ruling against the claimants, an automatic appeal goes to the Interior Board of Land Affairs (IBLA) in Washington. Such an appeal does not require a rehearing. It is simply a review of transcripts and other written evidence.[35]

After FLPMA, both Administrative Law Courts and the IBLA found itself with far more work than ever previously imagined. In addition to mining claims, a variety of cases involved leases, grazing rights, and other matters. However, mining claim contests have been by far the largest single group of such cases. Almost all such cases have been rather straightforward, hence the government won. In fact, any brief review of case reports of the IBLA shows that contests won by claimants are comparatively rare and usually draw special notice.

In one general class of cases, claimants were often more successful in appeals, though some of these eventually went beyond the IBLA to federal court. In such cases, claimants were economically working "nontraditional" materials. The government often felt that such activities were in violation of the Acts of 1947 and 1955 and maintained that the materials were simply "common varieties." Yet the combination of the "prudent man rule" and the phraseology of the original Act of 1872 allowing production of "valuable" deposits aided the claimants' cases before the courts.

The IBLA gave a comprehensive set of guidelines in a rather complex Idaho case of *Oneida Perlite* in which the claimants had filed for patent of 15 placer claims in a National Forest.[36] Much of the thrust of the decision was to determine how much perlite material could be claimed. The Board had ruled that some of the materials still did fall under the General Mining Laws. Too many claims could bring other problems and even promote a local monopoly, so the IBLA restricted the total by any party.

An important sequel case on appeal to the 9th Circuit was *Baker vs. U.S.*[37] The Court determined that a number of claims on volcanic "cinders" were valid even though the materials constituted at least 270 years' supply. This overturn of an IBLA decision proved most controversial. The U.S. Solicitor General attempted an appeal to the Supreme Court and obtained support from three justices, but these were not enough to convince the full court to hear the case.[38]

The owners of gemstone claims won an interesting contest that went to the U.S. Court of Appeals in the 1984 case of *Rogers vs. U.S.*[39] They produced competent witnesses who testified as to the uniqueness as well as the profitability of the Oregon operation.

An important case relating to the withdrawal process was *U.S.*

vs. *Alaska Limestone Corp.*[40] Claimants asserting "grandfathered" rights, had to prove a valid discovery at the date of withdrawal as well as the date of contest.

Similarly, in 1984 the 9th Circuit ruled that a claim for "common varieties" which predated the 1955 Act had to have a "valuable discovery" at the time of that Act as well as in the current market. Even so, the government might have been hard pressed to disallow the claim if the opposition had not conceded that the 1955 market was insufficient. This case was *Dredge Corp. vs. Conn.*[41]

Though the "common variety" cases were important to a few parties, the acreages involved were relatively trivial. The overall thrust of the times was toward greater protection of lands. BLM took a much greater role in this regard in the years following FLPMA. Again, there was some time lag between the passage of the Act and actual implementation of its provisions. The Code of Federal Regulations (CFR) includes Title 43, relating to the Bureau of Land Management. The Secretary of the Interior placed a new set of rules into 43 CFR, Section 3809 which took effect in late 1980. These were not the first regulations regarding surface protection and cleanup of mining operations. In 1974 the Secretary of Agriculture had issued regulations for claims on lands of the U.S. Forest Service, 36 CFR 228. For implementation of the Wilderness Act of 1964, the Secretary of the Interior had earlier issued special regulations in 43 CFR 3802, for BLM Wilderness Areas. However, neither of these sets of rules involved the extent of lands and standing claims as did 43 CFR 3809.

There is little doubt that the new regulations did make a difference. A case before the 9th Circuit Court of Appeals, *United States vs. Richardson*, (1979)[42] upheld restrictions on unnecessary surface blasting and bulldozing of unpatented claims. This case originated on Forest Service Lands, however the principle could apply to BLM as well.

By 1981 a federal District Judge, Ramon A. Ramirez in California, had ruled that BLM could invoke the regulations to evict "squatters" from spurious claims that they had filed to take advantage of the right of miners to live on claims. In this case, BLM could cite failure to provide a plan of operations (which had to include adequate reclamation of the lands) as well as lack of compliance with local sanitary regulations as ample grounds to evict the supposed "miners." Such cases were rather common, especially in the Pacific Northwest where a variety of "squatters" and even large scale drug producers used mining law as a ploy to occupy federal lands. The landmark case was *United States vs. Bales*.[43]

Claimants must submit a Notice to the local BLM office if a proposed operation involves less than 5 acres. If more than 5 acres are involved, the more detailed Plan of Operations is required. Those operators with work ongoing at the time the regulations took force submitted Notices and Plans at the end of 1980. Once again, BLM officials found themselves buried under a mass of paperwork. The problem was particularly severe because Plans of Operations required that BLM prepare an Environmental Assessment for each operation which affected over 5 acres.[44]

Moab, Utah, in the heart of uranium country, was then in the midst of the renewed interest in that material. Further, Moab had a scattering of active placer gold mines. By early 1981 the local BLM officials found themselves writing over a dozen Environmental Assessments. They also received over forty Notices for smaller operations. Lisbon Valley alone still had four large working uranium mines.[45]

The timing of the regulations with the increased activity had been a remarkable coincidence, though relatively short lived. The energy crisis of the 1970's tapered off in the early 1980's. An industrial accident at Three-Mile Island nuclear power plant in Pennsylvania captured considerable bad publicity so the industry moved away from new nuclear plants. Within little over a year, uranium prices had collapsed to below $20.00 per pound. Most of the mines closed within a few months. Two of the major operators decided to go on to patent on their claims. They believed that legal protection was necessary in the event of government contest in times of falling ore prices. It is interesting that they had no such fear of private parties in times of rising prices.[46]

The first of these involved six claims of the Small Fry Mine, an adit type underground mine which had previously produced a major volume of ore. Though the Small Fry Mine was then inactive, it still held considerable workable material. The BLM had to determine if the material met the traditional "prudent man test." The owners of the Small Fry held a long term contract with the government of the nation of Taiwan to supply uranium at $39.00 per pound of "yellow cake." At that price, there was little doubt that the Small Fry Mine was patentable, though it might not have been at the then collapsed market price of approximately $20.00. Rather than risk certain defeat in a legal contest action before an Administrative Law Court, the BLM granted the patents.[47]

Subsequently, nearby Rio Algom Corporation applied for patent on forty-one claims which were part of its deep underground operation. Rio Algom's mine is on the same uranium deposit as the Small Fry, but on a downthrown fault block so a shaft well over one thousand feet deep is required. When BLM examined the mine in 1983, it employed some 300 workers underground and in the adjacent mill. Since Kennecott Corporation's open pit copper mine at Bingham Canyon was then closed, Rio Algom was the largest active mine in the State of Utah. Ultimately BLM approved some twenty-seven claims for patent (the company withdrew applications on the remainder). Rio Algom continued underground production until late 1988, the last major uranium operation in the region. These were the last patents granted for uranium. Quite possibly they aided the company in keeping its doors open longer than any other. Significantly, other uranium mines in the area owned by such major firms as Homestake, Atlas Minerals, Union Carbide, Cotter Corp., and General Electric all closed long before Rio Algom.[48]

Even after uranium prices collapsed, the Colorado Plateau still has a mass of claims. The estimates are fully 250,000 in Utah alone with the entire region probably accounting for nearly one million. That is the majority of all the mining claims in the country, even including Alaska. Very few of these could stand validity examinations at the ore prices of the later 1980's. However, the manpower to conduct such examinations is severely lacking. In many cases BLM can not sell or otherwise dispose of "common materials" because they are on mining claims. This situation has proved to be a severe problem for the local road departments, however they rarely request that BLM conduct validity tests on such claims to release the materials. Overall, this is one of the most perplexing of the many current problems that the agency faces in adjusting to development in a once empty region.[49]

Outside the Colorado Plateau, BLM confronted other new problems with mining claims. In Nevada, some individuals have staked gold claims on extremely disperse materials which could be worked with modern technology. These are known as Carlin type deposits, profitable only at 1980's gold prices. As with uranium, claimants can tie up large amounts of lands with speculative claims.[50]

Also in the 1980's, a new series of mineral "scams" spread across the West. Of course, "salting" was nothing new, but some operators refined this time-worn practice to a fine art. At Moab, one local figure had years of uranium experience and profits. Even so, he fell prey to a "black box" scheme. He simply should have known better. The confidence game of selling a "secret process" goes back to pioneer days. In this case, the buyer first purchased placer gold claims for $250,000, then spent $800,000 more on a large mill and equipment to house the "secret process," only to see the inventor arrested on eighteen outstanding federal warrants from Idaho. There were several other mineral "scams" in the Moab area in the early 1980's. Such is the case when gold increases its value by several fold.[51]

Though "Mo" Udall's mishandling of the matter had killed any chance that Congress could further amend or repeal the Mining Laws for some years, a lobbying effort did develop to accomplish this end as the 1980's progressed. The Sierra Club's magazine periodically addressed the issue, then, in 1985, the organization went so far as to publish a hardbound book edited by Carl J. Mayer and George A. Riley entitled *Public Domain; Private Dominion*. As noted in an earlier section of the present discussion, Mayer and Riley viewed the Mining Laws as totally the work of the Comstock giants. They especially castigated Nevada's William Stewart as a classic Gilded Age figure. There is no need to restate the refutations of such a position at this point since much of the foregoing discussion has been aimed at just that. Mayer and Riley said nothing about continuation and maintenance of the law after 1872. They did address problems with enforcement of the leasing laws which are better documented but beyond our scope here.[52]

The environmentalist movement produced a second hardbound book on the topic in 1987. The Washington based organization Resources for the Future, employed attorney John Leshy to write *Mining Laws*. Leshy emphasized the fact that there were a number of attempts to amend the laws which came to naught over the years. He expressed a sense of utter shock that this could have been so, without giving any explanation. Regarding recent problems, he was on much firmer ground, but Leshy's historical interpretation simply attempted to apply modern environmentalist values throughout history to times when they were not widely accepted. In citing earlier suggestions for reform, such as the 1880 Public Lands Commission, he even ignored the fact that the contemporary problems were with the "apex rule" and the usage of local laws, not the principle of mining claims themselves.[53]

Other scholars focused on environmental disturbances from mining in the long-term historical context. Certainly, the landscape reflected activities of mineral removal, as Randall Rohe observed. However, veteran mining historian Duane Smith noted that reclamation was feasible and that many earlier champions of environmentalism were not necessarily opponents of mining, as noted earlier in the present study. Smith endorsed more compromise by both sides.[54] An added observation regarding the nineteenth century is that mining rushes would have undoubtedly occurred with resultant disturbances regardless of the claims system. The variety of rushes in other countries under a variety of legal systems clearly show the unstoppable psychology of the times.

Some local cases of mining and resultant protests gained publicity in the early 1980's. Work on a patented claim in the Grand Canyon naturally promoted controversy. A placer operation in Westwater Canyon on the Colorado River near the Colorado/Utah state line proved to be a "pet peeve" of the local BLM District Manager. He ordered the parties evicted on rather flimsy legal grounds prior to a validity examination. Had the placer miners possessed any cash for legal fees, they would have had an excellent court case. However, the site proved lacking in gold so they moved on peaceably, though they may have remained some extra weeks out of spite.[55]

In other areas, suburban development moved into mining locales, some of them predating the existence of the nearby cities. At Tucson, Arizona, such conflicts of development on unpatented claims had been an important factor in encouraging "Mo" Udall on his ill-fated proposal back in 1977. A continuation of such activity in the Tucson Mountains, an area which had seen mining since the first recorded claims in the Territory, brought protests from relative newcomers as new residential construction moved into the area. Much the same happened at Colorado Springs. In that locale the local government attempted to stop mining by invoking zoning ordinances. It was to no avail as determined in the case of *Brubaker vs. Board of Commissioners of El Paso County* (1982).[56] A unanimous Colorado Supreme Court ruled that the matter was solely within the jurisdiction of the federal government, which had expressed its will in the Act of 1872. So mining law had come full circle, from a function solely of the local community, to a federally endorsed right which could defy the overall wishes of a particular local community.

The ongoing controversies prompted the BLM itself to administratively address the situation by raising its fees, partly because of inflation, but partly to discourage filing and maintenance of frivolous claims. At the start of 1989 the fee for a new claim went from $5.00 to $10.00. The annual assessment record required $5.00 while no fee at all had previously been the case. The most marked change was with patent applications. The administrative fee went from $25.00 to $250.00, though the actual payment for the land could not be changed since it was specified in the Acts of 1870 and 1872.[57]

Despite BLM's own administrative changes, there was still an interest in reform in Congress by early 1989. Some critics might suggest that the Reagan Administration, including controversial Secretary of the Interior James Watt, would not have supported such a change. However, the fiasco of "Mo" Udall during the Carter Administration when executive support was present had effectively precluded action for some years anyway.

"Mo" Udall's Committee on Interior and Insular Affairs had a Subcommittee on Mining and Natural Resources. The Chairman of the Subcommittee, Nick Rahall of West Virginia, came from a state where the mining laws do not apply. Obviously "Mo" Udall still had an interest in the topic, especially after the 1977 episode, and knew that he could not serve much longer because of poor health. However, the formal record shows that Rahall requested the General Accounting Office (GAO) prepare one more study of the most studied subject in the long history of the public lands. The GAO issued its Report entitled *The Mining Law of 1872 Needs Re-*

Serious Movements for Reform   255

vision on March 10, 1989. The GAO briefly recognized the historic value of the mining laws in promoting settlement of the West. However, it primarily focused on the losses to the government of both lands and royalties from the claims/patent system. The GAO cited several examples of valuable properties which were patented and then resold for millions while the government received only the token payments unchanged since 1872. Further, the GAO noted similar cases then moving through the patent process. This time critics were going back to the traditional Progressive Era focus on monetary considerations that had produced the Leasing Act of 1920.[58]

The GAO report naturally attracted the attention of the news media. Several news stories appeared which stressed the value of mineral lands sold for less than $1000. Even Columnist Jack Kilpatrick, a well-known, highly experienced commentator on legal issues, sarcastically made this point in his regular column.[59]

Unfortunately the GAO Report itself, and the resultant news stories, had some serious flaws. Among the cases cited was a patent of lands known for oil shale which the owners then resold. What the GAO did not state was that such patents could only be granted for claims filed before 1920 since that issue had been addressed by the Mineral Leasing Act. Parties which had maintained such claims for all the intervening years should, and did, have some rights. Even so the government attempted to thwart the patents in a major court case which simply resulted in upholding of the actions. The GAO briefly mentioned this in a footnote in the Report but either did not grasp its significance, or chose to ignore it to further the primary thesis.[60]

Similarly, the GAO cited cases of gravel and stone production in the major urban areas of Phoenix and Las Vegas which were patented for a few hundred dollars. Both the values of the materials and the land itself were worth hundreds of thousands. However, the claims on these materials had to have been filed prior to 1955 because the Act of 1872 had been amended at that date to address just this type of situation. Again, rights existing at that date had "grandfathered" status. Again, the GAO slipped this point briefly into a footnote.[61]

The GAO also cited cases of patent applications near major skiing facilities in Colorado. However, such a patent would have to cite a valid discovery, certainly no easy proposition. Further, in the event of a repeal of the Act of 1872, court challenges would certainly result if such repeal attempted to end claims in existence at the date of repeal. In short, the GAO ignored the massive legal considerations of the Constitution's prohibition of *ex post facto* legislation which had a number of court precedents as enumerated in an earlier chapter.

Even so, the criticisms of the GAO in 1989 as well as two brief earlier reports and criticisms raised in earlier Congressional investigations were quite real. A repeal could ease problems in the long term management of federal lands, even though existing claims could stand.

However, the claims system still had some important political supporters as the issue gained momentum once again in 1989. Back in 1976 and 1977 the Senate had approved changes but the House had not. Now the positions were reversed. A member of the Senate from Arkansas, Democrat Dale Bumpers, was supporting legislation inspired by the recent GAO report that would allow claims to be held for a maximum of 15 years with the land then reverting to the government. Even this approach, clearly a compromise, met severe political and legal opposition.[62]

The most vocal supporter of maintaining the Act of 1872, even with the full patent provision, was Utah's Republican Jake Garn, a member of the Senate Energy Committee. Garn flatly stated that Bumpers's proposal:

> violates the federal government's promise that if you locate a claim and conduct a viable mining operation, you can receive title to that land. I don't want to see the government go back on its word on this issue.

Once again, the point arose that the Act of 1872 is a Far West version of homestead, a classic "little man's" measure. Garn spared no emotions or rhetorical skills in his emphasis of this point:

> In rural Utah thousands of people eke out a living by the revenues they earn from mining their claims, I don't want to see Congress pass a law which will deprive these people of those small, but critical revenues. The law has brought America the

Serious Movements for Reform 257

world's highest standard of living up until today. Entrepreneurs have risked their life savings and sacrificed their all to prospect and mine the mineral rich lands of this country. It has been the small miners who have made this system so valuable... Larger companies have also benefitted from the law, usually after buying out the little guy at the market price rate. There is nothing wrong with that because it encourages individual incentive. However, the proposal to amend the law takes away all of those incentives and essentially socializes all the public lands of the great American west. We don't need socialized mining laws, we need to continue with incentives. *The bill will wipe out small mom and dad prospectors and assure that only large corporations can engage in the mining business. The legislation is not necessary and it is an affront to western America and the hard working men and women who earn their living in the mining business.*[63]

Several other Senators from the West endorsed Garn's statement. Obviously a political battle was emerging with resultant regional antipathies that had previously been avoided in most of the earlier amendments and debates on changes, though such feelings had emerged to some extent in 1976. The 1977 incident involving "Mo" Udall had not even gotten very far in the legislative process.

At the end of the legislative session of 1990, amidst an epic conflict on the federal budget, the Senate once again considered a measure to suspend the full patent provision of the General Mining Laws for one year. This proposal was a "watered down" attack on the laws, but represented a more realistic move among their opponents to eliminate them piecemeal. Even so, the Senate voted 50 to 48 to maintain the full patent provision. Arkansas Senator Bumpers railed on, noting mining claims filed in National Forests in his own state for quartz crystals sought by "new age" followers. This trivial consideration failed to impress the Western Senators who stood firm. Though the vote split generally along party lines, a few Republican Senators from areas outside the West joined the opponents. These were more than compensated by Western Democrats who were among the 50. The long-standing pattern of Western unity on the issue regardless of partisanship still survived.[64]

Once again the points for and against the mining laws were emerging that were really indistinguishable from those expressed in the nineteenth century with periodic restatements right up to the present. Certainly the basic thesis of the Turner/Webb school of historians can find no better proof that the influence of the frontier is still a deep seated part of the contemporary American scene in law, politics, economics, and even psychology. The Turner/Webb thesis is the reason for the mining laws being the *Sacred Cow in the American West*, a status they have in early 1991 and could well retain long after that date.

Chapter Fourteen

Summary and Conclusions

The recent critics of the General Mining Laws, including John C. Leshy who wrote *Mining Law* (1987), and Carl Mayer and George Riley who wrote *Public Domain; Private Dominion* (1985), expressed a sense of shock that such laws existed at all, much less survived from 1866 into the 1980's. Yet for such survival, there had to be good explanations.

The early land policies of the United States were ambiguous in purpose. By the Civil War era Congress had finally agreed to easy distribution rather than profit to the government. The mining law was even more dramatic. The direct democracy of the mining camps naturally endeared the local law system to both the public and elected officials. Further, the local mining camps were able to exclude slavery, an abolition that carried over into the organization of California as a state in 1850. Thus the nation's leadership hesitated to interfere with all legal matters there. Indeed, Stephen A. Douglas picked up the method of "popular sovereignty" from California's success and disastrously attempted to apply the method to Kansas/Nebraska.

After the Civil War, comprehensive legislation finally gave federal sanction to local mining laws as well as providing a system for full private ownership of mines. This was a preemption rather than a direct land grant method since payment was required. However, the law specifically stated that lands be "free and open" to mineral development and removal without the full legal patent. Hence the focus of the General Mining Laws is free distribution of resources, if not the lands on which they are found. There can be no minimizing this consideration.

Though occasional suggestions to modify or repeal the laws did arise over the ensuing years, there were many officials as well as citizens who favored their continuation. The explanation for this continuity is simply the same as for the origin of the laws. Both situations strongly support the validity of the thesis of the "frontier school" of historians as originally summarized by Fredrick Jackson Turner and Walter Prescott Webb.

The General Mining Laws were only a part of the federal land distribution policies of the nineteenth century. However, an unusual combination of Mining Laws with other issues caused their perseverance after other land distribution was long ended.

Throughout the long history of the General Mining Laws, their defenders have made statements that have taken much the same tone over the years. The "little man" in the form of the "rugged individual" prospector still benefits from the continuation of the mining laws. Though the original Acts of 1866, 1870, and 1872 were the work of the Republican Party during the tumultuous Reconstruction period, the frontier element was strong enough to reverse partisanship during periods of Democratic political ascendancy. Major Democratic politicians were among the laws' strongest supporters in 1920, 1934, and 1946 when a surprising variety of other important reforms were enacted. Significantly, these reforms could proceed only within the basic confines required to maintain the General Mining Laws.

Political leaders of all persuasions saw the Mining Laws as integral parts of solutions to a wide range of severe national problems. Even the "popular soverignty" of mining camp meetings was an early example, prior to federal action on the issue. Subsequently, the Mining Laws survived because important political figures believed that they were useful in fighting two economic depressions and in preparing for a cold war. Though changes did appear imminent in 1977 and again in 1990, supporters again used the same frontier arguments as those of earlier times.

Another factor in the transformation of the Mining Laws into a "sacred cow" has been the thrust of many court decisions which have given unpatented mining claims the legal protection accorded all private property. Thus constitutional protections come into play

Summary and Conclusions

that protect standing claims and prohibit reform legislation from taking an *ex post facto* approach.

As a final concluding statement, some discussion is in order on what differences any of the currently demanded reforms would make. The fact that some previously sought changes are no longer of much consideration should be noted as significant background. The "apex rule" is of only trivial consideration today since almost all classic vein type deposits are long since depleted. Similarly, the use of local mining district law has long fallen by the wayside. Congress has addressed other problems as identified by previous official studies. Most notably, FLPMA remedied the government's lack of records for claims on its own lands and set requirements for rehabilitation of lands after ore removal.

Problems still standing as outlined by the BLM report at the time of passage of FLPMA can be summarized as following:

1. Cheap acquisition of other values through patent.
2. Loss of revenue to the government from mineral output from its own lands.
3. The prevention of other uses of some lands by the presence of mining claims (regardless of the intent of the claimant, either legitimate or nuisance).
4. The unusual shapes of lode claims which do not fit the rectangular survey system.
5. The encouragement of "scams" by the use of claims.

In examining these problems, this writer will once again emphasize the often overlooked legal factor that a repeal of the mining laws would not affect existing claims. Indeed, the courts would probably interpret Mining Laws as protected from amendments which allowed continuation of mining claims but attempted to raise the costs of ultimate patent or completely end that option for any standing claims. Thus, relating to point number 1 in the above list, the dramatic "horror stories" cited in the 1989 GAO report regarding patents of valuable property at nominal prices were foregone conclusions. Congress could have done nothing to stop them.

At the same time, government grants of valuable lands for nominal fees are problems that should be addressed, even if the net result is only on claims filed after a certain date. One option could be a simple amendment which set the patent price at an appraised value of the property in relation to its location. Of course, an end to the patent option would remove the problem for any claims after that date. However, the low rate of patent applications is a factor that should also be noted. In such cases as claims near existing Colorado skiing lodges, the government could thus recover genuine profit at full market price for similar future cases. Of course, the requirement that such claims meet full tests of validity for any minerals present would have to be met. (Recent drops in mineral prices probably account for the delay on the particular case in Breckenridge, Colorado, and show that those who may try to use patents in this way are on very shaky legal ground.)

Should the government attempt to collect royalties or other fees for the minerals themselves on new claims, as suggested in point number 2 above? The tales of bonanzas in the early days have obscured the fact that the vast majority of mining operations were rather marginal but did provide employment. The profits required for success in mining are notoriously thin, as a mass of ghost towns attest. Even so, some sort of sliding scale with field inspections could address this problem, again for claims filed after the date of such an amendment. A logistical problem that can be addressed more effectively regards the "tie up" of the "common varieties" of materials. Under the amendments of 1947 and 1955, such materials can be sold to private parties or even given to local governments for roads. However, the presence of a mining claim on a potential source for such materials precluded government authorized removal for any purposes. The legal justification is straightforward. The government has granted a form of property to claimants, even prior to patent. This point is so well established by a mass of court decisions that it is totally unrealistic to expect any alternate interpretation in future cases. Again, existing claims would have "grandfathered rights" but special exemptions for this matter could be written into an amendment that took effect at a certain date.

Regarding point 4, the mass of existing claims as well as patents has already made a surveying nightmare of the rectangular system, especially in highly mined areas. Even so, use of those designations as under the placer system would be advisable but, again,

Summary and Conclusions

would not apply to existing claims. Overall, this is a comparatively minor consideration.

Regarding point 5, it is true that mineral "scams" have operated on federal lands. Some of these have involved purely fictional deposits. Others have promoted "secret processes," some of the oldest tricks in the West. It is difficult to see how the General Mining Laws contribute to "black box" frauds. Even in the cases of overvalued claims, there are so many abandoned properties under patent that can be bought for small sums by unscrupulous parties that such "cons" would still operate.

The BLM itself has taken a stronger position with the higher fees for the various required records that it initiated in 1989. Perhaps some time should be allowed to see the difference that these changes may make. In other areas, the agency can take a yet more aggressive stand. Contest actions against nuisance claims, or claims that tie up road materials should become routine. Yet in some counties the local officials have been reluctant to even request such contests, even though they desperately need the materials. The owners of such claims are often local citizens with obvious interests in the opposite direction. The BLM can simply identify the locations on its own and perform validity inspections, with contest hearings if necessary. This could remove local officials from some of the community pressure that might result in such cases.

In Congress's ongoing attempts at revisions of the laws, certain lessons should be evident from "Mo" Udall's previous experience. Any attempt to overturn existing claims would arouse the most opposition. Though some supporters of change might wish to get a court test of a full repeal, the public reaction plus the probable overturn of the entire legislation makes this a foolish course. By contrast, the Wilderness Act of 1964 allowed a period of 19 years during which new claims could be staked, though under more restrictive conditions. This Act has been successful, though naturally it has attracted some critics. A "phased in" policy of some type would probably be more acceptable. In fact, that consideration probably accounts for the 48 votes that the most recent proposal did receive in the Senate.

In the final analysis, the mining laws still find support among the "little men" and any revisions should bear that fact in mind. The larger mining firms can afford royalty systems while the smaller ones can not. The larger firms can afford more intensive cleanup after completion of projects. The smaller firms are well-known in the BLM to "make messes and walk away from them." From the standpoint of pure protection of the environment, elimination of the smaller operators might be a good thing. However, the frontier heritage and the resultant Populist support for free economic markets and opportunities for all on the public lands still preclude such a restriction. In short, any future amendments of the General Mining Laws that the Congress may attempt will have to take into account the basic thrust of the frontier thesis regarding American politics and society. Since the nation is maturing, the frontier forces may be lessening over the years, yet they are still viable enough to merit common sense in dealing with a political issue that is so strongly linked to them. There have been very good historical reasons that the Mining Laws emerged as a "sacred cow." These historical forces produced a "psychological" outlook among much of the public in the Western United States that is ongoing. Even "Mo" Udall came to acknowledge this as a crucial fact in the politics of his own region. Yet changes still may be possible, even in a way as to avoid such a confrontation as occurred in 1977. Effective political compromises will have to acknowledge the continuation of the influence of the frontier. The Turner/Webb school is still of considerable importance even in understanding the politics of the end of the twentieth century.

NOTES TO THE CHAPTERS

Certain abbreviations are used throughout the section on documentation. For manuscript sources, the locations of papers are designated as follows.

Arizona Historical Society at Tucson: AZHS,
State Historical Society of Colorado at Denver: SHSC,
National Archives and Records Center facility at Suitland, Maryland, in suburban Washington D.C.: NARC,
Pima County, Arizona, courthouse at Tucson: PC,
Cochise County, Arizona, courthouse at Bisbee: CC,
Lake County, Colorado, courthouse at Leadville: LC,
San Miguel County, Colorado, courthouse at Telluride: SM,
Grand Resource Area of the Bureau of Land Management field office at Moab, Utah: BLM. (Other materials from this agency, either manuscript or published, are noted by the full title: Bureau of Land Management in the Notes.)

The documents at the National Archives and Record Center as used in this paper are of mineral patents. These are at a facility in Suitland, Maryland, rather than the main building in downtown Washington D.C. From the first of these types of government land grants in 1868 until 1908, the General Land Office issued a file number, beginning with 1. The materials submitted in application for the patent are in unbound file folders. Copies of the final documents issued to applicants are in a series of bound volumes. Patents can be referenced in these volumes either by file number or by volume and page numbers. Subsequent to 1908, mineral patents are in unbound file folders by number with no bound volumes at all and no distinction from other types of land grant patents.

A number of decisions of federal courts and agencies and a few from state courts are referenced. For U.S. Department of the Interior decisions, an example is 19 ID 239 in which the first number is a volume number, the "ID" simply means "Interior Decision," and the final number is the page number. In much the same manner, a notation of 27 IBLA 244 simply refers to a volume and page number of the Interior Board of Land Appeals.

For federal courts, a similar system is used. An example from a U.S. District Court would be 21 F. Suppl. 432. A set of volumes called the Federal Supplement has the texts of these decisions. In some cases the particular court and year may appear in parentheses after the volume and page number, but that information may be in the text. Typical Circuit Court of Appeals decisions would read 75 F. 99 or 277 F.2nd 331, the second example being from a second series of the Federal Reporter, the published volumes which contain these recent decisions. Finally, U.S. Supreme Court decisions appear in the United States Reports with much the same system. An example is 390 US 599. Citations for Acts of Congress appear in a similar format. The first number is a volume, the word Stat. refers to Statutes, and the final number is the page, as in 23 Stat. 27.

Several newspapers and newsmagazines are commonly cited so abbreviations are useful. These are as follows.

Arizona Republic, Phoenix, Arizona: AR
Arizona Daily Star, Tucson, Arizona: AS
New York Times, New York, New York: NYT
Newsweek, New York, New York: NW
Rocky Mountain News, Denver, Colorado: RMN
Times Independent, Moab, Utah: TI
Tucson Citizen, Tucson, Arizona: TC
The Western Historical Quarterly, a journal: WHQ.

Introduction

1. Clark Spence, "Western Mining," in Michael J. Malone, *A Bibliography of Frontier Literature* (Lincoln: University of Nebraska Press, 1983), p. 107.
2. Ray Allen Billington, *Westward Expansion* (Third edition, New York: Macmillan, 1967), pp. 9-10. It should be obvious that Billington generally supports Turner but does question the "safety valve."

Chapter One

1. C. D. Bowen, *Miracle at Philadelphia* (Boston: Little, Brown and Company, 1966), pp. 166-184.
2. United States, Library of Congress (editor, G. Hunt), *Journals of the Continental Congress, 1774-1789* (Washington: Government Printing Office, 1928), vol. 26, pp. 247, 275- 279, 324-331.
3. Public Land Law Review Commission (editor, P. W. Gates), *History of Public Land Law Development* (Washington: Government Printing Office, 1968), pp. 37-39, 62-63.
4. Hunt, *Journals of the Continental Congress*, vol. 28, pp. 251, 268, 284, 285, 375-381.
5. F. McDonald, *Novus Ordo Seclorum* (Lawrence: University Press of Kansas, 1985), pp. 19, 22.
6. C. Prieto, *Mining in the New World* (New York: McGraw-Hill, 1973), pp. 87-88.
7. *Ibid.*, pp. 90-94. R. J. Kerr (translator), *Mining Law of Mexico* (Chicago: Pan American Law Books, 1910). H. W. Halleck, *Collection of the Mining Laws of Spain and Mexico* (San Francisco: O'Meara and Painter, 1859). J. C. Lacy, "Early History of Mining in Arizona, Acquisition of Mineral Rights, " J. M. Canty and M. N. Greeley, *History of Mining in Arizona* (Tucson: Mining Club of the Southwest Foundation, 1987), pp. 3-5.
8. United States House of Representatives (editor, C. S. Tansill), *Documents Illustrative of the Formation of the Union of the American States* (Document 398 of the 69th Congress, 1st Session, Washington: Government Printing Office, 1927), pp. 4/-54.
9. United States, 1st Congress, 1st Session, *Debates and Proceedings of the Congress*, (Washington: Gales and Seaton, 1834), vol. I, Appendix, pp. 2159.
10. United States Constitution, Ammendment V. For origin see R. A. Rutland, *James Madison; The Founding Father* (New York: MacMillan, 1987) pp. 61-69.
11. Tansill, *Documents Illustrative,* pp. 596, 633, 726.
12. The politics of the first years of the United States are the subject of many monographs and biographies of major figures. A good overview is J.C. Miller, *The Federalist Era* (New York: Harper and Row, 1960).
13. Gates, *Land Law*, pp. 61-63.
14. *Ibid.*, p. 124.

15. H. C. Syrett (editor), *Papers of Alexander Hamilton* (New York: Columbia Press, 1966), vol. X, pp. 204-205.
16. *Ibid.*, pp. 318-319.
17. P. L. Ford (editor), *The Writings of Thomas Jefferson* (New York: Putnam, 1899), vol. X, pp. 3-12.
18. Gates, *Land Law*, p. 219.
19. The Act itself is 2 Stat. 448. See also, J.E. Wright, *The Galena Lead District* (Madison: State Historical Society of Wisconsin, 1966), pp. 6-11.
20. Ford, *Writings of Jefferson*, vol. V., p. 210.
21. Wright, *Galena*, pp. 14-20.
22. United States Congress. Senate, *Debates in Congress*, 2nd Session of the 20th Congress (Washington: Gales and Seaton, 1830), vol. V, pp. 8-9, 70 (December 18, 1828, and March 3, 1829).
23. *Ibid.*
24. A. C. Todd, *The Cornish Miner in America* (Glendale, California: Clark Co., 1967) shows the Cornish in all major mining areas starting with the lead mines.
25. Wright, *Galena*, pp. 20-28.
26. *Ibid.*, pp. 34-35.
27. Gates, *Land Law*, pp. 702-706.
28. Wright, *Galena*, pp. 100-101. United States Congress. House of Representatives, 22nd Congress, 1st Session, Executive Documents (Washington: Duff and Green, 1831), vol. I, document no. 3, p. 31.
29. Wright, *Galena*, pp. 101-102.
30. Ford, *Writings of Jefferson*, vol. V, p. 326.
31. *Ibid.*, vol. VI, pp. 32-34 (1790 letter in which Jefferson quoted Adam Smith).
32. Act of April 25, 1812, 2 Stat. 716.
33. Gates, *Land Law*, pp. 224-226.
34. *Ibid.*
35. *Ibid.*, p. 225. P. Temin, *The Jacksonian Economy* (New York: Norton, 1969), pp. 120-129, 136-138.
36. J. Whitney, *Metallic Wealth of the United States* (Philadelphia: Lippincott, 1854), pp. 115-116.
37. F. M. Green, "Gold Mining; a Forgotten Industry of Antebellum North Carolina," *North Carolina Historical Review*, vol. XIV, pp. 1-40. F. M. Green, "Georgia's Forgotten Industry: Gold Mining," *Georgia Historical Quarterly* vol. XIX, pp. 93-111, 210-228.
38. *Ibid.*
39. P. J. Bakewell, *Silver Mining and Society in Colonial Mexico; Zacatecas, 1546-1700* (Cambridge, England: The University Press, 1971). D. A. Brading, *Merchants and Miners in Bourbon Mexico; 1763-1810* (Cambridge, England: The University Press, 1971). T. A. Rickard, *Journey's of Observation* (San Francisco: Dewey, 1907).
40. A. Craven, *The Coming of the Civil War* (Chicago: University of Chicago Press, 1957), pp. 80-83.

41. R.S. Yeoman, *A Guidebook of United States Coins* (Racine, Wisconsin: Western Publications, 1971), pp. 6-12.
42. *Ibid.*

Chapter Two

1. C. H. Shinn, *Mining Camps* (New York: Knopf, 1948 reprint of 1885 edition), pp. 112-115.
2. *Ibid.*
3. Billington, *Westward Expansion*, p. 590.
4. Shinn, *Mining Camps*, pp. 181-182.
5. O. Howe, *The Argonauts of '49* (Cambridge, Massachusetts: Harvard University Press, 1923).
6. Shinn, *Mining Camps*, pp. 141-156.
7. United States Congress, *Congressional Globe*, 30th Congress, 2nd Session, pp. 1, 21, 37, 190, 340, 381, 435, 552-553.
8. W. Downie, *Hunting for Gold* (Palo Alto: American West Publishing Co., 1971 reprint of 1893 edition), pp. 80-82.
9. Shinn, *Mining Camps*, pp. 225-226. J. H. Jackson, *Anybody's Gold* (San Francisco: Chronicle Books, 1970 reprint of undated 19th century edition), pp. 90-91.
10. Jackson, *Anybody's Gold*, pp. 133-134, 204-207.
11. I. Stone, *Men to Match My Mountains* (New York: Doubleday, 1956), pp. 167-170. Downie, *Hunting for Gold*, p. 51.
12. Shinn, *Mining Camps*, pp. 226-228.
13. *Ibid.*, pp. 108-110.
14. *Congressional Globe*, 30th Congress, 1st Session, pp. 1072-1080.
15. Craven, *Coming*, pp. 259-264. David M. Potter, *The Impending Crisis* (New York: Harper, 1976), pp. 94-105.
16. Craven, *Coming*, pp. 251-256.
17. Billington, *Westward Expansion*, pp. 591-596.
18. Stone, *Men to Match*, pp. 167-170.
19. *Congressional Globe*, 31st Congress, 1st Session, pp. 244-247. C. M. Wiltse (ed.), *The Papers of Daniel Webster* (Hanover, New Hampshire: University Press of New England, 1988), pp. 515-519, 537-538, 556-562.
20. Stone, *Men to Match*, pp. 169-170.
21. *Congressional Globe*, 31st Congress, 1st Session, vol XXI, part 1, pp. 1793-4.
22. *Ibid.*, vol. XXII, part 1, pp. 1362-1373.
23. *Ibid.*, p. 1363.
24. *Ibid.*, pp. 1365-1367.
25. *Ibid.*, pp. 1368-1369.
26. *Ibid.*, p. 1373.
27. United States. Senate, 100th Congress, 2nd Session, *Biographical Directory of the United States Congress, 1774- 1989* (Washington: Government Print-

ing Office, 1989), p. 995. D. M. Potter, *The Impending Crisis, 1848-1861* (New York: Harper, 1976), pp. 106-114.
28. *Congressional Globe*, 31st Congress, 1st Session, Appendix, Messages of the President.
29. *Congressional Globe*, 32nd Congress, 1st Session, p. 290 and Appendix, Message of the President. Gates, *Land Law*, p. 712. R. W. Paul, *California Gold* (Cambridge, Massachusetts: Harvard University Press, 1947), pp. 220-221.
30. *Congressional Globe*, 32nd Congress, 1st Session, pp. 449-450.
31. United States Census (J. D. DeBow), *Seventh Census of the United States, 1850* (Washington D.C.: Robert Armstrong, 1853), pp. 969-982.
32. Craven, *Coming*, p. 250. Potter, *Impending*, pp. 108-110.
33. Craven, *Coming*., pp. 328-331. Potter, *Impending*, pp. 156-177.
34. Craven, *Coming*, pp. 357-365. Potter, *Impending*, pp. 156-177.
35. Craven, *Coming*, pp. 390-396. Potter, *Impending*, pp. 157-161.
36. R. Johannsen, *The Letters of Stephen A. Douglas* (Urbana: University of Illinois Press, 1961), pp. 182-183.
37. *Ibid.*, p. 183, footnotes.
38. "News from Australia," *NYT*, vol. I, no. 26, p. 4 (October 17, 1851). A similar series appeared in *Littleton's Living Age* through 1851.
39. "Australia," *NYT*, vol. I, no. 4, p. 1, (September 22, 1851).
40. "$2.1 Million Gold!" *NYT*, vol. I, no. 2, p. 2, "Address by Stephen A. Douglas at N.Y. State Fair," *NYT*, vol. I, no. 3, p. 4.
41. Billington, *Westward Expansion*, p. 605.
42. Craven, *Coming*, pp. 394-396.
43. C. B. Swisher, *Stephen J. Field* (Chicago: University of Chicago Press, 1930), pp. 84-88.

Chapter Three

1. M. Twain, *Roughing It* (New York: New American Library, 1980 reprint of 1868 edition), p. 164.
2. *Ibid.*, p. 151.
3. *Ibid.*, p. 168.
4. T. M. Marshall (ed.), *Early Records of Gilpin County, Colorado, 1859-1861* (Boulder: University of Colorado Press, 1920), pp. 7-8.
5. Since Colorado was officially part of "Bleeding Kansas" at the time of the 1860 Census, and was very remote, accurate figures are not available. However, some ideas are given throughout the contemporary account of O. J. Hollister, *The Mines of Colorado* (New York: Promontory, 1974 reprint of 1867 edition).
6. R. Paul, *Mining Frontiers of the Far West* (Albuquerque: University of New Mexico Press, 1963), pp. 90-92.
7. *Ibid.*, pp. 92-94.

8. "Territorial Acts," *RMN*, vol. I, no. 171 (March 13, 1861).
9. Twain, *Roughing It*, pp. 211-219.
10. D. DeQuille, *The Big Bonanza* (San Francisco: Bancroft, 1876, with many reprints), pp. 24-25, 40-41.
11. W. S. Greever, *Bonanza West*, (Moscow: University of Idaho Press, 1963), p. 105-106.
12. H. C. Hoover and L. H. Hoover, *De Re Metallica* (New York: Dover, 1950 reprint of 1912 translation), pp. 82-85 (extended footnote on history of mining law from Medieval times).
13. H. H. Bancroft, *Works of Hubert H. Bancroft* (New York: McGraw Hill, undated reprint of editions of 1883-1890), vol. 24, pp. 396-402.
14. Greever, *Bonanza West*, pp. 100-102.
15. Bancroft, *Works*, vol. 25, pp. 107-109, 121-128, 172-175.
16. *Ibid.*, pp. 74-75.
17. G. M. Ostrander, *Nevada; the Great Rotten Borough* (New York: Knopf, 1966), pp. 28-35. Bancroft, Works, vol. 25, p. 186.
18. Bancroft, *Works*, pp. 74-75.
19. Twain, *Roughing It*, p. 234. O. E. Young, *Western Mining* (Norman: University of Oklahoma Press, 1970), pp. 42-70.
20. Marshall, *Gilpin County*, pp. 1-5.
21. *Ibid.*, pp. 18-34.
22. *Ibid.*, pp. 34-47.
23. *Ibid.*, pp. 48-52.
24. *Ibid.*, pp. 53-68.
25. *Ibid.*, pp. 69-77.
26. *Ibid.*, pp. 178, 295.
27. *Ibid.*, pp. 175-176.
28. "Territorial Assembly," *RMN*, vol. 6, no. 225, p. 1 (May 8, 1866).
29. Stone, *Men to Match*, pp. 257-259, 277-281. M. S. Wolle, *Stampede to Timberline* (Denver: Sage Books, 1949), pp. 86-90.
30. Bancroft, *Works*, vol. 25, pp. 486-489.
31. United States Congress, *Congressional Globe*, 38th Congress, 1st Session (Washington. Congressional Globe Office, 1865), pp. 521, 693, 1209, 1228.
32. C. Ubbelohde, M. Benson, and D. Smith, *A Colorado History* (Boulder: Pruett Publishers, Fifth Edition, 1982), pp. 103-108.
33. United States Congress. *Congressional Globe*, 38th Congress, 1st Session, p. 1169. Billington, *Westward Expansion*, pp. 630-632.
34. S. Mowry, *The Mines of the West; Shall the Government Seize Them?* Rare pamphlet dated 1864, AZHS.
35. "The Mining Law Printed," *Arizona Daily Miner* (Ft. Whipple, Arizona), vol. I, no. 15, p. 1 (November 16, 1864). Mining Claims, vols. I-II, A-B, PC.
36. Gates, *Land Law*, pp. 362-367, 372-377, 379-381, 385-386.
37. *Ibid.*, pp. 335-339.
38. *Ibid.*, pp. 393-402.
39. *Ibid.*, 385-386, 799-802.

Chapter Four

1. A brief but good biographical sketch of Bennet is J.H. Silverman, "Making Brick Out of Straw," *Colorado Magazine*, vol. 53, pp. 309-327 (Fall 1976).
2. "Endorse Hiram Bennet," *RMN*, vol. I, no. 302, p. 1 (August 17, 1861).
3. United States Congress, *Congressional Globe*, 37th Congress, 2nd Session, pp. 133, 168.
4. United States Congress, *Congressional Globe*, 38th Congress, 2nd Session, pp. 1260-1262.
5. *Ibid.*, Acts, p. 258. *Congressional Globe*, 37th Congress, 2nd Session, p. 658, Appendix p. 349.
6. Yeoman, *Coins*, pp. 6-12.
7. United States. *Congressional Globe*, 38th Congress, 1st Session, Debates (1864) p. 495.
8. *Ibid.*, p. 232, 1184.
9. *Ibid.*, p. 1695.
10. *Ibid.*, p. 1696.
11. *Ibid.*
12. *Ibid.*
13. *Ibid.*, p. 1695.
14. *Ibid.*, pp. 1695-1696.
15. *Ibid.*, p. 1861.
16. *Ibid.*, p. 1914-1915.
17. *Ibid.*, p. 1916.
18. *Ibid.*
19. *Ibid.*, p. 3360. United States Senate, 100th Congress, 2nd Session. *Biographical Directory of the United States Congress, 1774-1989* (Washington: Government Printing Office, 1989), p. 818 (sketch of Conness).
20. United States Congress. *Congressional Globe*, 38th Congress, 2nd Session, p. 435.
21. *Ibid.*, pp. 1260-1262.
22. 13 Stat. 440.
23. United States Congress. *Congressional Globe*, 39th Congress, 1st Session, p. 2851.
24. United States Congress. Senate. *Reports of Committees*, 39th Congress, 1st Session (Washington: Government Printing Office, 1866), Report No. 105, to Accompany bill S. 257, p. 2.
25. *Ibid.*, pp. 1-2.
26. United States Congress. *Congressional Globe*, 39th Congress, 1st Session, pp. 3225.
27. *Ibid.*, pp. 3225-3227.
28. *Ibid.*, p. 3229.
29. *Ibid.*, p. 3231-3235.
30. *Ibid.*, p. 2965.
31. *Ibid.*, pp. 3141-3142.
32. *Ibid.*, pp. 3453, 4048-4054.

33. R. Elliott. *Servant of Power: A Political Biography of William M. Stewart.* Reno: University of Nevada, 1983, pp. 53-55.
34. United States Congress. *Congressional Globe*, 39th Congress, 1st Session, p. 49.
35. Gates, *Land Law*, pp. 719-720, 724-725.
36. Billington, *Westward Expansion*, p.624.
37. "Sherman Introduces Preemption Act," *RMN*, vol. 6, no. 210 (April 20, 1866). "Bills Coming Nearer Wants of Mining States," *RMN*, vol. 6, no. 212 (April 23, 1866). "Congress and the Mines," *RMN*, vol. 6, no. 282 (July 18, 1866). "Text of Act," *RMN*, vol. 6, no. 298 (August 6, 1866).
38. "Territorial Assembly," *RMN*, vol. 6, no. 225 (May 8, 1866).
39. United States Congress. *Congressional Globe*, 41st Congress, 2nd Session, pp. 314-319, 2027-2030.
40. *Ibid.*, pp.4918, 5043-5044.
41. *Ibid.*
42. United States Congress. *Congressional Globe*, 42nd Congress, 1st Session, pp. 67.
43. *Ibid.*, pp. 199, 775. See also, Paul, *Mining Frontiers*, pp. 187-189.
44. United States Congress. *Congressional Globe*, 42nd Congress, 2nd Session, pp. 532-535.
45. *Ibid.*, pp. 2456-2462.
46. T. Maley, *Mining Law*, (Boise: Mineral Land Publications, 1985), pp. 49-54.
47. 17 Stat. 465 and 17 Stat. 605.
48. The story of Sutro and his tunnel has been told and retold many times but most accounts omit the later part of his remarkable career. See Paul, *Mining Frontiers*, pp. 81- 83 for a brief account of the tunnel. Stone, *Men to Match*, pp. 313-322, 366-371, 394-396, gives more details. R. D. Dematier, C. F. McIntosh, and E. E. Waters, *The Rumble of California Politics*, (New York: John Wiley, 1970), pp. 140- 145 show Sutro's later career.
49. Webb, *Great Plains*, pp. 398-431 (a detailed discussion of land laws).

Chapter Five

1. Mineral Patents, folder 1, and vol. I, pp. 1-5, NARC.
2. United States Department of the Interior. General Land Office. *Instructions in Relation to Survey and Entry of Lode and Placer Claims* (Washington: Government Printing Office, August 8, 1870).
3. Checklist in Mineral Patents, folder 2, NARC.
4. Mineral Patents, vols. I-IV, folders 1-425, NARC.
5. Mineral Patents, vol. I, pp. 23, 291-296, vol. II, pp. 116-120, folders 5, 56, and 134, NARC.
6. Mineral Patents, vol. II, pp. 501-506, vol. III, pp. 26-30, folders 205, and 227, NARC.
7. Mineral Patents, vol. I, pp. 28-32, 286-290, folders 6 and 55, NARC.
8. Examples of sequences in the same locales are in Mineral Patents, folders 6-9,

13-24, 101-113 (Lander County, Nevada), folders 38-54 (Gilpin and Clear Creek Counties, Colorado), and 61-64 (the major Comstock Mines), NARC.
9. The Comstock mines in the Virginia District were vol. I, pp. 318-342, 357-61, folders 61-64, and 67. Gold Hill mines were in vol. I, pp. 362-375, vol. II, pp. 80-103, and 153-172, folders 68-69, 128-131, 141-143, NARC.
10. Greever, *Bonanza West*, pp. 124-127.
11. Jackson, W. Turrentine, *Treasure Hill; Portrait of a Silver Camp*, (Tucson: University of Arizona Press, 1963), pp. 5-6 (a good account of this lesser known area).
12. Mineral Patents, vol. I, pp. 53-63, folders 11 and 12, NARC. Ubbelohde, *Colorado*, pp. 143-148, 218-224.
13. Mining (Collection 117), folder 589, SHSC.
14. Frank Rearden papers (Collection 516), folder 5, SHSC.
15. Mineral Patents, folders 43, 44, 182-184, 357, NARC.
16. Mineral Patents, vol. XXX, pp. 84-96, folders 2486, 2487, NARC.
17. *U.S. v. V.A. Johnson*, General Land Office Contest No. 1704, NARC.
18. Mineral Patents, No. 063405 and 063789 (1943), NARC.
19. Mining Records, vol. 405, pp. 485-489, SMCO.

Chapter Six

1. Mineral Patents, vol. A, pp. 73-75, LC.
2. Paul, *Mining Frontiers*, p. 159. *Way Up Mining Co. vs. Tombstone Mining Co.*, decision by Commissioner of the General Land Office Nov. 28, 1881, NARC.
3. Paul, *Mining Frontiers*, pp. 180, 185.
4. C. C. Andrews, *The Story of Alaska* (Caldwell, Idaho: Caxton Publishing Co., 1953), p. 219. M. B. Sherwood, *Alaska and Its History* (Seattle: University of Washington Press, 1967), pp. 376-378.
5. R. G. Manguson, *Coeur d'Alene Diary* (Portland, Oregon: Metropolitan Press, 1968), pp. 16-19.
6. R. Brown, *Hard Rock Mines; the Intermountain West*, 1860-1920 (College Station: Texas A. and M. University Press, 1979), pp. 160-164.
7. Greever, *Bonanza West*, pp. 188, 196-197. Paul, *Mining Frontiers*, pp. 173-174.
8. *Ibid.*, pp. 274-278. H. Cook, "Too Little-Too Much; Water and the Tombstone Story," in *History of Mining in Arizona*, pp. 229-231.
9. Bancroft, *Works*, vol. 25, pp. 133, 486-489. Sprague, *Money Mountain* (Boston: L. Broon, 1953), pp. 298-300 (comparative production figures).
10. United States Department of Commerce. Bureau of the Census. *Historical Statistics of the United States, Colonial Times to 1970* (Washington: Government Printing Office, 1975), pp. 25, 31.
11. T.A. Rickard, "Across the San Juans" in *Journeys of Observation* (San Francisco: Dewey, 1907). This enitre section of 127 pages addresses the region. It was published separately as a small volume by the title *Across the San Juans* and is based on the author's own 1902 trek there.

Notes to the Chapters 275

12. Mineral Patents, vol. I, pp. 15-18, SMCO. R. L. Fetter and S. Fetter, *Telluride* (Caldwell, Idaho: Caxton Press, 1979), pp. 15-19.
13. Fetter, *Telluride*, p. 24. 49-51. Mineral Patents, vol. 54, p. 173, SMCO.
14. Ubbelohde, *Colorado*, pp. 185-186.
15. Greever, *Bonanza West*, pp. 127-130.
16. Gates, *Land Law*, pp. 417-419, 707-708. F. R. Wirth, "The Operation of the Land Laws in the Minnesota Iron District," *Mississippi Valley Historical Review*, vol. 13, pp. 438 (1927).
17. Gates, *Land Law*, pp. 550-555.
18. "Mine Jumping; the Maid of Erin Guarded by Armed Men," *Denver Republican*, vol. III, no. 54, p. 6 (Nov. 20, 1881). "Assessment Work," *Denver Republican*, vol. V, no. 9, p. 6 (January 9, 1882).
19. W. Ferril, manuscript, v. 3, p. 23 (1890), Denver Public Library.
20. R. McGrath, *Gunfighters, Highwaymen, and Vigilantes* (Berkeley: University of California Press, 1984), pp. 194-198, 228-232.
21. Mining Claims, vol. I, pp. 350, vol. K, pp. 215-216, PC. G. G. Boyer (editor), *I Married Wyatt Earp; the Recollections of Sarah Marcus Earp* (Tucson: University of Arizona Press, 1976), pp. 54, 59, 61-61, 83.
22. Boyer, Wyatt Earp, pp. 77-79.
23. *Ibid.*, pp. 107-114.
24. *Ibid.*, pp. 121-126.
25. Index to Mining Records, CC. Mining Records, vols. A-M, PC. Mineral Records vol. I, SM.
26. Mining Claim Contests, *Way Up Mining Co. vs. Tombstone Mining and Milling Co.*, files including letter of Oct. 25, 1881, from Robert Fletcher to the Commissioner of the General Land Office, NARC.
27. *Ibid.*, including written decision of November 28, 1881, by the Commissioner in favor of Tombstone Mining and Milling Co.
28. T. Heatwood, *Ghost Towns and Historical Haunts in Arizona* (Phoenix: Golden West Publishers, 1981), p. 5.
29. Mining Claims, vols. I and II, and Mineral Patents, vols. A-D, LC.
30. Schmuck, *Fourteeners*, pp. 22-29.
31. *Ibid.*, pp. 60-61.
32. Colorado Yule Marble Company (collection 159), Inventory pp. 4-5, SHSC.
33. Young, *Western Mining*, pp. 204-214.
34. I. Hale, *Electric Mining in the Rocky Mountain Regions* (pamphlet issued by American Institute of Mining Engineers, September, 1896), pp. 15-17. Mine and Smelter Supply Co., Catalogue No. 22 (New York: no publishing co. cited, 1912), pp. 954-957 (this is a rare volume at AZHS). Webb, *Great Plains*, pp. 167-179, 280-318, 333-365 (various technical adjustments to region).

Chapter Seven

1. Turner, *Frontier and Section*, pp. 5, 37-62.
2. D. A. Smith, *Rocky Mountain Mining Camps* (Lincoln: Universtiy of Nebraska Press, 1967), pp. 200-204.

3. Stanley L. Jones, *The Presidential Election of 1896* (Madison: University of Wisconsin Press, 1964), pp. 3-15.
4. *Ibid.*, pp. 16-35.
5. *Ibid.*, pp. 238-239.
6. *Ibid.*, pp. 332-351.
7. Wolle, *Stampede*, pp. 319-331. Census, *Historical Statistics*, p. 606.
8. S. Holbrook, *Rocky Mountain Revolution* (New York: Holt, 1956), p. 72.
9. V. Jensen, *Heritage of Conflict* (Ithaca, New York: Cornell University Press, 1950), pp. 74-87. See also R. E. Lingenfelter, *The Hardrock Miners: A History of the Mining Labor Movement in the American West, 1863-1893* (Berkeley: University of California Press, 1974).
10. Sprague, *Money Mountain*, p. 71.
11. *Ibid.*, pp. 131-132, 163-166.
12. *Ibid.*, pp. 174-176.
13. *Ibid.*, pp. 299-301. B. Levine, *Lowell Thomas's Victor* (Colorado Springs: Century One Press, 1982), pp. 3-15.
14. Bancroft, *Works*, vol. 25, pp. 226-228, B. Levine, *Cities of Gold* (Colorado Springs: Century One Press, 1981), pp. 12-15. Holbrook, *Rocky Mountain Revolution*, p. 72.
15. D. A. Smith, "Colorado's Urban Mining Safety Valve," *Colorado Magazine*, vol. 48, pp. 299-318. R.H. Peterson, *The Bonanza Kings* (Lincoln: University of Nebraska Press, 1977), pp. 78-79.
16. Manguson, *Coeur d'Alene*, pp. 153-154, 182-209. Peterson, *Bonanza*, pp. 71-72.
17. Fetter, *Telluride*, pp. 102-117. Rickard, *Journeys*, pp. 38-43.
18. "Horrible Catastrophe in Cripple Creek District," *Arizona Gazette*, vol. 23, no. 151, p. 1 (June 7, 1904). "Orchard Linked to Explosion," *Arizona Gazette*, vol. 23, no. 158, p. 1 (June 14, 1904).
19. W. Lord, *The Good Years* (New York: Harper Bros., 1960), pp. 140-146.
20. *Ibid.*, pp. 146-167.
21. *Ibid.*, pp. 166-167.
22. Yeoman, *Coins*, pp. 6-12.
23. S. Cohen, *The Streets Were Paved with Gold* (Missoula, Montana: Pictorial Histories Publishing Co., 1977), pp. 65-134. P. Berton, *The Klondike Fever* (New York: Knopf, 1958), pp. 8-12, 244-267.
24. Berton, *Klondike*, pp. 333-365.
25. Boyer, *Wyatt Earp*, pp. 158-191.
26. Andrews, *Alaska*, p. 219. Hulley, *Alaska*, pp. 264-266.
27. Boyer, *Wyatt Earp*, pp. 192-205.
28. Sprague, *Money Mountain*, pp. 299-301.
29. J. L. Benham, *Camp Bird and the Revenue* (Ouray, Colorado: Bear Creek Publishing, 1980), pp. 5, 11, 41-52.
30. Census, *Historical Statistics*, pp. 207-209.
31. United States. Works Projects Administration, Writers Program, *Copper Camp* (New York: Hastings House, 1943), pp. 32, 38-45. M. Malone, *The Battle for Butte* (Seattle: University of Washington Press, 1981), pp. 147-8.

32. W.P.A., *Copper Camp*, p. 45. Most of Malone's *The Battle for Butte* also addresses this theme.
33. "The Platform as Completed," *San Francisco Chronicle*, July 9, 1896, p. 4.
34. "The Repubican Platform Adopted at St. Louis," *San Francisco Chronicle*, June 19, 1896, p. 4. E. Ellis, *Henry M. Teller: Defender of the West* (Caldwell, Idaho: Caxton Press, 1941), pp. 17, 156-162.
35. W. Haywood, *Bill Haywood's Book; the Autobiography of William D. Haywood*, (New York: International Publications, 1929), pp. 29-33.
36. *Ibid.*, pp. 108-109.
37. T. A. Rickard, *Journeys*, pp. 38-43.

Chapter Eight

1. United States. House of Representatives, 46th Congress, 2nd Session. *Report of the Public Land Review Commission*, House Executive Document no. 46 (Washington: Government Printing Office, 1880), p. xxxv. Paul, *Mining Frontiers*, pp. 174-175.
2. Ostrander, *Nevada*, pp. 103-121.
3. United States. House of Representatives, 63rd Congress, 2nd Session. *Report No. 639 of the Commission to Amend the General Mining Laws* (Washington: Government Printing Office, 1914).
4. Shinn, *Mining Camps*, (J. H. Jackson introduction to 1947 reprint) pp. v-xxii.
5. P. Boller, *American Thought in Transition* (Lanham, Maryland: University Press of America, 1981), pp. 84-88, 214.
6. Shinn, *Mining Camps*, pp. 22-23.
7. *Ibid.*, p. 119.
8. *Ibid.*, pp. 66, 126-127, 167.
9. *Ibid.*, pp. 45, 95-99.
10. *Ibid.*, p. 208.
11. *Ibid.*, p. 5.
12. *Ibid.*, p. 104.
13. R. A. Billington, "Young Fred Turner," *Wisconsin Magazine of History*, vol. 46, no. 1, pp. 38-52 (1962).
14. Shinn, *Mining Camps*, pp. xiv-xxi, 250-256.
15. E. W. Teale, *The Wilderness World of John Muir* (Boston: Houghton Mifflin, 1954), pp. v-xx.
16. J. Muir, *The Mountains of California* (Place of publication not listed: 10 Speed Press, 1977 reprint of 1910 edition), pp. 326-328.
17. J. Muir, *Steep Trails* (Boston: Houghton Mifflin, 1918), pp. 198-203.
18. *Ibid.*, pp. 202-203.
19. *Ibid.*
20. *Ibid.*
21. H. Hawthorne and E. B. Mills, *Enos Mills of the Rockies* (Boston: Houghton Mifflin, 1935), p. 41.
22. W. E. Colby, "Grand Canyon as National Park," *Bulletin of the Sierra Club*,

vol. 10, p. 81 (1916). W. F. Bade, "Save the Redwoods League," and "Controlled Fires," *Bulletin of the Sierra Club*, vol. 11, pp. 89, 202 (1917).
23. H. C. Callahan, "Wanted: Australian Law," *Mining and Scientific Press*, vol. 108, p. 422. "Discovery vs. Permit System," *Mining and Scientific Press*, vol. 108, p. 244. G. Mason, "Revision of the Mining Law," *Mining and Scientific Press*, vol. 108, p. 98. F. P. Davis, "Revising Mining Law," *Mining and Scientific Press*, vol. 108, p. 982-983.
24. Hoover, *De Re Metallica*, pp. 82-85 (lengthy footnote).
25. Boyer, *Wyatt Earp*, pp. 212-213.
26. Mining Records, San Bernardino County, California, vol. 43, p. 13. Boyer, *Wyatt Earp*, pp. 236-237.
27. F. A. Crampton, *Deep Enough; a Working Stiff in the Western Mine Camps* (Norman: University of Oklahoma Press, revised 1982), pp. 21-26.
28. *Ibid.*, pp. 29-32.
29. *Ibid.*, pp. 55-61, 67-76.
30. *Ibid.*, pp. 85-99, 164-184, 238-240.
31. Manuscript collection No. 384 of Junius R. Lewis, Calendar of Papers, SHSC.
32. Manuscript collection No. 159 of the Colorado Yule Marble Co., Inventory, pp. 4-5, SHSC.
33. *Ibid.*
34. *Ibid.*

Chapter Nine

1. H. L. Copp, *Decisions of the Commissioner of the General Land Office* (San Francisco: Bancroft and Co., 1874), pp. 27-29.
2. *Ibid.*, pp. 23, 59.
3. *Ibid.*, pp. 77-79.
4. *Ibid.*, pp. 135-136.
5. *Ibid.*, p. 145.
6. *Ibid.*, p. 179.
7. House of Representatives. Land Review Document No. 46, pp. xxxv.
8. 175 US 571 (1900).
9. Federal Cases 13,413 and 13,414 (1879 citation).
10. 98 US 463 (1878).
11. 122 US 478 (1887).
12. 63 F 540 (1894).
13. 157 US 683 (1894).
14. 118 US 196 (1896).
15. 171 US 55, 88 (1898).
16. 101 F 518 (1900).
17. 171 US 293 (1898).
18. 108 F 189 (1900), affirmed 109 F 538.
19. 104 F 664 (1900), error dismissed 186 US 24, reversed other grounds 204 US 204.
20. 182 US 497 (1901).
21. 196 US 337 (1905).

22. 213 US 72 (1909).
23. Greever, *Bonanza West*, p. 188. Paul, *Mining Frontiers*, p. 173-174.
24. 254 F 630 (1918).
25. 50 F 588 (1892), rehearing 54 F 262, error dismissed 150 US 138.
26. 247 US 450 (1918).
27. 209 P 283 (1922), cert. denied 260 US 744.
28. 177 F 95.
29. Guilbert, *Ore Deposits*, pp. 547-553.
30. C. Spence, *Mining Engineer*, pp. 223-226.
31. Papers of several Arizona attorneys in the Medigovich Collection, AZHS, include good examples of the frequency of mining cases in the earlier twentieth century in Bisbee.
32. Shinn, *Mining Camps*, pp. 247-257. Crampton, *Deep Enough*, pp. 220-221.
33. H. P. Walker, "Arizona Land Fraud; Model 1880-Tombstone Townsite Co.," *Arizona and the West*, vol. 21, pp. 5-36.
34. Ibid., pp. 16-23.
35. 1 Arizona 404, 25 P. 793 (1881).
36. Walker, "Land Fraud," pp. 28-36.
37. Ibid.
38. 115 US 392, 404 (1885).
39. 139 US 507, 519 (1891).
40. 233 US 236 (1914).
41. Gates, *Land Law*, pp. 417-419, 707-708. F. R. Wirth, "The Operation of the Land Laws in the Minnesota Iron District," *Mississippi Valley Historical Review*, vol. 13, pp. 438 (1927).
42. 102 US 167 (1880).
43. 154 US 288 (1894).
44. 188 US 526 (1903).
45. 251 US 1 (1919).
46. 19 ID 455 (1894).
47. 197 US 313 (1905).
48. 249 US 337 (1919).
49. T. Maley, *Handbook of Mining Law* (Boise: Mineral Land Publications, 1980), pp. 389-392.
50. 130 US 630 (1889).
51. 16 Wallace 36 (1873, U.S. Supreme Court prior to use of United States Reports type of citations).
52. 140 F 854 (1905).
53. 212 US 389 (1909).
54. 176 US 221 (1900).
55. 236 US 459 (1915).
56. 253 US 330 (1920).
57. 252 US 450 (1920).
58. 280 US 306 (1930).
59. 182 F 685 (1910).
60. 113 Fed 273 (1901).

Chapter Ten

1. Gates, *Land Law*, pp. 725-738.
2. Maley, *Mining Law*, pp. 165, 188, 324.
3. Gates, *Land Law*, pp. 566-567.
4. *Ibid.*, pp. 568-569.
5. United States Senate, 58th Congress, 3rd Session, *Report of the Public Lands Commission*, Document 189 (Washington: Government Printing Office, 1905), pp. v-vi.
6. W. Johnson, *Gifford Pinchot; Forester-Politician* (New York: Garland Publishing Co., 1979), pp. 59-61.
7. 33 Stat. 628 (Part I).
8. W.W. Rostow, *The Stages of Economic Growth* (Cambridge, England: Cambridge University Press, 1960), chart facing page one.
9. United States Department of Commerce. Bureau of the Census, *Fourteenth Census of the United States for the Year 1920; Mines and Quarries*, vol. XI (Washington: Government Printing Office, 1922), pp. 21, 84-85. Department of Commerce. Bureau of the Census, *Thirteenth Census of the United States, 1910; Mines and Quarries*, vol. XI (Washington: Government Printing Office, 1913), pp. 22-27. M. Trimble, *Arizona* (New York: Doubleday, 1977), pp. 231, 238. Lynn R. Bailey treats developments at Bingham Canyon and Bisbee in *Old Reliable: A History of Bingham Canyon* (Tucson: Westernlore Press, 1988), and *Bisbee, Queen of the Copper Camps* (Tucson: Westernlore Press, 1983).
10. Census, *Mines and Quarries*, 1920, pp. 21, 84-85.
11. Census, *Historical Statistics*, p. 606.
12. United States Department of Commerce. Bureau of the Census, *Special Reports: Occupations at the Twelfth Census* (Washington: Government Printing Office, 1904), p. 232. Yeoman, *Coins*, pp. 10-11, 59.
13. Census, *Mines and Quarries*, 1910, pp. 22-23.
14. Census, *Occupations, Twelfth Census*, pp. 237-238.
15. Census, *Mines and Quarries*, 1920, pp. 84-85.
16. Census, *Mines and Quarries*, 1910, pp. 21-27, 58.
17. *Ibid.*
18. Young, *Black Powder*, pp. 84-112.
19. Census, *Mines and Quarries*, 1910, pp. 19-44.
20. Craven, *Coming*, pp. 100-102, 110-112.
21. Gates, *Land Law*, p. 731.
22. 23 ID 232.
23. Gates, *Land Law*, pp. 731-732.
24. W. Bean, *California; An Interpretive History*, (Second edition, New York: McGraw Hill, 1973), pp. 368-374.
25. *Ibid.*
26. Gates, *Land Law*, pp. 732-741.
27. 36 Stat. 847. The text of Taft's withdrawal is in 236 US 467 as part of the Supreme Court Decision which upheld it.

28. Gates, *Land Law*, pp. 740-741, 745-750.
29. United States Congress. Senate, 65th Congress, 2nd Session, 58 *Congressional Record*, p. 4112 (1919).
30. *Ibid.*, p. 4250.
31. *Ibid.*
32. *Ibid.*
33. *Ibid.*, pp. 4253-4254, 4285.
34. *Ibid.*, pp. 4161.
35. *Ibid.*, p. 4249.
36. *Ibid.*, p. 4162.
37. *Ibid.*, p. 4238.
38. *Ibid.*, p. 4285.
39. *Ibid.*, p. 4767-4779.
40. *Ibid.*
41. United States Congress. House of Representatives, 65th Congress, 2nd Sesson, 58 *Congressional Record*, pp. 7509-7513 (1919).
42. *Ibid.*, pp. 7516-7519.
43. *Ibid.*, pp. 7520-7521.
44. *Ibid.*, pp. 7539-7540.
45. *Ibid.*, pp. 7526, 7649, 7767.
46. *Ibid.*, p. 7590.
47. Gates, *Land Law*, pp. 743-745.
48. The Mineral Leasing Act of 1920 is at 41 Stat. 437.
49. Meyer and Riley, *Public Domain*, pp. 198-199.
50. Maley, *Mining Law*, p. 11.
51. R. Lacour-Gayet, *A History of South Africa* (London: Cassell Publishers, 1970), pp. 133-134. C. M. H. Clark, *A History of Australia*, vol. V, (Melbourne: Melbourne University Press, 1981), pp. 158-161. P. T. Flawn, *Mineral Resources* (New York: John Wiley, 1966), pp. 135-136, 203-209.
52. Clark, *Australia*, p. 158.
53. Lacour-Gayet, *South Africa*, pp. 153-159.
54. M.D. Bernstein, *The Mexican Mining Industry, 1890-1950* (Albany: State University of New York Press, 1964), pp. 18- 20. J.B. Romney, "American Interests in Mexico: Development and Impact During the Rule of Porfirio Diaz, 1876-1911," unpublished Ph. D. dissertation, University of Utah, 1969, pp. 42-58.
55. Bernstein, *Mexican Mining*, pp. 135-137.
56. Flawn, *Mineral Resources*, pp. 178-179. Greever, *Bonanza West*, p. 361.

Chapter Eleven

1. United States Department of Commerce. Bureau of the Census, *Census of Mines*, 1939 (Washington: Government Printing Office, 1941), pp. 337-359, 367-373 (figures for 1929 and 1939).
2. Census, *Historical Statistics*, p. 605.

3. United States. President, "First Inaugural Address of Franklin D. Roosevelt, March 4, 1933." Available in many sources.
4. United States. President, *Executive Order 6102 and Executive Order 6111* (Washington: Government Printing Office, 1933).
5. United States. Congress. House of Representatives, 73rd Congress, 1st Session, *Congressional Record*, pp. 4546- 4548 (May, 1933).
6. *Ibid.*, p. 4563.
7. *Ibid.*, Senate, p. 4929.
8. United States Congress. House of Representatives, 73rd Congress, 2nd Session, *Congressional Record*, pp. 963- 968, 1016. Senate, *Congressional Record*, pp. 1484 (January, 1934).
9. Census, *Historical Statistics*, p. 606.
10. J. T. Paterson, *Congressional Conservatism and the New Deal*, p. 114.
11. United States Congress. Senate, 73rd Congress, 2nd Session, *Congressional Record*, p. 1465 (January, 1934).
12. R. Moley, *The First New Deal* (New York: MacMillan, 1966), pp. 298-305.
13. United States Congress. House of Representatives, 73rd Congress, 2nd Session, *Congressional Record*, p. 107 (1933).
14. *Ibid.*, p. 10580 (June, 1934).
15. *Ibid.*, Senate, pp. 10678-10695.
16. A.M. Schlesinger, *The Coming of the New Deal* (Boston: Little Brown, 1957), p. 251.
17. United States. Congress. Senate, 73rd Congress, 2nd Session, *Congressional Record*, pp. 10921-11060 (June, 1934).
18. Schlesinger, *Coming*, pp. 244-252.
19. W. Leuchtenburg, *Franklin D. Roosevelt and the New Deal* (New York: Harper Bros., 1963), pp. 82-83.
20. "Treasury Outlining Silver Bill," AR, June 22, 1934, p. 1.
21. "Not More Gold But Figures," AR, June 22, 1934, Editorial page (unnumbered).
22. "Copper Mines Add 1000 to Payroll: Miami, Ajo, Scenes of Renewal in Activity; Silver is Aid," AR, June 30, 1934, p. 1.
23. Schlesinger, *Coming*, p. 252.
24. Gates, *Land Law*, p. 607.
25. United States. Congress. House of Representatives, 72nd Congress, 2nd Session, *Congressional Record*, pp. 3562- 3569 (February, 1933).
26. United States. Congress. House of Representatives, 73rd Congress, 2nd Session, *Committee Hearings, Use, Improvement, and Development of the Public Range*, (Washington: Government Printing Office, 1934), pp. 21-22.
27. United States Congress. House of Representatives, 73rd Congress, 2nd Session, *Congressional Record*, pp. 11142- 11143. Senate, *Congressional Record*, p. 11162 (June, 1934).
28. "Growth of Gold Mining," AR, June 25, 1934, p. 8.
29. Bureau of Land Management, *Placer Examination*, pp. 73-84.
30. Census. *Census of Mines, 1939*, pp. 337, 344, 368, 381-382, 392-394.
31. *Ibid.*, pp. 381-382.

Notes to the Chapters 283

32. *Ibid.*, pp. 383-384.
33. D. P. Morgan, *Steam's Finest Hour* (Milwaukee: Kalmbach Publishing, 1959), pp. 1-8.
34. A. H. Carhart, "Homemade Gold," *Saturday Evening Post*, September 17, 1932, pp. 21, 31-32. S. G. Blythe, "The Argonauts of '32," *Saturday Evening Post*, October 15, 1932, pp. 10-11, 33-34. F. R. Bechdolt, "Stampede, 1936 Model," *Saturday Evening Post*, November 14, 1936, pp. 14-15, 53-54.
35. Ubbelohde, *Colorado*, pp. 316-317.

Chapter Twelve

1. Heatwole, *Ghost Towns*, pp. 26-27.
2. General Land Office, Patent Application 063789, NARC.
3. Section 505 of the Soldiers and Sailors Relief Act of 1940 makes this a standing rule for persons who own claims while actually in the military. During World War II all claims were exempted from annual assessment under 56 Stat. 271, which was subsequently extended through the 1940's.
4. United States. National Archives and Records Service, *Public Papers of the Presidents; Harry S Truman* (Washington: Government Printing Office, 1961), pp. 362-365.
5. United States. National Archives and Records Service, *Code of Federal Regulations; Title 3, the President, 1943-1948* (Washington: Government Printing Office, 1957), Executive Order 9613, pp. 425-426. (Hereafter abbreviated as 3 CFR 1943-1948.)
6. *Ibid.*, Executive Order 9701, pp. 510-511.
7. Archives, *Truman*, pp. 362-366.
8. *Ibid.*
9. 3 CFR 1943-1948, Executive Order 9639, pp. 440-441, Executive Order 9727, pp. 531-532. Steel Mills in 3 CFR 1952, Executive Order 10340.
10. United States Atomic Energy Commission (AEC), *Prospecting for Uranium* (Washington: Government Printing Office, 1949), pp. v-vi.
11. United States Congress, *Hearings Before the Special Committee on Atomic Energy*, 79th Congress, 2nd Session, Part I, (Washington: Government Printing Office, 1946), pp. 93-95.
12. *Ibid.*, pp. 315-317.
13. *Ibid.*, p. 318.
14. *Ibid.*, pp. 318-319.
15. *Ibid.*, p. 319.
16. *Ibid.*, pp. 319-320.
17. *Ibid.*, pp. 324-325.
18. *Ibid.*, pp. 327-328.
19. United States Congress. Senate, 79th Congress, 2nd Session, *Congressional Record*, pp. 6085-6087 (June, 1946).
20. *Ibid.*, pp. 6090-6092.
21. *Ibid.*, pp. 6086-6088.

22. *Congressional Quarterly* (Washington: Press Research Inc., 1946), vol. II, pp. 505-514.
23. Atomic Energy Commission, *Prospecting*, pp. 39-42, 72-74.
24. 59 Stat. 613.
25. 3 CFR 1946, Reorganization Plan No. 3, p. 1068.
26. Gates, *Land Law*, pp. 632-634. Maley, *Handbook*, pp. 444-458.
27. Atomic Energy Commission, *Prospecting*, pp. 40-41.
28. "High Powered Rush for Uranium Claims," *Life*, vol. 41, no. 12, p. 57 (September 17, 1951).
29. Atomic Energy Commission, *Prospecting*, pp. 28-35.
30. Nash, "Uranium Deposits," in the *Seventy-Fifth Anniversary Commemorative volume at the Society of Economic Geologists* (El Paso; Economic Geology Publishing, 1980), pp. 96-104.
31. "Navajos Go Into Uranium Business," *Life*, June 4, 1951, pp. 61-65.
32. "Charlie Steen," NW, vol. XLIII, no. 15, p. 100 (April 19, 1954). "Mining; the Cisco Kid," *Time*, vol. 62, pp. 60-61 (August 3, 1953).
33. "Frontier Days, 1954," NW, vol. XLVIII, no. 12, p. 27 (March 22, 1954).
34. P. Reed, "Prospector Left Legacy of Sorrow," RMN, vol. 123, no. 158, p. 4 (September 27, 1981).
35. R. Coughlin, "Vernon Pick's Struggle to Be Himself," *Life*, March 19, 1956, p. 179.
36. "Pennies for Uranium," *Time*, vol. LXIII, no. 14, p. 89 (April 5, 1954).
37. "Frontier Days," NW, p. 27.
38. Peters, *Exploration*, p. 540.
39. BLM's policy of "multiple use" dates from its creation by President Truman with a strengthening of the concept for lands covered by mining claims under 69 Stat. 367 and further strengthening under 90 Stat. 2743.
40. Maley, *Mining Law*, pp. 282-311.
41. 61 Stat. 681.
42. 69 Stat. 681.
43. 69 Stat. 367.
44. E. Wayburn and M. Barnum, "Some Mining Law Conflicts Ended", *Sierra Club Bulletin*, January, 1956, pp. 23-24.
45. United States. Congress. Committee on Energy and Natural Resources, 95th Congress, 2nd Session, *Report on Revision of the Mining Law of 1872* (Washington: Government Printing Office, 1977), pp. 55-57.
46. Bureau of Land Management. Patent No. 120000, NARC.
47. Bureau of Land Management. Patent application No. 04543, NARC.
48. Wayburn and Barnum, "Conflicts Ended."
49. Nash, "Uranium Deposits," pp. 89-96.

Chapter Thirteen

1. Commission on Organization of the Government (Herbert Hoover, Chairman), *Concluding Report to Congress* (Washington: Government Printing Office, 1949).

2. *Ibid.*, Appendix L, pp. 53-55.
3. *Ibid.*
4. *Ibid.*, pp. 44-47 (including reorganization chart).
5. Peters, *Exploration*, pp. 193-199.
6. S. L. Udall, *The Quiet Crisis*, (New York: Holt, Rinehart, and Winston, 1963), pp. 188-191.
7. M. Frome, *National Park Guide*, (16th edition, Chicago: Rand McNally, 1981), pp. 17, 83-84.
8. 88 Stat. 577.
9. Land Law Review Commission. *One Third of the Nation's Land* (Washington: Government Printing Office, 1971), preface. This was the cumulation of several years of work which had included *History of Public Land Law Development* (Gates).
10. "Hardrock Mining on the Public Lands Under a Century Old Law" (Washington: Sierra Club Pamphlet, 1977).
11. 83 Stat. 852.
12. J. McPhee, *Encounters with the Archdruid* (New York: 1971), central theme of the first chapter.
13. United States Congress. Senate. *Legislative History of FLPMA*, Publication 95-99 (Washington: Government Printing Office, 1978), pp. 157-158.
14. *Ibid.*, p. 201-202 (reprint of debates in Congressional Record).
15. *Ibid.*, pp. 202, 212.
16. *Ibid.*, pp. 257-258, 668-716.
17. 90 Stat. 2743, sec. 204.
18. Senate, *Revision of Mining Law*, pp. 1-21.
19. *Ibid.*, pp. 22-23.
20. *Ibid.*, pp. 1-21.
21. Senate. *Biographical Directory*, p. 1965.
22. *Congressional Quarterly Almanac* (Washington: Congressional Quarterly, 1976), p. 186. "Mo Defends Mining Bill," TC, vol. 107, no. 139, p. 3C (June 15, 1977).
23. "Udall to Face Mine Operators and Discuss Bill," TC, vol. 107, no. 161, p. 16A (July 7, 1977).
24. *Ibid.*
25. "Small Mine Operators, Udall Clash," TC, vol. 107, no. 163, p. 1B (July 9, 1977).
26. A. Bushnell, "Asta and Co. Head for Rocky Mountain Mixer," TC, vol. 107, no. 161, p. 2C (July 7, 1977).
27. "Mo Yielding on Mining Law-Or Is He?" TC, vol. 107, no. 208, p. 1 (August 31, 1977). "Udall Opposes Carter Mining Law Reform," TC, vol. 107, no. 209, p. 15A (September 1, 1977). C. Collins, "Udall Reversal Stirs Doubting Thomases," TC, vol. 107, no. 214, p. 3C (September 7, 1977).
28. Collins, "Reversal." D. Robinson, "Editorial," AS, vol. 136, no. 248, p. 10A (September 5, 1977).
29. "Prospectors Hunt Mo's Scalp," TC, vol. 107, no. 135, p. 1B (June 11, 1977).
30. United States. Department of the Interior. Bureau of Land Management.

Opportunity and Challenge; the Story of the Bureau of Land Management. (Washington: Government Printing Office, 1988), Appendix, table of employment.
31. BLM, internal memoranda, description of training at Phoenix facility.
32. *Ibid.*
33. The rise in metals prices during 1979 can be found in any regular listing of commodities prices, usually with stocks and bonds in business publications.
34. From FLPMA, 90 Stat. 7743, section 314. Maley, *Handbook*, pp. 172-208.
35. Maley, *Mining Law*, pp. 588-590.
36. 57 IBLA 167 (1981).
37. 613 F2nd 224 (1980).
38. Maley, *Mining Law*, pp. 270-272.
39. 726 F2nd 1376 (1984).
40. 66 IBLA 316 (1982).
41. 733 F2nd 704 (1984).
42. 599 F2nd 290 (1979), cert. denied 44 US 1014.
43. 522 F 150.
44. Maley, *Mining Law*, pp. 452-458.
45. BLM, Surface Protection under 43 CFR 3809, files.
46. Uranium prices as reported in TI 1980-1983.
47. BLM, Patent Application for Small Fry Mine (1982).
48. BLM, Patent Application of Rio Algom Corporation (1983).
49. BLM, internal report on gravel sales and records of mining claims.
50. Guilbert, *Ore Deposits*, pp. 558-563.
51. BLM, internal files on Perkins placer claims. See also, State of Arizona. Department of Mines and Mineral Resources (M. N. Greeley), *Mining Scams* (Circular No. 11, January, 1986).
52. Mayer, *Public Domain*. J. Hooper, "The Mining Law of 1872," *Sierra Club Bulletin*, vol. 67, no. 4, p. 32 (July, 1982). D. Dagget, "Yellowcake National Park," *Sierra Club Bulletin*, vol. 70, no. 3, pp. 28-31 (July, 1985).
53. J. C. Leshy, *Mining Law* (Washington: Resources for the Future, 1987).
54. R. Rohe, "Man and the Land; Mining's Impact on the Far West," *Arizona and the West*, vol. 28, pp. 299-339 (1986). D. Smith, *Mining America; the Industry and the Environment, 1800-1980* (Lawrence: University of Kansas Press, 1987).
55. "Hold Up Grand Canyon Mine Removal," TC, February 29, 1988, p. 2C.
56. A brief overview of this extremely complex situation is in the publication by the State of Arizona. Department of Mines and Mineral Resources (L. D. Clark and V. H. Verity), *Laws and Regulations Governing Mineral Rights in Arizona* (9th edition, Phoenix: 1986), pp. 2-4. The Colorado Supreme Court Decision is in 652 P.2nd 1050 (1982).
57. United States. Bureau of Land Management. BLM-AA-GI- 89-007-4130 (agency internal directive raising fees).
58. United States. General Accounting Office. *The Mining Law of 1872 Needs Revision* (Washington: Government Printing Office, 1989).

59. J. Kilpatrick, "Taxpayers Should Get a Share of the Gold," regular editorial column distributed nationally, March 30, 1989, reprinted in Conservative Chronicle, vol. 4, no. 15, p. 25 (April 12, 1989).
60. General Accounting Office, *Revision*, p. 12 footnote.
61. *Ibid.*, p. 23 footnote.
62. "Garn Opposes Changes in Historic Mining Law," TI, vol. 96, no. 25, p. B7 (June 22, 1989).
63. *Ibid.*
64. B. Schulte, "Rush for Crystals Puts Century-Old Mining Law On Spot," AS, November 4, 1990, pp. 1-2G.

INDEX

Act of Congress of 1866 (terms and passage), 70–73, 84–86, 88
Act of Congress of 1870 (Placer Mining Act, terms and passage), 79–80, 84–86, 88, 128, 131–132, 180–183
Act of Congress of 1872 (final Act of General Mining Laws, terms and passage, 80–86, 88, 128, 131, 132, 183–188, 207
Act of Congress, 1945 (Government Reorganization), 221
Act of Congress, 1947 (salable minerals), 228–229
Act of Congress, 1955 (salable minerals), 228–229
Adams, Herbert Baxter (professor), 137, 139
Adams, John Quincy, 11
Alcorn, James (Sen., Mississippi), 82
American Flat District, Nevada, 94
American Smelting & Refining Corp. (ASARCO), 176–177
Anaconda Corp. (Amalgamated), 130–131, 196
Antero (Ute Chief), 114
"Apex rule," 48–51, 57, 72, 94, 100, 122, 130, 135–136, 152–160, 169–171, 242, 253
Appalachians (gold rushes), 16–19, 21
Army, U.S., 11–14, 27–28, 31, 36, 58–60
Articles of Confederation, 1, 4–5
Ashurst, Henry F. (Sen., Arizona), 183
Aspen, Colorado, 100
Atomic Energy Act (1946), 213–220
Atomic Energy Commission (A.E.C.), 214, 219, 221–222

Aurora, Nevada, 46, 48, 91, 108
Australia (gold rush), 39–40, 72, 127, 188–191

Bancroft, Hubert H., 50
Bank of California, 90–91, 106
Barnum, M. M., 229
Barringer, Daniel (mining engineer), 136
Barton, David (Sen., Missouri), 11–12
Bennet, Hiram P. (Colorado delegate), 64–76, 85
Benton, Thomas Hart (Sen., Missouri), 11, 32–33
Billington, Ray Allen (historian), xi
Bingham Canyon, Utah, 99–100, 147, 176, 206, 211
Bisbee, Arizona, 144, 147
Black Hills, Dakota Territory, see Deadwood, Lead
Bland Allison Act, 118
Blanding, Utah, 226
Blutelier, Robert (mining attorney), 112
Bodie, California, 108
Bonanza Four (on Comstock), 106
Borah, William (Idaho prosecutor), 126, 197
Bradley, Joseph P. (U.S. Supreme Court Justice), 154
Branch, John (Sen., N.C.), 11
Brandeis, Louis (U.S. Supreme Court Justice), 168
Branscome, Edwin (mining company official), 216
Brewer, David (U.S. Supreme Court Justice), 154, 164, 166

[289]

British Mining Law, 2, 48
Brower, Dave, 236, 239
Bryan, William Jennings, 81, 119–120, 195–198
Buffalo, preservation of, 65–66
Bumpers, Dale (Sen., Arkansas), 256–257
Bureau of Land Management, xii, 170, 221, 227–228, 235, 237, 240, 246–247, 249–250, 253–254
Burkhart, Glynn, 245
Butte, Montana, 130–131
Byers, William, 64, 78

California (gold rush to), 22
Camp Bird Mine (Colorado), 129–130
Canadian uranium rush, 231
Carleton, col. James, 60
Carlin Gold deposits, 252
Carter, Jimmy, 242
Carter, Vincent, 202
Census, U.S., (1850), 36; (1870), 101; (1880), 103; (1890), 103, 117, 134; (1900), 123, 134; (1910), 117–178; (1920), 177, 179; (1930), 193, 204; (1940), 204–205
Central City, *see* Gilpin Co., Colorado
Chafee, Jerome (delegate, Colorado), 81
Chandler, Zachariah (Sen., Michigan), 68
Charles III (King of Spain), 3
Charlotte, N.C., 18–19
Churchill, Winston, 221
Chilean miners (in California), 25–26
Chinese (miners), 25, 33, 47
Civil Rights Act, 1964, 185
Claim jumping, 71, 107–108
Clagett, William Horace (delegate, Montana, mining attorney), 80–81, 85, 160
Clancy, William (judge), 130–131
Clay, Henry, 29–31, 36–37
Cleveland, Grover, 198
Clum, John (editor *Tombstone Epitaph*), 60–61, 161
Cochise County, Arizona, 109, 112–113, 161–162
Coeur d'Alene, 99, 101, 109, 121, 125–126, 133, 158
Coinage Act, 1873 ("Crime of '73"), 118
Cole, Cornelius (Rep. & Sen., California), 69, 79, 82
"Cold War," 221–233
Collins, Christina, 244
Colorado School of Mines, 122, 225
Colorado Springs, Colorado, 254

Colton, Don Byron (Rep., Utah), 200
Compromise of 1850, 29–31, 36–37
Comstock, Henry, 50, 100, 102–103
Comstock Lode, *see* Virginia City, Nevada
Confederate States, 19, 58–60
Conness, John (Sen., California), 69, 70–74, 76, 85, 87
Connor, Patrick (U.S. Army officer), 99–100
Constitution, United States, 4–5, 185
Cornish miners, 12, 120, 121, 134, 147, 178
Cornwall, England, 2
Coughlin, Charles, 197
Court Cases:
Argentine Mining Co. vs. Terrible Mining Co., 153; *Baker vs. U.S.*, 248; *Barden vs. Northern Pacific R.R.*, 164; *Blackburn vs. Portland Gold Mining Co.*, 153; *Bradford vs. Morrison*, 167; *Brubaker vs. Board of Commissioners of El Paso County*, 254; *Banker Hill and S. Mining vs. Empire State of Idaho Mining*, 156; *Calhoun Gold Mining Co. vs. Ajax Gold Mining Co.*, 156; *Cameron vs. U.S.*, 168; *Castle vs. Womble*, 165–166; *Christman vs. Miller*, 166, 168; *Colorado Central Mining Co. vs. Turck*, 158; *Consolidated Wyoming Gold Mining Co. vs. Champion Mining Co.*, 154; *Cosmopolitan Mining vs. Foote*, 154; *Creede and Cripple Creek Mining Co. vs. Unita Tunnel*, 156; *Deffenback vs. Hawke*, 163, 167; *Del Monte Mining and Milling Co. vs. Last Chance Mining Co.*, 154; *Diamond Coal and Coke Co. vs. U.S.*, 163, 165; *Dredge Corp. vs. Conn*, 249; *E. Field et al. vs. M. Gray et al.*, 161; *Flagstaff Silver Mining Co. vs. Tarbet*, 153; *Iron Silver Mining Co. vs. Elgin Mining Co.*, 154; *Ivanhoe Mining Co. vs. Consolidated Mining Co.*, 164; *Jones vs. Wild Goose Mining Co.*, 159; *Mammoth Mining Co. vs. Grand Central Mining Co.*, 157; *McKinley vs. Wheeler*, 167; *Northern Pacific R.R. vs. Soderberg*, 164; *O'Connell vs. Pinnacle Gold Mines*, 167; *Oneida Perlite*, 248; *Original Sixteen to One MIne vs. Twenty-One Mining Co.*, 158; *Roberts vs. U.S.*, 167; *Rogers vs. U.S.*, 248; *St. Louis Mining Co. vs. Montana Mining Co.*, 156; *Stevens vs. Williams*, 153; *Teller vs. U.S.*, 170; *Tom Reed Gold Mines Co.*

Index

vs. *United Eastern Milling Co.*, 159; *Tyler Mining Co. vs. Last Chance Mining Co.*, 154, 157; *U.S. vs. Alaska Limestone Corp.*, 248–249; *U.S. vs. Bales*, 249; *U.S. vs. Midwest Oil Co.*, 167; *U.S. vs. North American Transportation Co.*, 167–168; *U.S. vs. Richardson*, 249; *U.S. vs. Rizzinelli*, 169–170; *U.S. vs. Southern Pacific R.R.*, 165; *Union Oil Co. of California vs. Smith*, 166, 180; *Walrath vs. Champion Mining Co.*, 156; *Wilbur vs. U.S. ex. rel. Krushnic*, 168
Crampton, Frank, 145–148
Creede, Colorado, 103, 119, 159
Cripple Creek, Colorado, 121, 129, 133, 145
Curie, Pierre and Marie, 178

Dahlonega (Georgia gold rush site), 16–17, 21
Darrow, Clarence, 126
Davis, Jefferson, 33
Deadwood, Dakota Territory, 162–163
DeQuille, Dan (William Wright), 46–47, 51
Diaz, Porfirio, 189–190
Dickinson, Clement C., 197
Dodge, Augustus (Sen., Iowa), 33
Dohery, Harry F., 185
Douglas, Dr. James, 136, 176–177
Douglas, Stephen A., 37–41
Downie, William, 24, 26
Dyers, Martin (Rep., Texas), 195

Earp brothers, 108–109, 162
Earp, Wyatt, 108–109, 127–129, 144–145
Earp, Josephine Sarah Marcus, 109, 127–129, 144–145
Elston, John A. (Rep., California), 185
Ely, Richard, 137, 139
Englebright, Harry (Rep., California), 201
Environmental Analyses and Environmental Impact Statements, 238
Esmeralda District, Nevada, *see* Aurora
Ewing, Thomas (Sen., Ohio), 32

Fairbanks, Alaska, 99, 128–129, 190
Fairplay, Colorado, 58, 114, 207
Fall, Albert, 182, 184, 187
Farland, N.C. (Commissioner, Gen. Land Office), 112
Federal Land Policy and Management Act of 1976 (FLPMA), 239, 241, 245–247
Federalists (Hamiltonian), 6–8

Felch, Alphens (Sen., Michigan), 33
Ferril, Will C., 107
Field, Edward, 161–162
Field, Stephen, 35, 41, 136, 153–155, 163–164, 170–171
Ford, President Gerald, 239–240
Forest Service, U.S., 170, 174–176, 183, 185, 201–202, 222, 229–230, 235, 237, 240
Forrest, Sir John, 188
Forks of the Yuba (California placer camp), 24–25
Fillmore, President Millard, 34–36
Free black miners, 26, 114, 148
"Free Silver," 118–120, 126, 131–132, 195–198
Frémont, John C., 31–34, 42

Galena, Illinois, 9–14, 67, 76–77
Gallatin, Albert, 6, 9
Gamboa, Francisco Xavier, 3
Garn, Jake (Sen., Utah), 256–257
General Accounting Office (1989 report), 254–256, 261
General Land Office (U.S.), 15, 66, 70, 77, 87–96, 112–113, 151–152, 173–175, 211, 221, 227
Geological Survey, U.S., 174, 181, 235
Gilpin, Governor William, 59
Gilpin Co., Colorado, 53–56, 91, 94
Gold Hill, Nevada, *see* Virginia City
Gold Standard (Acts 1933, 1934), 194–195
Grand Canyon, 168, 173
Grand Junction, Colorado, 226
Grant, President Ulysses S., 82, 85, 202
Grants, New Mexico, 222, 227
Gratiot Brother's smelter, 13–14
Grazing Service, U.S., 200–202, 221
Great Lakes Copper Rush, 21
Greeley, Horace, 54
Greever, William S., (author, *Bonanza West*), 75
Gregory, John, H., 53
Gwin, William (Sen., California), 31

Hamilton, Alexander, 6–9, 78, 197
Hammond, John Hays, 136, 160
Hargreaves, Edward, 39
Harding, President Warren G., 182
Harlan, James (Sen., Iowa), 79–80
Harris, Richard, 99
Haskell, Floyd (Sen., Colorado), 240
Hatch, Carl A. (Sen., New Mexico), 218–219

Haywood, William "Big Bill", 125–126, 132
Hays, President Rutherford B., 135
Hearst, George, 51, 97
Hearst, William Randolph, 51
Heinricks, Grover, 243
Heinze, F. Augustus, 130–131, 147
Hernandez, Benigno Cardenas (Rep., New Mexico), 185
Hickenlooper, Bourke (Sen., Iowa), 216
Hickock, "Wild Bill", 162
Higby, William (Rep., California), 68, 75–76
"High grading," 123
Hill, Nathaniel P., 58, 101
Holliday, "Doc", 108–109, 162
Holman, Williams (Rep., Indiana), 69
Holmes, Oliver Wendell, Jr., 157
Homestead Act (1862), i, 61–62, 66, 85, 163
Hook, George, 97
Hoover, President Herbert, 48–50, 143–144, 160, 233
Hoover Commission, 233–236, 240

Ickes, Harold, 201, 215, 218
Ingram, J. B., 103–104, 110–111.
Interior, U.S. Dept. of, x, 15, 151–152, 168, 181, 246–248
Interior, Secretary of, 151, 161, 165, 201, 236–237, 249, 254
International Workers of the World (IWW), 147
Ionaville District, California, 89
Iron ore (Great Lakes region), 84, 106–107, 163, 179, 190
Iron Ore, Utah, 230

Jackling, D. C., 212
Jackson, President Andrew, 11, 15
Jackson, Henry M. (Sen., Washington), 239, 241
Jefferson, Thomas, 1, 8–10, 78, 197
Johns Hopkins University, 137–139
Johnson, President Andrew, 75, 77, 78, 85
Johnson, President Lyndon, 237
Johnson, V. A., 95
Julian, George W. (Rep., Indiana), 63, 73–78
Juneau, Joseph, 99

Kansas-Nebraska Act, 37–38, 243
Kasson, John (Rep., Iowa), 66
Kearns, Tom, 100

Kellogg, Noah, 99, 109
Kennecott Corp., 176, 206, 211
Kennedy, President John F., 236–237
Kett, Fredrick F., 216–218
Khoumeni, Ayatollah, 247
Kilpatrick, Jack, 255
King, Rufus, 2
King, William H. (Sen., Utah), 183, 196
Kirby, William (Sen., Arkansas), 184
Klondike, *see* Canadian Yukon
Koch, Walter, 211

LaFollett, Robert M. (Sen., Wisconsin), 184
Lake County (Colorado), 113–114
LaMar, L. Q. C., 167
Land Ordinances, 1784 and 1785, 1, 4, 6, 61
Lander Co., Nevada, 91
Lead, Dakota Territory, 97, 106
Lead Leasing, 9–16, 21, 67, 76–77
Leadville, Colorado, 53, 97, 100, 104–105, 107, 113–114, 153, 158
Lewis, Junius, 148
Legate, Thomas, 13
Leshy, John, 252–253, 259
Lincoln, President Abraham, 41, 58
Lincoln Memorial, 148–150
Long, Huey (Sen., Louisiana), 198

McClure, James (Sen., Idaho), 239–240
McClure, L. C., 104
McFadden, Louis T. (Rep., Pennsylvania), 194
McGrath, Roger, 108
McMahon, Brian (Sen., Connecticut), 215–218
McPhee, John, 238–239
Madison, President James, 4–6, 15, 75
Maldanardo, Gabriel, 47
Manhattan Project, 212–213, 219
Marble, Colorado, 114–115, 148–150
Marsh, George (Rep., Vermont), 28–29
Marshall, James, 17
Mason, William R., 27–28, 31
Mayor, Carl, 75, 91, 135–136, 252, 259
Mears, Otto, 105–106
Metcalf, Lee (Sen., Montana), 240
Mexico, 3, 189–191
Mexico, miners from, 25, 33, 47, 60–61, 138, 178
Miller, Sidney, 95
Milliken, Eugene (Sen., Colorado), 217, 226
Mills, Enos, 142, 173
Mineral Leasing Act (1920), 182–188

Index

Miners' meetings, 22, 24–26, 34–39, 53–58, 71, 80, 128
Mining equipment and techniques, 12–13, 17–18, 45, 115–116, 146, 179, 205–207, 222, 224
Mints, U.S., 18–19, 36, 65, 178, 208
Moab, Utah, 226, 250–252
Moley, Dr. Raymond, 196
Mondell, Frank W. (Rep., Wyoming), 185
Monroe, President James, 2
Monterrey, California, Quick Silver Mining District, 87
Monticello, Utah, 226
Morgenthau, Henry, 197
Mormons, 30, 99–100
Morrill, Justin S., 61–62, 68
Moyer, Charles H., 125–126
Muir, John, 140–142

Nashville Convention (1850), 29
National Aeronautics and Space Administration (NASA), 222
National Environmental Policy Act of 1969 (NEPA), 238
National Parks, see also specific parks, 173–174, 237, 242
Navajo Indian Reservation, 223
New Deal, see Franklin D. Roosevelt
New Orleans, 18–19
Nixon, President Richard, 238
Nobel, Alfred, 115
Nome, Alaska, 99, 128–129, 159, 167–168, 190
Norris, Frank, 165
Norris, George (Sen., Nebraska), 197
Northwest Ordinance, 1787, 4, 5

Oddie, Tasker, 144
Oil, 180–188
Oil Leasing Act, 180–188, 222
O'Mahoney, Joseph C. (Sen., Wyoming), 219, 222
Oppenheimer, Robert, 215
Orchard, Harry, 125–126
Oro Fino Gulch District, Montana, 89
Osgood, John, 115
Ouray, Colorado, 103, 129

Park City, Utah, 99–100
Patents, mineral, 87–96
Phelan, James D. (Sen., California), 184
Phelps Dodge Corp., 176–177, 199
Pick, Vernon, 225–226
Pickett Act 1910, 181–182, 185–186

Pikes Peak region (colorado rush, 1859), 44, 122
Pima County, Arizona, 60–61, 109, 112, 244
Pinchot, Gifford, 174–175
Pitney, Mahlon, 66
Pittman, Key (Sen., Nevada), 196
Polk, President James K., 22–23, 220
Pomeroy, Samuel (Sen., Iowa), 82
"Popular Sovereignty," 29–31, 36–41, 71–72
Poston, Charles, 61
Preemption, 15–16, 62
Prescott, Arizona, 60
Proclamation of 1763 (British), 77
Public Land Law Review Commission, 237–238

Rahill, Nick (Rep., West Virginia), 254
Railroad land grants, 61
Raker, John E. (Rep., California), 184–185
Ralston, William, 90–91
Ramirez, Ramon A., 249
Reagan, President Ronald, 254
Rearden, Frank, 93
Reconstruction (post Civil War), 77–78
Reese River District, Nevada, 90
Republican Party (Jeffersonian), 6
Republican Party (post-Civil War), 77–78
Rhodes, Cecil, 189
Rich, Sylvester, 114
Rickard, T. A., 17–18, 134, 143, 160
Riley, George A., 75, 91, 135–136, 252, 259
Rio Algom Corp., 251
Rische, August, 97
Robinson, Don, 244
Robinson, James W. (Rep., Utah), 201
Rockefeller, John D., 181
Rohe, Randall, 253
Roosevelt, President Franklin D., 194–203
Roosevelt, President Theodore, 168, 174, 186
Rostow, Walt W., 176

Saegart, William, 243
"Salable minerals", 228–229
Salting (mine scams), 53, 252, 263
San Juan Mountains, Colorado, 103, 129–130
Sargent, Aaron A. (Rep., California), 79–80
Sawatch Mts., Colorado; Mt. Antero, 114; Mt. Elbert, 104–105; Mt. Massive, 104
Schieffelin, Ed, 97, 98, 112
Schlesinger, Arthur M., 198–199

Schurtz, Carl, 161
Schwartzwalder, Fred, 225
Senzel, Irving, 241–242
Seward, William, 33
Shannon, Thomas B. (Rep., California), 66, 68
Sharon, William, 90–91
Shell Oil Co., 181
Sherman, John (Sen., Ohio), 70, 72, 78
Sherman Silver Purchase Act (1890), 118–119
Sherman, William T., 27
Shinn, Charles Howard, 137–140
Sierra Club, 75, 135–136, 142–143, 220, 229, 236–237, 239, 252
Silver City, New Mexico, 61
Silverton, Colorado, 103, 129
Silver Purchase Act (1934), 195–200
Sioux Indians, 103
Skagway, Alaska, 127
Slavery in mines, Georgia, 17–18, 21, 30; Latin America, 17–18
Smith, Adam, 14
Smith, Duane A., 133, 253
Smith, Marcus A. (Sen., Arizona), 183–184
Smith, Martin F. (Rep., Washington), 194
Smith, "Soapy," 119, 127
Smoot, Reed (Sen., Utah), 182–184, 187
Smuggler Mine, Telluride, Colorado, 103–105, 110–111, 159
South African mining, 189, 191
Spanish Mining Law, 2–3, 32, 48
Spence, Clark, ix
Spoilers Gang (Nome, Alaska), 129, 167–168
Springfield District, California, 27
Standard Oil Company, 181
Stanton, Irving, 92
Steen, Charlie, 210, 223, 225–227
Sterling, Thomas (Sen., South Dakota), 184
Stewart, William H. (Sen., Nevada), 51–53, 63, 69, 71–76, 78, 82, 85, 135, 160
Stratton, Winfield Scott, 122–124
Strikes (labor disputes), 1877, 117; 1890s, 117, 121, 123–126, 1331; post 1900, 144
Supreme Court, U.S., 151–171, 215
see "Court Cases" for specific decisions.
Surveys, Western, 65, 70
Sutro, Adolph, 84, 152
Sutter, John, 17, 22
Swenson, Robert W., 75, 219

Tabor, H. A. W., 87, 102, 109, 113, 122, 223, 225
Tabor, "Baby Doe," 109
Taft, President William Howard, 181–182, 186
Talmadge, James (Rep., New York), 29
Taylor, Edward T. (Rep., Colorado), 185, 200–202, 221
Taylor, President Zachary, 34
Teapot Dome, Wyoming, 182, 187
Teller, Edward, 215
Teller, Henry, 91–92, 132, 167
Telluride, Colorado, 103–105, 125, 129, 159
Ten Mile/Mosquito Mountains, Colorado, 114
Thomas, Charles S., 183
Thomas, Elmer, 197
Thomas, Lt. Martin, 11–14
Timber and Stone Act (1878), 106–107
Tomb of Unknown Soldier, 149–150
Tombstone, Arizona, 97–98, 100–101, 109, 112–113, 161
Tonopah/Goldfield, Nevada, 127, 133, 144–147, 176, 178
Townsites (conflicts with mining claims), 161–163
Truman, President Harry S., 213–215, 219
Turner, Fredrick Jackson, xi, 41, 96, 117, 133–134, 138–139, 149, 217, 220, 231, 258, 260–264
Twain, Mark (Samuel Clemmens), 43–44, 51, 80, 147, 156, 161

Udall, Morris "Mo" (Rep., Arizona), 242–246, 253–254, 263–264
Udall, Stewart, 236–238
Union Carbide Corp., 218
Union Oil Co., 181
Uranium, 178, 212–227, 230–231
Uranium geology (Chinle and Morrison formations), 223
Uravan, Colorado, 222
Ute Indians, 103, 114
Utex Corp., 230

Vanadium Corp., 215–218
Van Buren, President Martin, 16
Virginia City, Nevada, 44–53, 90–91, 100, 106

Wallace, Henry A., 201
Wallace, William, 68

Index

Walsh, Thomas, 129–130
Wannemaker, Nathaniel, 114
Washburne, Elihu (Rep., Illinois), 67
Watt, James, 254
Wayburn, Dr. Edgar, 229
Webb, Walter Prescott, xi, 19, 41, 85–86, 96, 115, 133, 138–139, 149, 217, 220, 231, 258, 260–264
Webster, Daniel, 29–31, 36–37
Western Federation of Miners (WFM), 123–126, 147
Wheeler, Burtonk, 195–196
Wickenburg, Arizona, 60
Wilderness Act, 1964, 237–238, 263
Wilmot, David, 28–30
Williams, George (Sen., Oregon), 73
Willard, Charles (Rep., Vermont), 82

Wilson, President Woodrow, 182, 186
Wood, Fernando (Rep., New York), 66–68, 73, 76
Works Progress Administration (WPA). 204, 208
World War I, 177, 184
World War II, 211

Yellowstone National Park, 81, 174
Yetman, David, 244
Young, Brigham, 99
Young, Otis, 115
Yukon (Canadian Territory), 99, 127, 188, 190
Yule, George, 114–115, 148–149, 228
Yuma, Arizona, 60

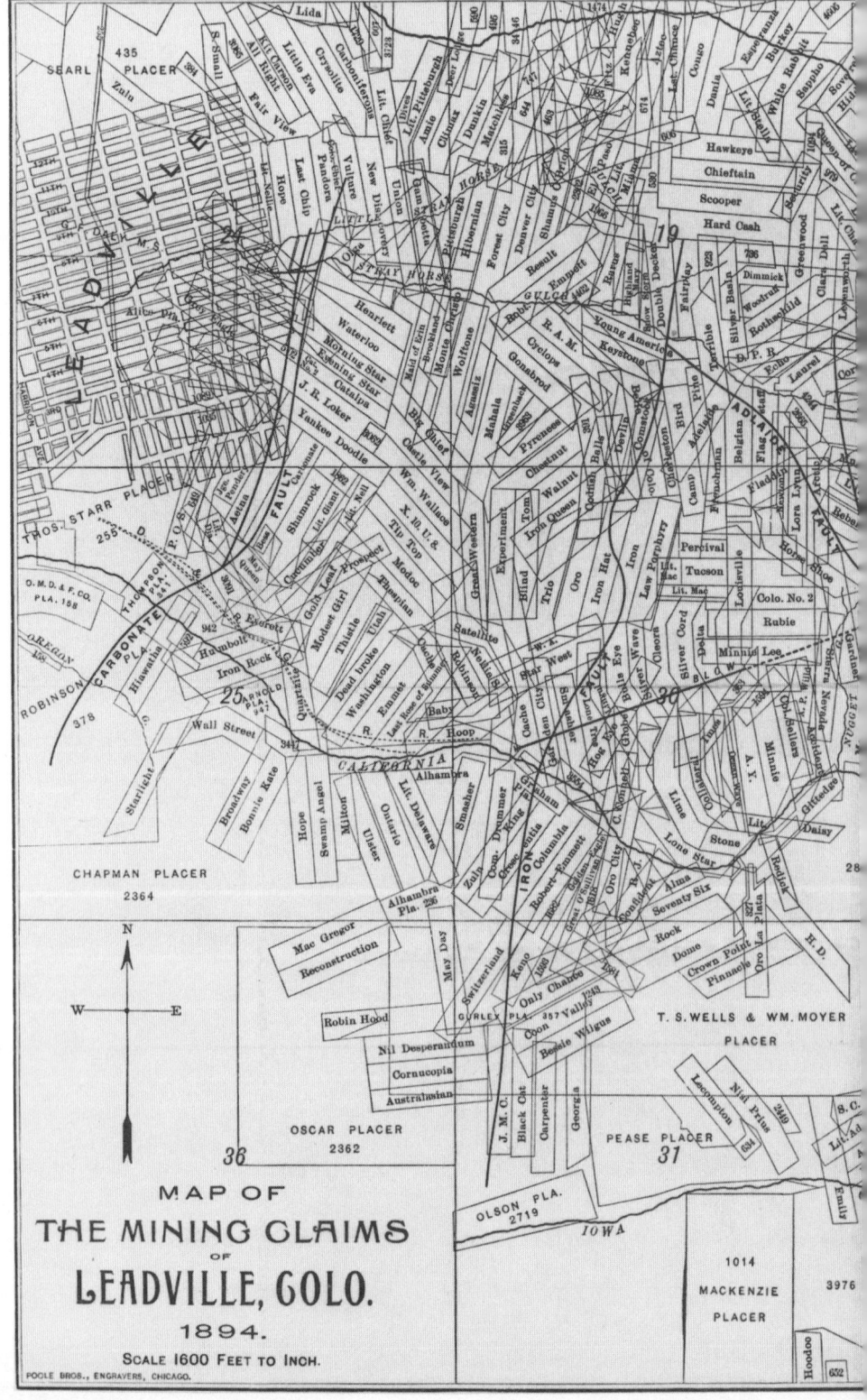